VOYAGES IN ENGLISH

Writing and Grammar

Elaine de Chantal Brookes

Patricia Healey

Irene Kervick

Catherine Irene Masino

Anne B. McGuire

Adrienne Saybolt

LOYOLAPRESS.

CHICAGO

Cover Design/Production: Loyola Press
Cover Illustration: Jeff Parks, Anni Betts
Interior Design/Production: Loyola Press, Think Design Group

Acknowledgements to copyright holders appear on page 326, which is to be
considered a continuation of the copyright page.

ISBN-10: 0-8294-2361-3
ISBN-13: 978-0-8294-2361-7

LOYOLAPRESS.

3441 N. Ashland Avenue
Chicago, Illinois 60657
(800) 621-1008
www.loyolapress.com

09 10 11 12 13 14 15 Web 10 9 8 7 6 5 4 3 2

VOYAGES IN ENGLISH
WRITING AND GRAMMAR

Welcome to

Inside the Student Book

The Teacher Planning Pages

Inside the Teacher Guide

Parent Letter

Scope and Sequence of Skills

Grade 2 Contents

CHAPTER 5 Contractions and Book Reports 144

CHAPTER 6 Word Study and Research Reports 176

CHAPTER 7 Research Tools   210

Grammar Review   222

Step-by-Step Teaching   T-224

Proofreading Marks Chart   inside back cover

Welcome to VOYAGES IN ENGLISH

WRITING AND GRAMMAR

A SIXTY-YEAR LEGACY

Sixty years ago a handful of highly experienced grammar and writing teachers set out on a quest—to develop a curriculum for teaching English to immigrant children. They knew that language is critical to finding a place in the world. They knew that communication cannot be separated from critical thinking. They knew that fluency, creativity, communication, and elaboration cannot be successfully separated from grammar, mechanics, syntax, and semantics.

Today our eyes are filled with color television and computer graphics. Our minds are filled with ever-changing information. Our e-mails carry important news of business and too often serve as the only connection to our extended families. Still, as it was six decades ago, our first impression of a person's skills and intelligence is firmly set in how well the person communicates—in conversation and in writing.

VOYAGES IN ENGLISH IN THE 21ST CENTURY

We at Loyola Press worked with the Sisters, Servants of the Immaculate Heart of Mary, Immaculata, Pennsylvania, the program authors, for two years to conceptualize this edition of *Voyages in English*. We realized that more than ever students and teachers need the values of the past to carry us all into the future. Through that collaboration, we forged this shared vision to

- uphold the strength and rigor of the original *Voyages* program,

- provide all students (and teachers) with proficiency in the foundations of grammar; and to provide the tools needed to master each writing genre, enabling them to communicate successfully with any audience, and

- reintegrate the writing process with its structural underpinnings at the word level, the sentence level, and the idea level (beyond the paragraph level).

We bring the best values of the past to the 21st century, empowering students as critical thinkers who can achieve their full potential.

FOCUS ON GRAMMAR

In every grade, growth in oral and written language skills is of paramount importance. Language is a vehicle for expressing wonder and delight, a tool for exchanging ideas, a medium for transmitting information, and a resource for bridging the differences among people. It is the underlying philosophy of *Voyages in English* to help students recognize these goals of language and to provide them with the skills to attain these goals.

Voyages in English includes the major areas of grammar: correct usage, mechanics, and dictionary skills. Each chapter incorporates a grammar concept with one of the following writing genres: personal narratives, friendly letters, how-to writing, descriptions, book reports, and research reports. For purposes of instruction, the grammar skills are often taught in isolation, but they should not be considered separate and distinct from one another.

Students at the primary level are just becoming acquainted with the tools of language. They are eager to express themselves orally and in written form. In these activities, spontaneity and creativity are encouraged. Grammar, correct usage, mechanics, and spelling are taught primarily to enhance the students' oral and written expression. Becoming proficient in language is a process. As students mature, their knowledge and use of the language should mature as well.

Voyages in English will provide a foundation for the further development of language skills. A textbook, coupled with a teacher's own love of language, is a vehicle for transmitting to the students an appreciation for the written word.

<!-- signatures -->

INSIDE THE STUDENT BOOK

Grammar Study

Each chapter of the student book provides comprehensive practice of each grammar concept. These practice pages can be used to introduce and reinforce concepts in class, or can be sent home with students as homework.

8 Grammar Skills

sentences
nouns
verbs
pronouns
adjectives
contractions
synonyms and antonyms
homophones

Grammar Practice:
Students practice each grammar skill using a variety of activities.

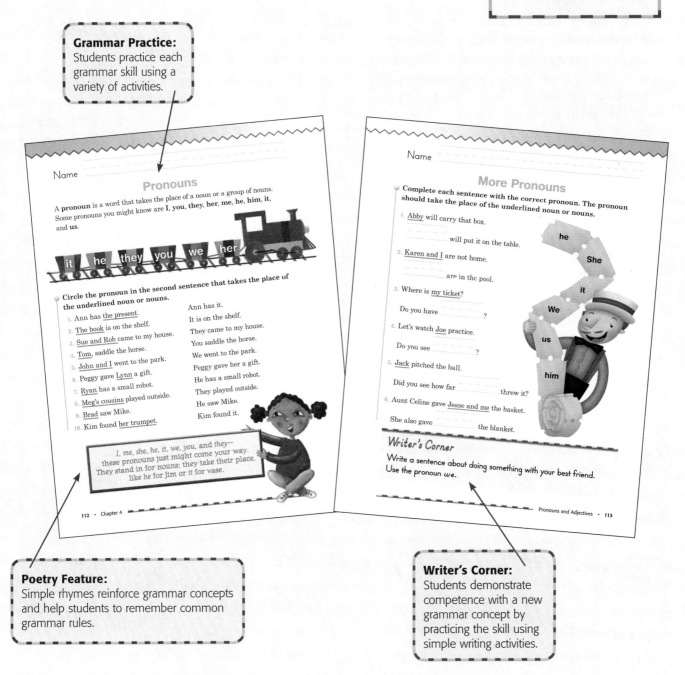

Poetry Feature:
Simple rhymes reinforce grammar concepts and help students to remember common grammar rules.

Writer's Corner:
Students demonstrate competence with a new grammar concept by practicing the skill using simple writing activities.

Grammar Assessment

Two Show What You Know pages are provided at the end of each grammar chapter and can be used as reinforcement or as review. A Cumulative Review is offered at the end of the book to test students' mastery of the primary grammar concepts they must know at the end of the year.

Show What You Know:
Use as a review of the chapter's major concepts or to test students' mastery of the chapter's grammar skills.

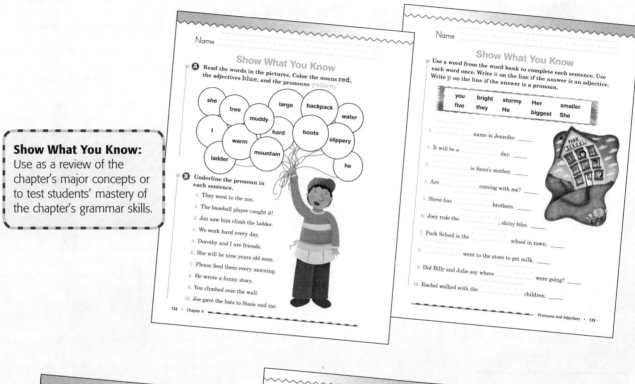

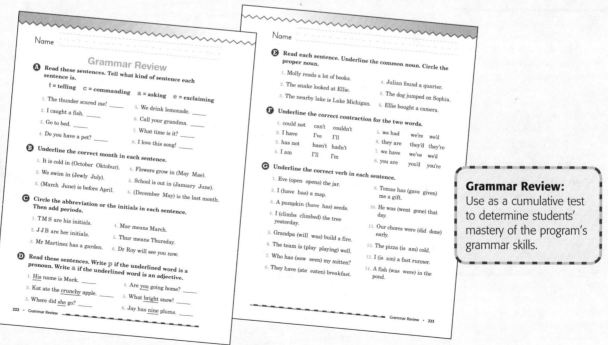

Grammar Review:
Use as a cumulative test to determine students' mastery of the program's grammar skills.

Get Ready to Write

Get Ready to Write introduces students to each chapter's writing genre. Students learn about the elements and characteristics of each genre, and workbook practice helps to illustrate how those elements and characteristics are applied to writing.

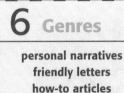

6 Genres

personal narratives
friendly letters
how-to articles
descriptions
book reports
research reports

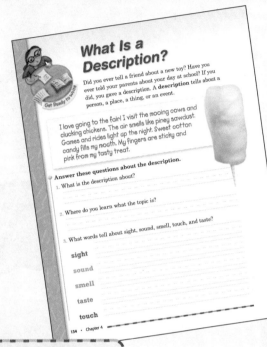

What Is a Description?

Did you ever tell a friend about a new toy? Have you ever told your parents about your day at school? If you did, you gave a description. A **description** tells about a person, a place, a thing, or an event.

I love going to the fair! I visit the mooing cows and clucking chickens. The air smells like piney sawdust. Games and rides light up the night. Sweet cotton candy fills my mouth. My fingers are sticky and pink from my tasty treat.

Answer these questions about the description.

1. What is the description about?

2. Where do you learn what the topic is?

3. What words tell about sight, sound, smell, touch, and taste?

sight

sound

smell

taste

touch

134 • Chapter 4

What Is a . . . ?:
Students learn clear definitions of the elements and the characteristics of the genre.

Topic Sentences

A description begins with a topic sentence. The **topic sentence** tells what you are describing. A topic sentence grabs a reader's attention.

Topic Sentence

I love to wake up to the sounds and smells of breakfast. The smell of bacon tickles my nose. I hear the pop of the toaster and the hiss of spattering butter. Soon I hear eggs cracking against a bowl. I am up before the eggs hit the pan.

Which is a better topic sentence? Write an **X** next to the better sentence in each pair.

1. I like lemonade. ☐

Cold lemonade is perfect on a hot day. ☐

2. My bedroom is nice. ☐

My bedroom is my favorite place to be. ☐

3. My sister is the cutest baby ever. ☐

This is what my sister looks like. ☐

4. We have Movie Night every week. ☐

We watch movies. ☐

Descriptions • 135

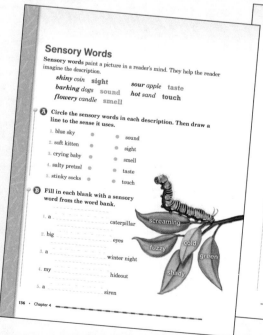

Sensory Words

Sensory words paint a picture in a reader's mind. They help the reader imagine the description.

shiny coin **sight**   *sour* apple **taste**
barking dogs **sound**   *hot* sand **touch**
flowery candle **smell**

A Circle the sensory words in each description. Then draw a line to the sense it uses.

1. blue sky   • sound
2. soft kitten   • sight
3. crying baby   • smell
4. salty pretzel   • taste
5. stinky socks   • touch

B Fill in each blank with a sensory word from the word bank.

1. a _____ caterpillar
2. big _____ eyes
3. a _____ winter night
4. my _____ hideout
5. a _____ siren

screaming   fuzzy   cold   green   shady

136 • Chapter 4

Sensory Words in a Description

A Look at each topic. List three sensory words for each.

recess   a thunderstorm   pizza

B Write one sentence that describes each thing. Use the sense next to each thing.

1. a fireworks show (**sight**)

2. a farm (**sound**)

3. a campfire (**smell**)

4. hot cocoa (**taste**)

5. tree bark (**touch**)

Descriptions • 137

Genre Practice:
On subsequent pages, students practice the skills they will need to write a complete portfolio piece for each genre.

Writer's Workshop

The Writer's Workshops are the writing process in action. The stages of the workshop illustrate how the writing process moves the work forward. Prewriting, Drafting, Revising, and Publishing help young writers develop and express their ideas. Editing and Proofreading help students check their work for clarity, logic, and accuracy.

Learn by Example: A virtual student guides students through the writing process. Achievable examples are modeled to illustrate the process in action.

Prewriting: By using the same prompts the virtual student uses to generate brainstorming ideas, students are able to brainstorm focused, age-appropriate topics. They are then challenged to use a graphic organizer to put thoughts and ideas into a coherent order.

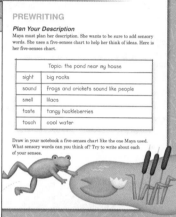

Drafting: An age-appropriate first draft allows students to see the relationship between prewriting and drafting. This "sloppy copy" helps emphasize the importance of capturing ideas at this stage of the writing process.

Editing and Revising: Students use a professional, yet achievable checklist to edit the ideas and the flow of their draft. They are then guided to develop a new draft to better catch errors and to improve the draft as a whole.

Proofreading: Students use a second checklist to edit the grammar and conventions in their draft.

Publishing: Students create a final portfolio piece that is both audience- and age-appropriate. A variety of publishing suggestions are offered in each chapter.

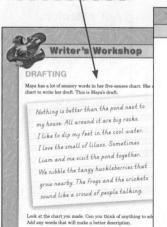

THE TEACHER PLANNING PAGES

Preceding each chapter is a brief seminar for teachers. These planning pages provide background, activities, and guidance for each grammar skill and writing genre. The guidance of curriculum planners and grammar experts helps teachers approach each chapter with confidence.

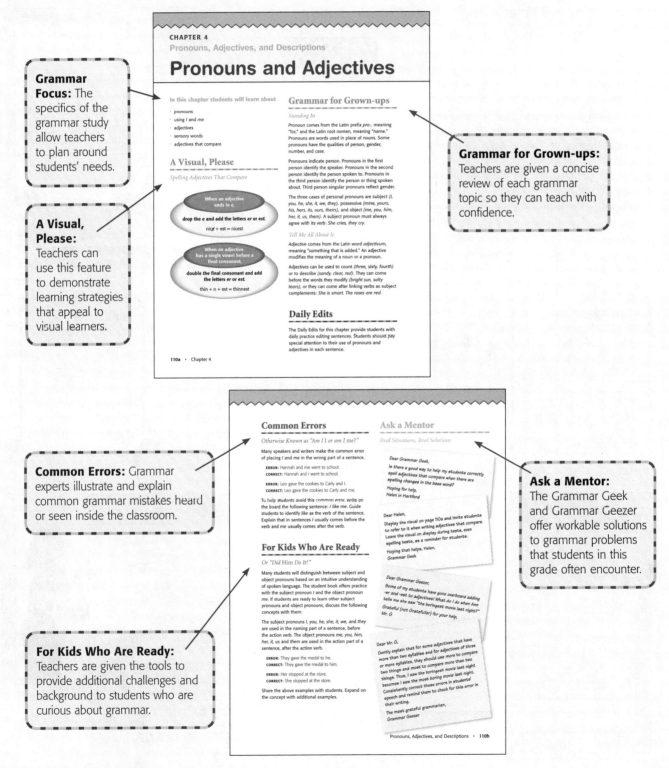

Grammar Focus: The specifics of the grammar study allow teachers to plan around students' needs.

A Visual, Please: Teachers can use this feature to demonstrate learning strategies that appeal to visual learners.

Grammar for Grown-ups: Teachers are given a concise review of each grammar topic so they can teach with confidence.

Common Errors: Grammar experts illustrate and explain common grammar mistakes heard or seen inside the classroom.

For Kids Who Are Ready: Teachers are given the tools to provide additional challenges and background to students who are curious about grammar.

Ask a Mentor: The Grammar Geek and Grammar Geezer offer workable solutions to grammar problems that students in this grade often encounter.

CHAPTER 4
Pronouns, Adjectives, and Descriptions

Descriptions

"When you described it as a remote house in the country........."

Genre Characteristics

At the end of this chapter, students will write a description. They will then be guided through the writing process in the Writer's Workshop. The completed description will include the following:

- a beginning that names the topic
- a middle that describes a person, a place, a thing, or an event
- vivid adjectives
- sensory words
- correct grammar, spelling, capitalization, and punctuation

Daily Story Starters

Some Daily Story Starters for this chapter provide students with practice brainstorming topics for descriptions, real or imaginary. Other Daily Story Starters provide students with practice writing sentences that describe the familiar or imaginary. This daily practice helps students understand how to choose topics and also broadens students' understanding of how descriptions are useful in all kinds of writing.

Begin each day by writing on the board the Daily Story Starter. Allow time for students to complete the sentence. Then discuss the results as a class.

110c • Chapter 4

Talk with students about what topic is suggested by the completed sentence. Help students determine when a topic is a good topic for a description. Allow students to compare sentences in order to demonstrate the varied ways the same topic can be described.

Describe It for Me

An effective description is like a photograph—an image that seems almost real. Whether it is part of a longer piece of writing or complete in itself, its focus on the topic is sharp and distinct, so the reader always knows exactly what is being described. Its content is illustrative, developing and printing a picture in the reader's mind.

The writer of an effective description captures the reader's attention with an informative beginning, keeps the reader engaged in a middle with logical connections, and crafts a summarizing ending that leaves a lingering impression. Rich sensory details make the piece both satisfying and informative. The language is always appropriate for the audience.

The description may be organized using time order, spatial order, or order of importance. A description is well constructed, and the sentences flow from one to the other in a logical progressive order. These sentences are correct in grammar, spelling, capitalization, and punctuation.

Teacher's Toolbox

Try the following ideas to help your students get the most out of the Writer's Workshop:

- Encourage students to keep a journal or picture journal to write or draw their impressions of interesting people, places, things, or events.
- Add to your classroom library literature rich in descriptive language.
- Create a bulletin-board display of descriptive marketing materials, such as descriptions of appealing vacation spots, toys, or food.

Reasons to Write

Share with students the following list of people who write descriptions. Discuss why it is important to become a good writer of descriptions.

- video game creators
- movie or book reviewers
- scientists who study volcanoes

Literature Links

You can add to your classroom library the following titles to offer your students examples of descriptions:

Alice Ramsey's Grand Adventure by Don Brown

Frog and Toad All Year by Arnold Lobel

Abuela by Arthur Dorros

Pronouns, Adjectives, and Descriptions • 110d

Genre Characteristics:
Explicitly stated genre characteristics help to define the genre and allow teachers to teach with confidence and consistency.

Genre Description:
A comprehensive explanation of the elements and characteristics of the writing genre helps teachers understand the relationship between grammar, mechanics, and writing.

Teacher's Toolbox:
Suggestions from professional educators offer ways to help students get the most out of their writing experience.

Literature Links:
Teachers can offer their students relevant and age-appropriate examples of the genre.

Reasons to Write:
Drawing on the practical applications of each genre, Reasons to Write offers examples of people who use writing in their jobs and everyday lives.

Assessment

The student's scoring rubrics guide students to practice self-evaluation, as well as to see how well they understand the elements and characteristics of each writing genre. The teacher's scoring rubric provides teachers with a targeted and balanced tool for assessing student writing at the idea level, the sentence level, and the word level.

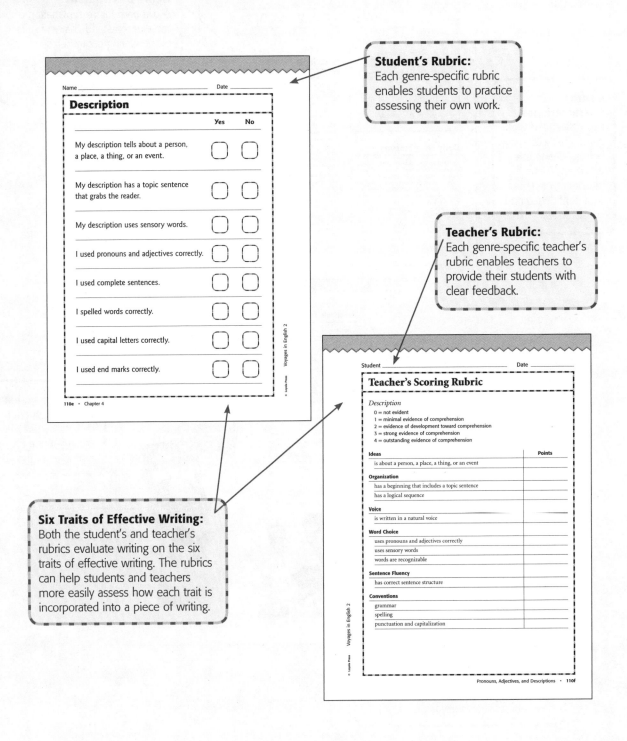

Student's Rubric:
Each genre-specific rubric enables students to practice assessing their own work.

Teacher's Rubric:
Each genre-specific teacher's rubric enables teachers to provide their students with clear feedback.

Six Traits of Effective Writing:
Both the student's and teacher's rubrics evaluate writing on the six traits of effective writing. The rubrics can help students and teachers more easily assess how each trait is incorporated into a piece of writing.

Name _____ Date _____

Description

	Yes	No
My description tells about a person, a place, a thing, or an event.		
My description has a topic sentence that grabs the reader.		
My description uses sensory words.		
I used pronouns and adjectives correctly.		
I used complete sentences.		
I spelled words correctly.		
I used capital letters correctly.		
I used end marks correctly.		

110e • Chapter 4

© Loyola Press   Voyages in English 2

Student _____ Date _____

Teacher's Scoring Rubric

Description
0 = not evident
1 = minimal evidence of comprehension
2 = evidence of development toward comprehension
3 = strong evidence of comprehension
4 = outstanding evidence of comprehension

Ideas	**Points**
is about a person, a place, a thing, or an event	
Organization	
has a beginning that includes a topic sentence	
has a logical sequence	
Voice	
is written in a natural voice	
Word Choice	
uses pronouns and adjectives correctly	
uses sensory words	
words are recognizable	
Sentence Fluency	
has correct sentence structure	
Conventions	
grammar	
spelling	
punctuation and capitalization	

© Loyola Press   Voyages in English 2

Pronouns, Adjectives, and Descriptions • 110f

Extensions

The Daily Edits, Daily Story Starters, and Chapter Adaptors provide teachers with a variety of ways to extend and reinforce each chapter's concepts. Teachers can use these features as class activities or as additional practice for students who are having trouble. Each chapter's extensions are tailored to the grammar skills and the writing genre that students are learning about, giving teachers a way to reinforce the connection between writing and grammar.

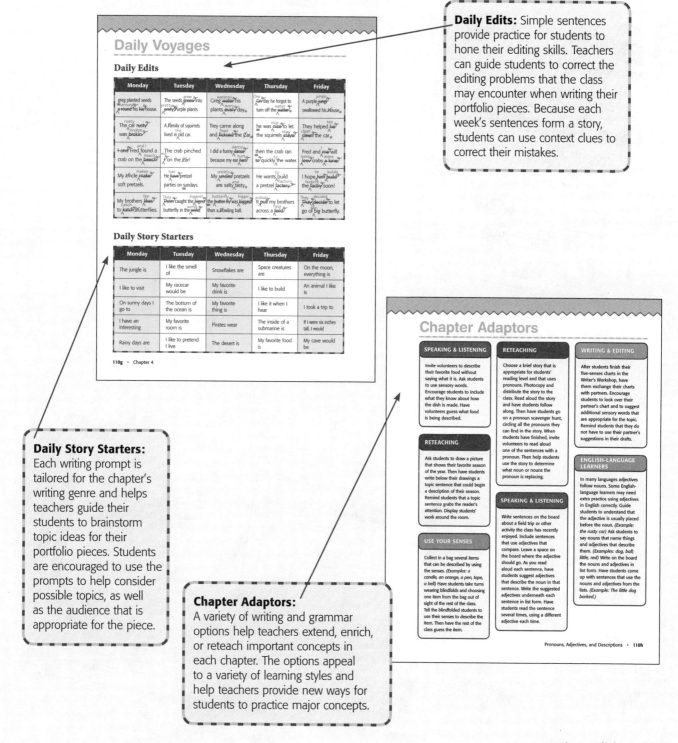

Daily Edits: Simple sentences provide practice for students to hone their editing skills. Teachers can guide students to correct the editing problems that the class may encounter when writing their portfolio pieces. Because each week's sentences form a story, students can use context clues to correct their mistakes.

Daily Story Starters: Each writing prompt is tailored for the chapter's writing genre and helps teachers guide their students to brainstorm topic ideas for their portfolio pieces. Students are encouraged to use the prompts to help consider possible topics, as well as the audience that is appropriate for the piece.

Chapter Adaptors: A variety of writing and grammar options help teachers extend, enrich, or reteach important concepts in each chapter. The options appeal to a variety of learning styles and help teachers provide new ways for students to practice major concepts.

INSIDE THE TEACHER GUIDE

Annotated Student Pages

The Teacher Edition of *Voyages in English* provides annotated student pages
for quick reference and easy correction. Each clearly marked page can be
easily referenced to its corresponding teaching at the back of the book.

Step-by-Step Teaching

The step-by-step teaching at the end of the Teacher Guide runs parallel to each student book chapter. The step-by-step teaching provides guidance, suggestions, and activities for the implementation of each chapter. Teachers are also equipped with flexible modeling ideas to ease the integration of grammar and writing. The teaching is clearly marked for easy reference to the annotated student book pages.

Teaching Grammar: Teachers can guide students through the elements of each grammar lesson, using the suggested activities and modeling techniques.

Introducing the Chapter: Each chapter opens with an age-appropriate model of the genre. Teachers can use the step-by-step plan to introduce the elements and characteristics of the genre and to show how grammar relates to writing.

Get Ready to Write: Teachers can use these activities and modeling techniques to deepen students' understanding of the writing genre.

Writer's Workshop: This guide offers specific definitions of each stage of the writing process, as well as concrete examples and modeling activities. Teachers can use these suggestions to guide students as they work on their portfolio pieces.

Parent Letter

The reproducible parent letter on page xxii, which is intended to be sent home with students at the beginning of the school year, provides teachers with a way of informing parents about the writing process. It guides parents to understand that the development and exploration of ideas is as important as a polished final piece and a definitive grade. The parent letter also offers advice for how parents can become involved in guiding their children by assuming the roles of editor and advisor.

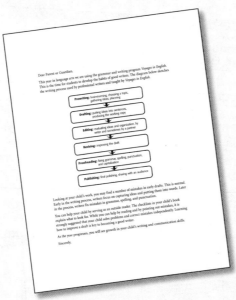

Blackline Masters

In addition to the comprehensive grammar practice provided in each student book, Loyola Press is proud to offer online additional practice pages for the grammar skills. The Blackline Masters can be used to reinforce or to assess the grammar concepts taught in the program.

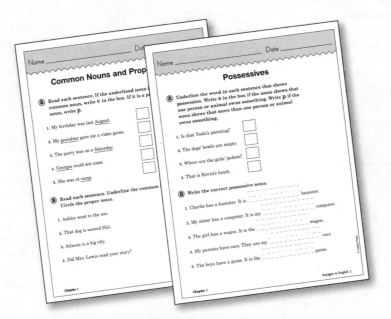

One Chapter, One Month

Each chapter in *Voyages in English* is a study of a grammar concept and a writing genre. The chapters are designed to cover about 25 class days—a chapter opener, grammar lessons presented across 22 days, and the genre Writer's Workshop across 18 days. By the final week, students should have a clear understanding of how the structure of grammar supports the expression of writing.

	MONDAY	TUESDAY	WEDNESDAY	THURSDAY	FRIDAY
WEEK 1	Grammar	Grammar	Grammar	Grammar	Grammar
WEEK 2	Grammar	Grammar	Grammar **Get Ready to Write**	Grammar **Get Ready to Write**	Grammar **Get Ready to Write**
WEEK 3	Grammar **Get Ready to Write**	Grammar **Prewriting**	Grammar **Prewriting**	Grammar **Drafting**	Grammar **Drafting**
WEEK 4	Grammar **Editing**	Grammar **Editing**	Grammar **Revising**	Grammar **Revising**	Grammar **Proofreading**
WEEK 5	Grammar **Proofreading**	Grammar **Publishing**	**Publishing**	**Presentations**	**Presentations**

Dear Parent or Guardian,

This year in language arts we are using the grammar and writing program *Voyages in English*. This is the time for students to develop the habits of good writers. The diagram below sketches the writing process used by professional writers and taught by *Voyages in English*.

Prewriting: brainstorming, choosing a topic, gathering ideas, planning

Drafting: putting ideas into sentences, producing the working copy

Editing: evaluating ideas and organization, by writer and sometimes by a partner

Revising: improving the draft

Proofreading: fixing grammar, spelling, punctuation, and capitalization

Publishing: final polishing, sharing with an audience

Looking at your child's work, you may find a number of mistakes in early drafts. This is normal. Early in the writing process, writers focus on capturing ideas and putting them into words. Later in the process, writers fix mistakes in grammar, spelling, and punctuation.

You can help your child by serving as an outside reader. The checklists in your child's book explain what to look for. While you can help by reading and by pointing out mistakes, it is strongly suggested that your child solve problems and correct mistakes independently. Learning how to improve a draft is key to becoming a good writer.

As the year progresses, you will see growth in your child's writing and communication skills.

Sincerely,

Scope and Sequence of Skills

Grammar	Grade Level		
	1	**2**	**3**
NOUNS			
common/proper	I	T	T
singular/plural	I	I	T
irregular			T
possessive		I	T
collective			T
as subjects			T
used in direct address			I
words used as nouns and verbs			I
words used as nouns and adjectives			I
PRONOUNS			
singular/plural	I	I	T
subject	I	I	I
object	I	I	I
possessive			I
as compound subjects			I
agreement with antecedent			I
ADJECTIVES			
descriptive	I	I	T
positive/comparative/superlative	I	I	T
articles			T
demonstrative			I
that tell how many	I		I
common/proper			I
as subject complements			I
position of			I
words used as nouns or adjectives			I
little, less, least			I
ADVERBS			
manner		I	I
time			I
place			I
negation			I

I = Introduced, **T** = Taught

Grammar (continued)	Grade Level		
	1	2	3
VERBS			
subject/verb agreement	I	I	T
action	I	I	T
being/linking	I	I	T
words used as nouns/verbs			I
regular/irregular	I	I	I
simple present	I	I	I
simple past	I	I	I
future with *will*			I
future with *going to*			I
helping (auxiliary)		I	I
principal parts			I
present progressive		I	I
past progressive		I	I
CONJUNCTIONS			
coordinating			I
SENTENCES			
declarative	I	I	I
interrogative	I	I	I
exclamatory	I	I	I
imperative	I	I	I
simple	I	I	I
compound (conjunctions)			I
PARTS OF SENTENCES			
subject and predicate		I	I
simple subject		I	I
simple predicate		I	I
compound sentence elements			I
subject complement			I
PUNCTUATION/CAPITALS			
end punctuation	I	I	T
capital letters	I	I	T
periods/capital letters in abbreviations		I	T
periods/capital letters in titles and initials		I	T
titles of books, stories, etc.	I	I	I
commas in series			I
commas in compound sentences			I
apostrophes	I	I	T
writing addresses			T
writing direct quotes			I
commas in direct address			I
commas after initial phrase			I

I = Introduced, **T** = Taught

Writing	Grade Level		
	1	2	3
GENRES			
Personal Narratives	X	X	X
Descriptions	X	X	X
Book Reports/Expository Writing	X	X	X
How-to Articles	X	X	X
Friendly Letters	X	X	X
Creative Writing			X
Persuasive Writing			X
Research Reports	X	X	X
GENRE SKILLS			
Plot Development			X
Organization	X	X	X
Ideas and Outlines	•	•	•
Spatial Order			•
Chronological Order	•	•	•
Comparing and Contrasting			•
Title	X	X	X
Topic	X	X	X
Introduction	X	X	X
Body	X	X	X
Conclusion	X	X	X
Audience	X	X	X
Purpose	X	X	X
Voice/Tone/Word Choice	X	X	X
Sentence Fluency	X	X	X
WRITING PROCESS			
Prewriting	X	X	X
Brainstorming	•	•	•
Free Writing	•	•	•
Organizing Ideas	•	•	•
Choosing a Topic	•	•	•
Drafting	X	X	X
Content Editing	X	X	X
Proofreading	X	X	X
Revising	X	X	X
Publishing	X	X	X

X = skill taught at grade level, • = topic taught at grade level

Writing (continued)	Grade Level		
	1	**2**	**3**
WRITING SKILLS			
Revising Sentences			X
Adjectives	X	X	X
Graphic Organizers	X	X	X
Five-Senses Chart	•	•	•
Idea Charts	•	•	
Storyboards	•	•	
Sentence Strips/Note Cards	•	•	•
Word Maps/Word Webs/Idea Webs			•
Expanding Sentences			X
Combining Sentences			X
Verbs			X
Dialog			X
Sentence Types			
Simple Sentences	•	•	•
Compound Sentences			•
Transition Words		X	X
WORD STUDY			
Prefixes			X
Number Prefixes			X
Antonyms	X	X	X
Synonyms	X	X	X
Exact Words	X	X	X
Nouns	•	•	•
Verbs	•	•	•
Adjectives	•	•	•
Adverbs			•
Homophones	•	•	•
Contractions	X	X	X
Transition Words		X	X
Suffixes			X
Noun and Adjective Suffixes	•	•	•
Adverb and Verb Suffixes	•	•	•

X = skill taught at grade level, • = topic taught at grade level

Writing	Grade Level		
	1	2	3
STUDY SKILLS LESSONS			
Dictionary	X	X	X
Pronunciation			•
Word Definition	•	•	•
Entry Words		•	•
Guide Words		•	•
Taking Notes	X	X	X
Library and Internet Sources	X	X	X
Parts of a Book	X	X	X

X = skill taught at grade level, • = topic taught at grade level

Sentences

In this chapter students will learn about

- writing a complete sentence
- capital letters
- end marks
- telling sentences
- commanding sentences
- asking sentences
- exclaiming sentences
- naming parts (subjects)
- action parts (predicates)

A Visual, Please

Is It a Sentence?

Does it have a *naming part*?

The boys played hockey.

↓

Does it have an *action part*?

The boys played hockey.

↓

Then it is a sentence.

The boys played hockey.

Grammar for Grown-ups

Strictly Sentences

The word *sentence* is derived from the Latin *sententia,* meaning "feeling" or "opinion." A sentence consists of several parts of speech organized into a pattern that expresses a complete thought.

A declarative (telling) sentence makes a statement and ends with a period. An interrogative (asking) sentence asks a question and ends with a question mark. An imperative (commanding) sentence gives a command and ends with a period. An exclamatory (exclaiming) sentence expresses strong emotion and ends with an exclamation point.

Every sentence has two basic parts: the subject (naming part), which is the explicit or implied person, place, or thing talked about; and the predicate (action part), which is what the subject is, has, or does.

Daily Edits

The Daily Edits provide students with daily practice in editing sentences. Prior to assigning the first Daily Edit, go over the Proofreading Marks chart on the inside back cover of the student book.

Begin each day's grammar lesson by writing on the board the Daily Edit. Help students correct the sentence. Then discuss the results as a class. Help students understand what corrections are necessary to make the sentence accurate and complete.

Consider leaving on the board the corrected sentences. Because each week's sentences form a story, there will be context clues to help students find and correct mistakes.

Common Errors

Or "Where is the action part?"

Some developing writers, by mistakenly omitting the action part (predicate), write sentence fragments rather than complete sentences. This error occurs because young writers often forget that all sentences must have a naming part (subject) and an action part (predicate).

> **ERROR:** Many children.
> **CORRECT:** Many children play soccer.
>
> **ERROR:** The funny dog.
> **CORRECT:** The funny dog does tricks.

As students revise their writing, remind them to check each sentence for an action part. Explain that the action part tells what something is or does.

For Kids Who Are Ready

Or "Doing Two Things at Once"

For students who are ready to apply the finer points of grammar to their writing, discuss the following concept:

If two sentences have the same naming part but different action parts, the sentences can be combined. The two sentences can be made into one sentence by using the naming part only once and combining the two action parts.

> **SENTENCES:** The cat sits. The cat purrs.
> **COMBINED:** The cat sits and purrs.
>
> **SENTENCES:** The dogs barked. The dogs howled.
> **COMBINED:** The dogs barked and howled.

Encourage students to combine action parts if two sentences share the same naming part.

Ask a Mentor

Real Situations, Real Solutions

Dear Grammar Geek,

Some of my students don't understand how to write complete sentences. How can I help them?

Help me,
Maria K.

Dear Maria,

Display the visual on page 6a. Review it often with students. Use other simple sentences to illustrate the concept.

Completing sentences around the world,
Grammar Geek

Dear Grammar Geezer,

Some of my students forget to include a naming part (subject) or an action part (predicate) when they write "sentences." How can I help them express complete thoughts?

Fragmented,
Jo in Jersey

Dear Jo,

Write the following fragment on the board: The kittens. Ask your students the following questions: Who is this sentence about? (The kittens) Can you tell what the kittens are doing? (no) How can we change this so we answer these questions: Who is this about? What did they do?

Work with the class to fill in the missing information. Repeat the activity with other sentence fragments, such as The other players. Ran around. and Hears the phone. Then remind students that they should be able to answer the same questions with their own sentences.

Defragmenting lives,
Grammar Geezer

I THINK I'LL KEEP A DIARY

THE END OF PREHISTORY

David Cooney: www.CartoonStock.com

Personal Narratives

Genre Characteristics

At the end of this chapter, students will write a personal narrative. They will be guided through the writing process in the Writer's Workshop. The completed personal narrative will include the following:

• a topic about something that really happened to the writer
• a first-person point of view
• a beginning that tells what the story is about
• a middle that tells what happened
• an ending that finishes the story
• time order
• correct grammar, spelling, capitalization, and punctuation

Daily Story Starters

The Daily Story Starters for this chapter provide students with practice writing about themselves. This daily practice helps to prepare students for writing their personal narratives.

Begin each day by writing on the board the Daily Story Starter. Allow time for students to complete the sentence. Then discuss the results as a class. Because the purpose of this activity is to practice brainstorming, talk to students about their ideas and whether the ideas are appropriate for the genre.

Taking It Personally

Personal narratives are written to share significant events in writers' lives. They are personal to the core, and at their best they are revealing and relevant to others.

A personal narrative has a clear focus on a particular topic. The topic is always a true story or event that the writer experienced. First-person point of view indicates to the reader that the writer is telling the story about himself or herself. The ideas in the narrative help express the importance of the topic to the writer.

Effective personal narratives are well organized. Ideas are usually presented in order. The main idea is often clearly explained in the beginning, while the ending of a personal narrative gives a sense of resolution.

The writer of an effective personal narrative knows how to let his or her personality shine through with the use of humor, phrasing, dialog, or a combination of these characteristics. Personal narratives have an honest voice—one that is authentic and true. Throughout a personal narrative, the writing is correct in grammar, punctuation, capitalization, and spelling.

Teacher's Toolbox

Try the following ideas to help your students get the most out of the Writer's Workshop:

- Encourage students to keep a picture journal to record important or interesting personal experiences.

- Invite students to bring in pictures or drawings of favorite family events. Discuss how these events might make good personal narrative topics.

- Invite local officials (such as the mayor, an entertainer, or the principal) to tell the class about an event they remember from their own childhood.

Reasons to Write

Share with your students the following times in which people write personal narratives. Talk about why it is important to become a good writer of personal narratives.

- an astronaut writing a report about a recent space mission

- a songwriter writing a song about something that happened in his or her life

- a police officer writing a speech to give to second graders about what she does each day

Literature Links

You can add the following titles to your classroom library to offer your students examples of well-written personal narratives:

Tar Beach by Faith Ringgold

There's an Alligator Under My Bed by Mercer Mayer

Celia's Island Journal by Celia Thaxter

Personal Narrative

	Yes	No
My story is about me.	☐	☐
My story has a beginning, a middle, and an ending.	☐	☐
I used the words I, me, and my.	☐	☐
I used complete sentences.	☐	☐
I spelled words correctly.	☐	☐
I used capital letters correctly.	☐	☐
I used end marks correctly.	☐	☐

Voyages in English 2

© Loyola Press

Teacher's Scoring Rubric

Personal Narrative

0 = not evident
1 = minimal evidence of comprehension
2 = evidence of development toward comprehension
3 = strong evidence of comprehension
4 = outstanding evidence of comprehension

	Points
Ideas	
topic relates to a real event	
Organization	
has a logical sequence	
has a beginning	
has a middle	
has an ending	
Voice	
is written from the writer's point of view	
Word Choice	
uses appropriate words	
words are recognizable	
Sentence Fluency	
has correct sentence structure	
Conventions	
grammar	
spelling	
punctuation and capitalization	

Daily Voyages

Daily Edits

Monday	Tuesday	Wednesday	Thursday	Friday
Sam woke up to a loud ~~noiz~~. (noise)	Something was ~~xploding~~! (exploding)	Sam ran out the ~~bak~~ door. (back)	the loud noise (was) fireworks.	Sam sat down and ~~injoyed~~ the show. (enjoyed)
Ruby loves her tree ~~hous~~. (house)	one night a storm ~~nocked~~ it down. (knocked)	ruby cried over the smashed wood.	Then she heard a ~~truk~~ drive up? (truck)	her dad already had new boards (and) nails.
i led the Thanksgiving Day parade.	I wore (a) shiny uniform.	I even had a silver baton.	then I took a wrong ~~tern~~. (turn)	We marched all (the) way to the ~~rivir~~! (river)
john had a colorful ~~flowar~~ garden. (flower)	Winter (was) coming ~~was~~ soon.	John did not want to ~~lus~~ his garden. (lose)	so he bought paints and painted a picture.	Now ~~hiz~~ garden hangs (his) on the ~~the~~ wall.
Why did Jack and Ann go to the ~~streem~~ ? (stream)	They wanted to ~~cach~~ fish. (catch)	Ann ~~brougt~~ fishing poles. (brought)	jack forgot to bring the ~~werms~~. (worms)	They ~~desided~~ to swim with the fish instead. (decided)

Daily Story Starters

Monday	Tuesday	Wednesday	Thursday	Friday
I once found	Last Saturday I	My first day of school was	I tripped and laughed when	I once dressed up as
I went with my friends to	I was nervous when I	I ate outside when	My favorite day was when	I helped make
It was strange when I saw	It was raining when I	I met my friend at	I had an adventure when	I helped someone when
It was fun when I	My favorite meal was	I stayed up late when	I liked going to	I wish I hadn't
I sang a song at	I once rode in a	I got wet when	I once shared my	I was proud when I

Chapter Adaptors

SPEAKING & LISTENING

Have partners ask one another questions using asking sentences and answer using telling sentences. Remind students to speak in complete sentences. Tell partners to listen closely to each other. As students talk, walk around the room to assist them.

RETEACHING

Read aloud a story. Ask students to tell the events that happened in the beginning, the middle, and the ending. Remind students that a personal narrative must have a beginning, a middle, and an ending in order to be complete.

ENGLISH-LANGUAGE LEARNERS

Some English-language learners may feel more comfortable with their speaking ability than with their writing ability. Invite students who share the same primary language or the same English-language level to work together. Encourage them to help one another when they pick topics and plan their stories.

ROBOT COMMANDER

Ask students to imagine that they have a robot. Tell them that the robot understands only commanding sentences. Have students draw pictures of their robots and write at least three commanding sentences for the robot. *(Examples: Make me a snack. Do my chores. Walk the dog.)* Walk around the room and make sure that students are writing complete sentences and using correct capitalization and punctuation. Invite volunteers to share their drawings and commanding sentences.

RETEACHING

Think of sentences that might begin with one of the six question words. *(Who, What, When, Where, Why, How)* Then create asking sentence strips, leaving off the first word of each sentence. Write the six question words on the board. Distribute the incomplete sentence strips to students. Then ask students to match their question with the correct question word on the board and have them read aloud the completed sentence.

WRITING & EDITING

Make a poster to display in the classroom that includes the following peer-conferencing tips:

1. Always begin by saying what you liked about your partner's writing.
2. Be polite when talking about your partner's writing.
3. Listen to your partner's ideas.
4. Think about which of your partner's ideas you will use in your writing.

SENTENCE SUPERHIGHWAY

Draw on the board a highway with four exit ramps. On the highway, write *Types of Sentences*. Label the ramps *Asking, Commanding, Exclaiming,* and *Telling*. Then draw a road sign at the beginning of each ramp with the corresponding questions: *Does it ask a question? Does it tell people to do something? Does it show excitement? Does it tell about something?* Say aloud a sentence and ask a volunteer to drive a toy car along the highway and to choose the correct exit ramp. Repeat with other volunteers and kinds of sentences.

CHAPTER 1

Sentences and Personal Narratives

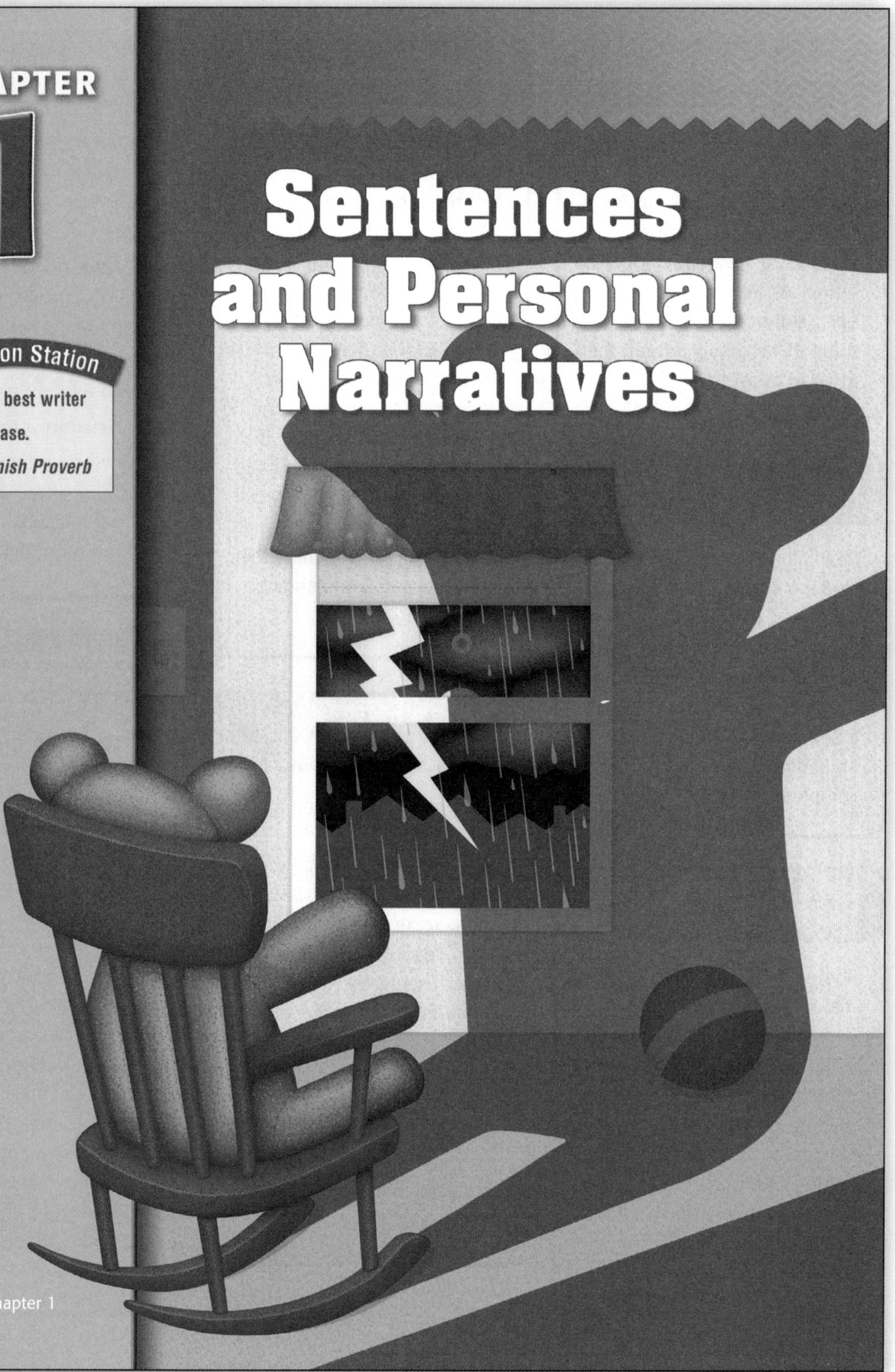

Quotation Station

Even the best writer has to erase.

–Spanish Proverb

Stormy Night

It was a loud, rainy night.
Scary shadows were everywhere.
My chair looked like it had a
monster on it! So I turned on
the light. Then I laughed.
It was just my fuzzy bear.
It is funny to be scared
of a little, fuzzy bear.

Name _____

The Sentence

A **sentence** is a group of words that expresses a complete thought.

This is not a complete sentence.

> *The bear*

This group of words is not a sentence because it does not tell anything about the bear. A period is not placed after these words.

This is a complete sentence.

> *The bear ate the honey.*

This group of words is a sentence because it tells what the bear did. A sentence always ends with an end mark. A period (.) is a kind of end mark.

Write an **S** next to each group of words that is a sentence. Put a period at the end of each sentence.

__S__ 1. I made a cake .

_____ 2. A kite

__S__ 3. Jill gave the ball to Jenny .

__S__ 4. Run and hide, Bill .

_____ 5. My desk

__S__ 6. I rode my bike .

_____ 7. The dog

_____ 8. At home

__S__ 9. We made our beds .

__S__ 10. This is a holiday .

A little black dot that you can see.
Period is my name.
A telling sentence ends with me,
I play a telling game.

8 • Chapter 1

Name

More About Sentences

A sentence begins with a **capital letter.** It ends
with an **end mark.**

Write these sentences correctly.
Begin each sentence with a
capital letter. Put a period at
the end of each sentence.

1. the dog eats its dinner

The dog eats its dinner.

2. i love to go fishing

I love to go fishing.

3. amal kicks the ball

Amal kicks the ball.

4. we walk to school

We walk to school.

5. brandon sweeps the floor

Brandon sweeps the floor.

Sentences • 9

Name _____

Capital Letters and End Marks

Unscramble each group of words to make a sentence. Remember to add capital letters and periods.

1. sing to she likes

   She likes to sing.

2. sit sofa the on we

   We sit on the sofa.

3. book the reads he

   He reads the book.

4. eats cookies jesse the

   Jesse eats the cookies.

5. dog i give bath the a

   I give the dog a bath.

6. runs dog the fast

   The dog runs fast.

7. pretty pony that is a

   That is a pretty pony.

8. flowers they fresh bring

   They bring fresh flowers.

Name _____

Words Working Together

Words work together to build a sentence. Remember, a sentence is a group of words that expresses a complete thought.

A Color the check mark next to each complete sentence.

 1. Aki goes to school.

 2. gets rabbits

 3. Kylie sings with the radio.

 4. Mario watches the movie.

 5. eats an apple

 6. Andy stops the

B Match the words in the first list with the words in the second list to build a complete sentence.

1. The kids   rises.

2. My mom   plays hockey.

3. The moon   fly.

4. Birds   go to the park.

5. Kenji   wears a green apron.

Name _____

More Words Working Together

A Match the words in the first list with the words in the second list to build a sentence. Put the correct letter on the line. The first one is done for you.

1. The happy children   __d__   a. crashed against the rocks.

2. The baseball player   __e__   b. howled through the treetops.

3. A bitter cold wind   __b__   c. blazed in the fireplace.

4. Two large pine logs   __c__   d. clapped their hands.

5. The big white waves   __a__   e. hit a home run.

B Match the words in the first list with the words in the second list to build a sentence.

1. Three baby robins   chased the little mouse.

2. The big red truck   sped across the sky.

3. My playful kitten   hung in the closet.

4. Jeff's winter coat   slept in a nest.

5. A shiny silver plane   rumbled down the street.

Name _____

Telling Sentences

A **telling sentence** tells about something.
A period (.) is placed at the end of a
telling sentence.

The honey is in the jar.
The honey is sticky.

● Underline the complete telling
sentence in each pair.
Put a period at the end of
each telling sentence.

1. Bob likes to fish .
   Does Bob like

2. Parks his blue car
   Dad parks his car .

3. Sings in the morning
   My pet bird sings .

4. Beth holds the cat .
   The furry cat

5. Down the busy street
   Joe runs down the street .

6. The bunny is soft .
   The soft little bunny

7. Leslie talks on the phone .
   On the phone

8. Type on
   I type on the computer .

Writer's Corner

Write a telling sentence about something you did this morning.

Sentences • 13

Name _____

Making Telling Sentences

Use the words on the right to make telling sentences.
Put a period at the end of each sentence.

Puppets

writing

tire

flowers

skateboard

cards

rain

park

help

shoes

birds

plates

1. We go to the *park* .

2. They feed the *birds* .

3. Kira will not *help* .

4. Jason dries the *plates* .

5. Mae rides her *skateboard* in the park .

6. Erin and Shawn play *cards* .

7. Macon thinks *writing* is fun .

8. Grandma plants *flowers* in her garden .

9. *Puppets* scare my sister .

10. Your *shoes* look new .

11. Today it will *rain* .

12. This *tire* would make a good swing .

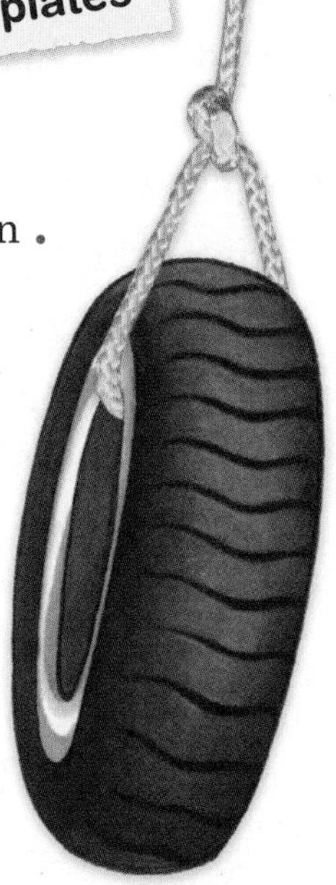

Name _____

Commanding Sentences

A **commanding sentence** tells people what to do. A commanding sentence begins with a capital letter. A period (.) is usually placed at the end.

Stop at the red light.   Wait for me.

A Color each sign that has a commanding sentence on it.

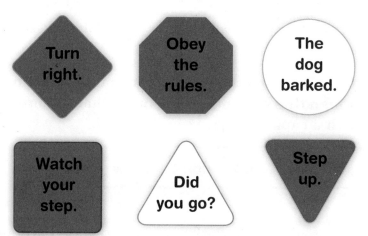

B Put a period at the end of each commanding sentence. Underline the capital letter in the first word of each sentence.

1. Turn off the light .   5. Ride your bike .

2. Open the door, please .   6. Blow the whistle .

3. Work quietly .   7. Water the flowers .

4. Swim across the pool .   8. Write the answer on the line .

Writer's Corner

Write a commanding sentence that you might say to someone crossing the street.

_____

Name _____

More Commanding Sentences

A Underline the commanding sentence in each pair.

1. The dog is named Bear.
   <u>Walk the dog.</u>

2. <u>Help your little brother.</u>
   Your little brother plays baseball.

3. <u>Give Shen the cookie.</u>
   The cookie tastes good.

4. These bags are heavy.
   <u>Carry these bags.</u>

B Choose the word from the word bank that best completes each commanding sentence. Remember that a sentence begins with a capital letter.

go	put	stop	don't	mow	eat

1. *Go* to the kitchen.

2. *Put* on your shoes.

3. *Mow* the lawn.

4. *Eat* the orange.

5. *Stop* banging the drum.

6. *Don't* pet the tiger.

> Commanding Sentence is my name.
> Giving directions is my aim.
> I help you know the things to do
> at home, at play, and in school too!

Name _____

Sentence Review

A **telling sentence** tells about something. A **commanding sentence** tells people what to do.

● **Write t beside each telling sentence. Write c beside each commanding sentence.**

1. The team is ready. __t__

2. Play ball. __c__

3. The boats are moving. __t__

4. Turn off the light. __c__

5. My house is on King Street. __t__

6. My brother works at night. __t__

7. Please sit down. __c__

8. Nan likes to draw. __t__

9. I read that book. __t__

10. Listen to the story. __c__

11. Your desk is neat. __t__

12. Color the picture. __c__

Name _____

More Sentence Review

A Write **t** next to each telling sentence. Write **c** next to each commanding sentence.

1. Give Molly your hand. __c__

2. She can help you cross the street. __t__

3. Josh likes to read. __t__

4. Take him to the library. __c__

5. Let Josh pick a book. __c__

6. Josh loves books about dinosaurs. __t__

7. Don't let him get a scary book. __c__

8. Josh also likes movies. __t__

9. Josh can get one movie. __t__

10. Be home by five o'clock. __c__

B Write your own telling sentence.

_____

_____

_____

C Write your own commanding sentence.

_____

_____

_____

Name _____

Asking Sentences

An **asking sentence** asks a question. Some asking sentences begin with **question words.** An asking sentence ends with a question mark (**?**).

● **Complete each sentence with a question word from the word bank. You may use some words more than once. Answers will vary.**

How	What	Who
Why	When	Where

1. _____ are you doing?

2. _____ old are you?

3. _____ did Mary laugh?

4. _____ is the picnic?

5. _____ is Pete?

6. _____ gave Ren that daisy?

7. _____ do we leave for the park?

8. _____ do you feed your parrot?

I am a squiggle on your page
with a little dot below.
At the end of each asking sentence,
please place me just so.

Name _____

More Asking Sentences

A Complete each sentence with one of the question words on the right. Use each word one time.

1. *Are* you going to the circus?

2. *Has* Jonah popped his balloon?

3. *Do* you like popcorn?

4. *Did* you see the clown?

5. *Have* the elephants done any tricks?

6. *Is* there enough popcorn for everyone?

Do

Has

Have

Are

Is

Did

B Write the letter that tells what each sentence is. Put the correct end mark at the end of each sentence.

t = telling   **c** = commanding   **a** = asking

_a_ 1. Will you go with me **?**

_t_ 2. All fish need water **.**

_t_ 3. Today is cold **.**

_a_ 4. Does John know the way **?**

_c_ 5. Jump over the fence **.**

Name

Exclaiming Sentences

An **exclaiming sentence** shows surprise or excitement. An exclamation
point (!) is placed at the end of an exclaiming sentence.

What a hot day it is!   *The sun is coming out!*

**Underline the capital letter at the beginning of each sentence.
Then put an exclamation point at the end.**

1. Watch your step !

2. I am so excited !

3. He can hardly wait !

4. What a surprise !

5. Watch out for the ball !

6. The storm is coming !

7. Today is my birthday !

8. Look at her run !

9. The bus is coming !

10. This tastes delicious !

My name is Exclamation Point.
Now if you are very wise,
you will put me at the end
of each sentence of surprise.

Name _____

More Exclaiming Sentences

Write your own exclaiming sentence for each picture. Remember to use an exclamation point (!). Sample answers shown.

1. What a funny monkey!

2. This is a great gift!

3. This is a cute puppy!

4. That clown is silly!

5. I see a scary jack o'lantern!

Writer's Corner

Write an exclaiming sentence that you might say during a thunderstorm.

Name

Asking and Exclaiming Sentences

Read the sentences. Put a question mark at the end of each asking sentence. Put an exclamation point at the end of each exclaiming sentence.

1. How old are you **?**

2. Can you see the clowns **?**

3. It is so hot today **!**

4. That is a funny mask **!**

5. Where is my hat **?**

6. Hurry, Paige **!**

7. Where is the squirrel **?**

8. Watch out **!**

9. I had the best birthday **!**

10. Did you read the story **?**

Name

More Asking and Exclaiming Sentences

Read the sentences below. Put an **X** in the Exclaiming box for each exclaiming sentence. Put an **X** in the Asking box for each asking sentence. Add the correct end mark to each sentence. The first one is done for you.

	Exclaiming	Asking
1. Where is your house **?**		**X**
2. Mary did well on her test **!**	X	
3. I love my dog **!**	X	
4. How are you **?**		X
5. It is really hot **!**	X	
6. This game is fun **!**	X	
7. Is it raining **?**		X
8. Do you have a scooter **?**		X
9. Who brought the kittens **?**		X
10. When are you going home **?**		X

Name _____

The Naming Part of a Sentence

A sentence has two parts. The **naming part** of a sentence tells who or what the sentence is about.

> *Sari* *likes to sing.*

In this sentence the naming part is **Sari** because the sentence is about Sari.

> *The stars* *are very bright.*

In this sentence the naming part is **The stars** because the sentence is about the stars.

Underline the naming part of each sentence.

1. We play in the snow.

2. Talia has red mittens.

3. I have a fast sled.

4. Kim makes a snow angel.

5. They make a snowman.

6. Our neighbors come over.

7. Chad makes snowballs.

8. The puppy eats snow.

9. We get cold.

10. Aunt Debbie gives us hot cocoa.

Name

The Action Part of a Sentence

The **action part** of a sentence tells what a person or a thing does.

We ran home.

In this sentence the action part is **ran home** because it tells what We did.

Jake cleaned his room.

In this sentence the action part is **cleaned his room** because it tells what Jake did.

Underline the action part of each sentence.

1. The sisters watch TV.

2. Miss Burke opens the book.

3. Emil washes the dishes.

4. They play hopscotch.

5. Mr. Smith sells ice cream.

6. Kathy answers the telephone.

7. Brian plays a video game.

8. Marc runs to second base.

9. Ally helps wash the car.

10. We water the plants.

Name _____

Naming Parts and Action Parts

Remember that a sentence has two parts. Together, the naming part and action part form a complete sentence.

Ⓐ **Match the naming part to the action part. The first one is done for you. Then say each complete sentence.**

1. She   has a pretty dress.

2. The doll   make a sandcastle.

3. The baby   sleeps in his stroller.

4. I   goes to the store.

Ⓑ **Draw a line under the naming part. Draw a circle around the action part.**

1. We go to the beach.

2. My father brings a picnic.

3. I bring a pail and a shovel.

4. Grandma brings a blanket.

5. Leo makes a sandcastle.

6. Taylor and Paul go swimming.

7. My mother teaches Carly how to surf.

8. We go home after sunset.

Name _____

Show What You Know

Put the correct end mark at the end of each sentence.
Then write the letter telling what kind of sentence it is.

t = telling   **c** = commanding

a = asking   **e** = exclaiming

__t__   1. Some fish swim in the ocean **.**

__a__   2. Will you go with me **?**

__e__   3. It is so cold **!**

__a__   4. Does Tim know how to swim **?**

__c__   5. Write your name in the book **.**

__t__   6. The green frog hopped across the pond **.**

__c__   7. Plant the seed in the ground **.**

__e__   8. That was a great game **!**

__a__   9. Do you know your teacher's name **?**

__c__   10. Don't step in that puddle **.**

Name _____

Show What You Know

A **Read the sentences below. Underline the naming part. Circle the action part.**

1. <u>I</u> (like peanut butter.)

2. <u>Jamal and Nico</u> (eat lunch.)

3. <u>They</u> (know where we are going.)

4. <u>Lucy and Avril</u> (pet the puppies.)

5. <u>He</u> (sees a huge spider.)

B **Write a telling sentence.**

_____
_____

C **Write a commanding sentence.**

_____
_____

D **Write an asking sentence.**

_____
_____

E **Write an exclaiming sentence.**

_____
_____

Get Ready to Write

What Is a Personal Narrative?

We use sentences to write stories. A personal narrative is a story about you.

A personal narrative has a **beginning**, a **middle**, and an **ending**. A personal narrative uses the words **I**, **me**, and **my**.

The Beginning

The **beginning** is the first sentence or sentences in a story. The beginning tells what the story is about.

beginning

The wind played a trick on me today. *A brisk breeze took my hat and tossed it across the ground. I chased my hat and grabbed it. Would you like to have the wind treat your favorite hat this way?*

Match each beginning to its story. Write the letter on the line.

a. This morning I had my first skating lesson.

b. I had fun yesterday with a cardboard box.

c. Last week I was riding my bike.

__c__ Dad said it was time to take off my training wheels. I got scared. I started slowly. I pedaled once. I pedaled twice. I couldn't believe it. I was riding all by myself!

__a__ As soon as I moved onto the ice, my feet slid out from under me! My coach helped me up and we started over. I wonder if penguins have this much trouble.

__b__ I made it into a sled. Down a hill I zoomed on my simple sled. What an exciting ride!

The Middle

The **middle** tells what happens in the story.
A story usually has more than one middle sentence.

middle

It was my very first balloon ride. The giant, colorful balloon began to float. People waved to me from the ground. The balloon went higher and higher. *Someday I'd like to go around the world in a balloon.*

Read the beginning and ending sentences below. Write your own middle sentences. Use the word bank for help.

splash	sun	turtle	fish	swim	boat

My Day at the Lake

I had a great day at the lake. _____

_____

_____

_____

_____

_____

_____

_____

I had so much fun that I can't wait to go back again.

The Ending

The **ending** is the last sentence or sentences in a story. The ending finishes the story. It may tell the last thing that happens, ask a question, or tell about a special feeling the writer has.

My brother and I were making cookies. He challenged me to an egg-cracking contest. He neatly cracked an egg with one hand. Then it was my turn. The whole egg, shell and all, plopped into the cookie dough. ⌐I lost the contest, but the cookies were still delicious!⌐

ending

● **Choose the correct ending for each story. Write the letter on the line.**

Nothing tastes better than lemonade on a warm day. My brother and I decided to make some. He cut up the lemons. I squeezed the lemons into a jar. Then I added sugar and water. Dad tasted it and made a funny face. __c__

a. I cannot wait to ride again.

b. I learned that the forest is a noisy place to sleep!

I learned a lot about camping last summer. Owls were hooting all night. Chirping birds woke me up in the morning. __b__

c. I think I will add more sugar next time!

Today was my first time on a subway train. We moved so fast that I could barely stand. I had to hold on tight. In the tunnel it got dark. __a__

Write a Story

A personal narrative is a story about you. You are the star in your story. Remember to use the words **I**, **me**, and **my** to show that the story is about you.

○ **Write a story about a day you remember well. Remember to include**

a **beginning** that tells what the story is about.

a **middle** that tells what happened in the story.

an **ending** that tells the last thing that happened, asks a question, or tells a special feeling.

Beginning   I remember the day I _____

_____

_____

Middle   _____

_____

_____

Ending   It was the _____ day ever.

Writer's Workshop

PREWRITING

Pick a Topic

A personal narrative is a story about you. The topic can be anything that happened to you.

my trip to Florida

my first day of school

my very scary night

the time I won the contest

Raj needs to pick a topic for a personal narrative. Look at his notes.

Write a personal narrative about you. It should be a real story that happened to you. Jot down ideas in your notebook. Think about a time that

- **you were happy**

- **you were really surprised**

- **something funny happened**

- **you were scared by something silly**

Write down as many ideas as you can. Then circle the idea you like best. This will be your topic.

PREWRITING

Plan Your Story

Now Raj must plan his personal narrative. He draws pictures to help him plan his story. He draws pictures of the beginning, the middle, and the ending of his story.

Beginning

Middle

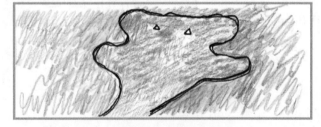

Ending

What pictures come to mind when you think of your story? Draw in your notebook pictures of the beginning, the middle, and the ending. Write **Beginning** next to the beginning pictures. Write **Middle** next to the middle pictures. Write **Ending** next to the ending pictures.

Writer's Workshop

DRAFTING

When you first write your narrative, you are drafting. This is Raj's draft.

> My chair looked like it had a monster on it! So I on the light. Then I laughed. It was just my fuzzy bear. It is funny to be scared of a little, fuzzy bear.

Look at the pictures you drew. Make sure that they are in the right order. Draw more pictures if you need to. Then write a sentence to go with each picture.

Write your draft in your notebook. Use your pictures and sentences to help you. You can also use the words in the word bank if you need help. Remember to write a beginning, a middle, and an ending.

surprise	happy	loud	shiny
scary	warm	fuzzy	laugh

EDITING

When you check your draft, you are editing. Raj uses this Editing Checklist to check his draft.

I don't have a beginning.

Editing Checklist

- ☐ Do I have a beginning?
- ☐ Do I have a middle?
- ☐ Do I have an ending?
- ☐ Is my story about me?
- ☐ Is my story in order?

It was a loud, rainy night. Scary shadows were everywhere. ∧My chair looked like it had a monster on it! So I on the light.

Look at the mistake Raj finds. How does he fix it?

Look at your draft. Then use the checklist. If you spot a mistake, fix it. You might ask a friend to read your story. Friends can help spot mistakes.

REVISING

Raj copies his draft. He adds changes that make the draft better.

Copy your story. Add any changes that will make it better. Fix any mistakes that you find. Make your story the best it can be.

Personal Narratives • 37

Writer's Workshop

PROOFREADING

When you check your words and sentences, you are proofreading. Raj uses this Proofreading Checklist to check his draft.

Proofreading Checklist

☐ Are all the words spelled correctly?

☐ Did I use capital letters?

☐ Did I use the right end marks?

☐ Are the sentences complete?

It was a loud, rainy night.

Scary shadows were everywhere.

My chair looked like it had a monster on it! So I∧on the light.
                                        turned

Look at the mistake that Raj finds. How does he fix it?

Use the checklist to check your draft. Put an **X** next to the questions you can answer yes to. Use these proofreading marks to mark your changes.

Proofreading Marks		
Symbol	**Meaning**	**Example**
∧	add	We∧books. (read)
⟋	take out	~~the~~ the park
⊙	add period	She is smart⊙
≡	capital letter	c̲a̲rl j̲ones
⁄	lowercase letter	He likes S̸occer.

PUBLISHING

When you share your work, you are publishing it. It is an exciting time. Your readers are seeing your very best work.

How will Raj publish his draft?

Are you ready to share your work? Copy your story onto a sheet of paper. Print as neatly as you can. Be sure to copy it exactly. Leave room to draw a picture.

You can share your story in many ways. How will you share yours?

I want to read my story to my mom!

Make a book.

Give it to my parents.

Put it on the bulletin board.

Stormy Night
It was a loud, rainy night.
Scary shadows were everywhere.
My chair looked like it had a
monster on it! So I turned on
the light. Then I laughed.
It was just my fuzzy bear.
... funny to be scared
... e, fuzzy bear.

Make it into a skit.

Read it to a friend.

Frame it.

Decide with your class how to share your story. Come up with new and fun ways.

Remember to keep thinking of new story ideas!

Nouns

In this chapter students will learn about

- nouns
- common nouns
- proper nouns, including days of the week and months of the year
- abbreviations and initials
- singular nouns and plural nouns
- singular possessive nouns
- plural possessive nouns
- compound words

A Visual, Please

Types of Proper Nouns

Commonly Used Proper Nouns	
names of days	Monday
names of months	July
names of holidays	Christmas
family names used as names	Father
titles of respect	Mrs.

Grammar for Grown-ups

What Are You Talking About?

The word *noun* comes from the Latin word *nomen,* meaning "name." A noun is a word that names a person, a place, a thing, or an idea.

Nouns can be categorized in several ways. Common nouns name general people, places, things, or ideas *(boy, church, van, love).* Proper nouns name particular people, places, things, or ideas *(John, Holy Name Church, Ford Windstar, New Deal).*

A singular noun names one person, place, thing, or idea. A plural noun names more than one person, place, thing, or idea. Add *-s* to form the plural of most nouns *(cars).*

Nouns can be made possessive to show ownership. A singular possessive noun is a singular noun that shows ownership *(pet's cage).* A plural possessive noun is a plural noun that shows ownership *(voters' ballots).*

Daily Edits

The Daily Edits for this chapter provide students with daily practice editing sentences. Students should pay special attention to the use and capitalization of nouns.

Begin each day's grammar lesson by writing on the board the Daily Edit. Help students correct the sentence. Then discuss the results as a class. Help students understand what corrections are necessary to make the sentence accurate and complete.

Consider leaving on the board the corrected sentences. Because each week's sentences form a story, there will be context clues to help students find and correct mistakes.

Common Errors

Otherwise Known as "Quit Being So Possessive"

Some developing writers use an apostrophe in a plural noun, unintentionally making it possessive.

ERROR: Some boy's wear blue hats.
CORRECT: Some boys wear blue hats.

ERROR: The apple's are red
CORRECT: The apples are red

Remind students to check all words with apostrophes as they revise their writing. Students should be able to tell whether these words are meant to show ownership or are meant to show more than one person, place, thing, or idea. Have students work together to check and change any errors.

For Kids Who Are Ready

Or "Is It a Compound Word?"

For students who are ready to apply the finer points of grammar to their writing, discuss the following concept:

Not all compound words are written as one word. Some compound words are written as two words. Other compound words are hyphenated.

ONE-WORD COMPOUND: firefighter
TWO-WORD COMPOUND: air bag
HYPHENATED COMPOUND: half-dollar

Share with students the examples above. For extra practice, have students find additional examples of each type of compound word. Tell students to check a dictionary to be sure whether they should write a compound word as one word, two words, or a hyphenated word.

Ask a Mentor

Real Situations, Real Solutions

Dear Grammar Geek,

Are there specific proper noun categories that a second grader should know?

I like lists,
Marguerite

Dear Marguerite,

Display and review the visual on page 40a. Your students might find it helpful when deciding which words to treat as proper nouns.

A fellow list liker,
Grammar Geek

Dear Grammar Geezer,

Many of my students misplace apostrophes when writing possessive nouns. How can I help them understand where to put apostrophes?

My students' (not student's) friend,
Leah from Lynchburg

Dear Leah,

Sometimes the best way to remember how to write a word is to memorize what the word looks like. The possessive forms of irregular plurals such as children's and women's often need to be studied carefully and memorized. One good way to do this is to create and display a special spelling list that consists of tricky possessives.

Taking a trip down memory lane,
Grammar Geezer

"Hey—Cool! I've never
seen a 'dear John' email before."

Friendly Letters

Genre Characteristics

At the end of this chapter, students will write a friendly letter. They will be guided through the writing process in the Writer's Workshop. The completed friendly letter will include the following:

- the date the letter was written
- a greeting that names the recipient
- a body that shares the writer's message
- a closing followed by the writer's name
- correct grammar, spelling, capitalization, and punctuation

Daily Story Starters

The Daily Story Starters for this chapter provide students with practice generating messages for friendly letters. This daily practice helps to prepare students for writing their friendly letters.

Begin each day by writing on the board the Daily Story Starter. Because the audience, or recipient, of a letter often determines the message, help students choose an audience before composing their sentences. Allow time for students to complete their sentences. Help students determine whether their messages are appropriate for the audiences and purposes of their letters. Discuss the results as a class.

Taking It Personally

Friendly letters, or personal letters, are perhaps the most common form of writing for most people. As a genre, friendly letters are unique in almost every way.

While many genres speak to a wide audience, the audience for a friendly letter is usually one person or a small group of people. The purpose of a friendly letter is variable. It might be to share a story or a message, to say thank you, or to ask a favor. Whatever the purpose, ideas in friendly letters reflect a writer's own experience and often share sentiments that forge a personal connection between the writer and reader.

Effective friendly letters follow a standard form that includes the date, a greeting that usually begins with *Dear* and the person's name, a body, a closing, and a signature. The body of a friendly letter shares ideas in a natural voice, often using informal language.

Effective friendly letters have a variety of sentence types for emphasis and impact. These sentences are correct in grammar, spelling, capitalization, and punctuation.

Teacher's Toolbox

Try the following ideas to help your students get the most out of the Writer's Workshop:

- Have students share personal letters, e-mails, or cards with personal messages that they have received.

- Consider taking the class on a field trip to the local post office.

- Create a bulletin-board display of personal letters that you have received, including both e-mails and those sent through the Postal Service.

Reasons to Write

Share with your students the following times at which people write friendly letters. Talk about why it is important to become good writers of letters.

- sharing good news about a grade, an athletic triumph, or a recital

- thanking someone for a gift

- inviting a friend or relative to visit

Literature Links

You can add the following titles to your classroom library to offer your students examples of letters:

Dear Mr. Blueberry by Simon James

Yours Truly, Goldilocks by Alma Flor Ada

The Jolly Postman by Janet and Allan Ahlberg

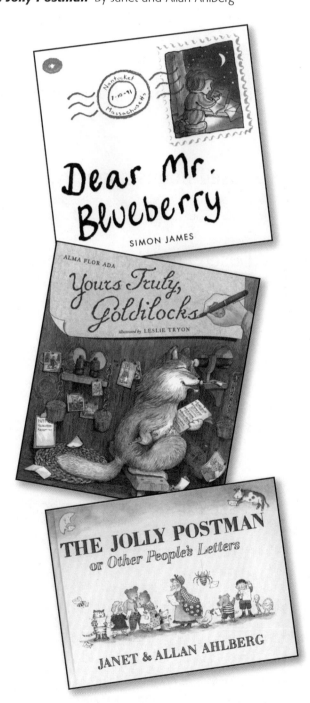

Friendly Letter

	Yes	No
My letter shares a story or a message, says thank you, or asks a favor.	☐	☐
My letter has all the necessary parts.	☐	☐
I used nouns correctly.	☐	☐
I used complete sentences.	☐	☐
I spelled words correctly.	☐	☐
I used capital letters correctly.	☐	☐
I used end marks correctly.	☐	☐

Voyages in English 2

Teacher's Scoring Rubric

Friendly Letter

0 = not evident
1 = minimal evidence of comprehension
2 = evidence of development toward comprehension
3 = strong evidence of comprehension
4 = outstanding evidence of comprehension

	Points
Ideas	
communicates a coherent message, such as a story, an expression of gratitude, or a request	
Organization	
has a date	
has a greeting	
has a body	
has a closing	
has a signature	
Voice	
is written in a natural voice	
Word Choice	
uses nouns correctly	
uses appropriate words	
words are recognizable	
Sentence Fluency	
has correct sentence structure	
Conventions	
grammar	
spelling	
punctuation and capitalization	

Voyages in English 2

Daily Voyages

Daily Edits

Monday	Tuesday	Wednesday	Thursday	Friday
Rain Rane poured down, and Lightning flashed.	lights the lites went out!	searched my mom serched for candles	My dad searched for a flashlite flashlight	i used my light-up robot to see.
chickens The chikens heard a growl	rooster the red ruster gathered the hens.	hurried They huried into the hen house	the A wolf ran into farmyard	The Chickens shut the hen house dor. door
Did you hear about robert's aple? apple	he found a talking werm. worm	what did the Worm say?	Please Plez do not Eat my house	robert did not eat the worms house. worm's
Dr. Grim drove to the Airport on wednesday.	He wanted to fly to london.	dr. Grim got on the wrong air plane. airplane	He landed in japan on thursday.	Dr. Dcr. Grim desided decided he liked Japan.
We traveled to Six lighthouses lighthouse.	Which wich was your favorite?	lighthouse i liked the light house with the ghost.	ghost Did the gost scare you?	The Ghost sang a song four me. for

Daily Story Starters

Monday	Tuesday	Wednesday	Thursday	Friday
This week I made	Today I learned	Thank you for helping me	May I borrow	I want to show you
Thank you for telling me	Will you help me	I like to practice	Thank you for giving me	Can you come to
I heard a joke about	Don't forget to	Can you teach me to	Say hello to	Thank you for making me
I enjoyed your	Yesterday I played	Will you send me	Thank you for taking me	Can you tell me
May I use your	Thank you for sharing your	My favorite toy is	My teacher gave me	My friend is

Chapter Adaptors

WRITING & EDITING

To improve their editing skills, encourage students to check their work one line at a time for each item on the Editing and Proofreading Checklists. Have students take two sheets of paper and place them on the page they are editing so that they can see only one line of text at a time.

DEAR MISS TOOTH FAIRY

Ask students to write a short friendly letter to the tooth fairy. Tell them to include any personal experiences they have had with losing their teeth. Remind students to include all the necessary parts of a friendly letter. Have students draw a picture of the tooth fairy at the bottom of their letters.

RETEACHING

Have students choose a favorite character from a story. Ask students to imagine what that character's home might look like. Then invite students to draw pictures of their characters' homes. Ask students to label the items in their pictures with possessives. (Example: Cinderella's glass slipper)

WISH YOU WERE HERE

Have students make a post card from a fantastic place. (Examples: outer space, land of dinosaurs) Ask students to draw a picture of their imaginary place on one side of a sheet of paper. Then have them write on the other side a short letter to a friend or family member telling about the place they are visiting. Remind students to include all the necessary parts of a friendly letter. Invite students to share their post cards with the class.

RETEACHING

Draw a 3 x 3 grid on a sheet of paper and label the columns Days, Months, and Titles. Photocopy the grid and distribute to partners. Ask partners to fill in each column of the grid with the appropriate abbreviations. For example, under Months students might write Feb., Oct., and Aug. When students have finished, call out a day, month, or title. Tell students that if they have the abbreviation for that word on their grid to draw an X through it. Explain that the first person to complete a row of Xs horizontally, vertically, or diagonally should call out Bingo!

SPEAKING & LISTENING

Read aloud a friendly letter you have received. Be sure to incorporate the elements and characteristics given in the sections Get Ready to Write and Writer's Workshop. Remind students of the elements and characteristics of a friendly letter and what their letters should include. Then invite the class to write a thank-you letter to the principal, school nurse, or a recent class visitor. Write on the board their ideas and the specific parts of a friendly letter. Then guide students to write the thank-you letter. Have students tell which parts were the date, greeting, body, closing, and signature.

ENGLISH-LANGUAGE LEARNERS

English-language learners may need extra help understanding the possessive form of nouns because 's is not used to form possessives in many languages. Have students draw pictures of something they own, such as a pencil, a book, or a toy. Then help students write below the picture the possessive form of his or her name before each noun. (Example: Mario's book)

Nouns and Friendly Letters

Quotation Station

Words have no wings, but they can fly thousands of miles.

—Korean proverb

June 1, 2007

Dear Grandma,

We have a new puppy. Her name is Buttercup. Buttercup's fur is soft and yellow. She likes to swim in the lake. I cannot wait for you to meet her.

Love,
Ava

Nouns and Friendly Letters • 41

Name

Nouns

A **noun** can name a person. A noun can name a place. A noun can name a thing.

Write each noun in the word bank under the correct heading.

farmer	lunch	brother	zoo	farm
Tom	ball	radio	park	

Person	**Place**	**Thing**
farmer	zoo	lunch
brother	farm	ball
Tom	park	radio

A noun names a person, a place, or a thing—
a friend, the park, or a bell that rings,
a boy, a building, a bat, or a ball.
Nouns are words that name them all.

Name _____

More Nouns

Does the underlined noun name a person, a place, or a thing? Circle the answer.

1. Earth is a <u>planet</u>.   **person**   **place**   (**thing**)

2. The <u>rooster</u> crowed at dawn.   **person**   **place**   (**thing**)

3. The boats sail on the <u>lake</u>.   **person**   (**place**)   **thing**

4. The <u>robot</u> belongs to me.   **person**   **place**   (**thing**)

5. We pick flowers in the <u>garden</u>.   **person**   (**place**)   **thing**

6. <u>Tito</u> saw a skunk.   (**person**)   **place**   **thing**

7. A <u>comet</u> has appeared.   **person**   **place**   (**thing**)

8. My <u>dad</u> plays basketball.   (**person**)   **place**   **thing**

9. I took a walk in the <u>park</u>.   **person**   (**place**)   **thing**

10. My <u>sister</u> likes to read.   (**person**)   **place**   **thing**

Writer's Corner

Write a sentence about a person you know. Use a noun.

Nouns • 43

Name _____

Proper Nouns

A **proper noun** can name a special person. A proper noun can name a special place. A proper noun can name a special thing. A proper noun always begins with a capital letter.

*Who is that **girl**?*   *Oh, that is **Maya**.*

A Write each proper noun from the word bank under the correct heading.

| Mayflower | United States | Liberty Bell |
| Florida | Julie | Steve |

Person	Place	Thing
Julie	United States	Mayflower
Steve	Florida	Liberty Bell

B Find the name of the special person, place, or thing in each sentence. Underline the proper noun. Circle the capital letter that begins each proper noun.

1. Miami is a big city.

2. Tara had a birthday party.

3. Did you see the Statue of Liberty?

4. When did you visit Italy?

5. Jory is my brother.

6. Do they like Texas?

Name

The Days of the Week

The names of the days of the week are proper nouns. The name of each day begins with a capital letter.

Sunday	Monday	Tuesday	Wednesday	Thursday	Friday	Saturday

Write the day that answers the question.

1. What is the last day of the week? *Saturday*

2. On what day does the week begin? *Sunday*

3. What is the third day of the week? *Tuesday*

4. On what day do you start school? *Monday*

5. What day comes after Thursday? *Friday*

6. What is the fourth day of the week? *Wednesday*

7. What day comes before Friday? *Thursday*

Nouns • 45

Name

Practice the Days of the Week

Look at the weather forecast. Answer the questions about the weather. Remember, the names of the days of the week are proper nouns. A proper noun begins with a capital letter.

Sunday Monday Tuesday Wednesday Thursday Friday Saturday

20° 27° 33° 30° 33° 40° 50°

1. On which day will it snow? *Wednesday*

2. Which will be the warmest day of the week? *Saturday*

3. Which day will be very cloudy? *Tuesday*

4. Which is the last day it will be 33°? *Thursday*

5. Which day will be a little cloudy? *Monday*

6. Which day will reach 40°? *Friday*

7. Which day of the week will be the coldest? *Sunday*

Name _____

The Months of the Year

The months of the year have special names. They are proper nouns. The name of each month begins with a capital letter.

Trace the names of the months of the year. Begin with January and work down.

January	July
February	August
March	September
April	October
May	November
June	December

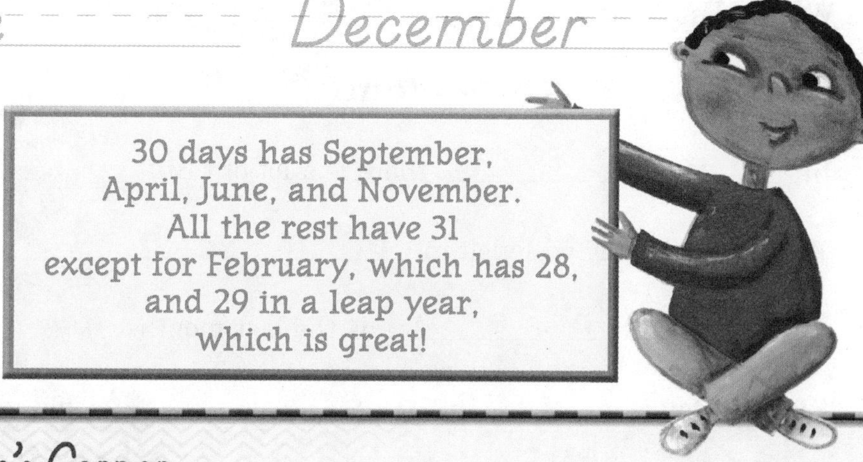

30 days has September,
April, June, and November.
All the rest have 31
except for February, which has 28,
and 29 in a leap year,
which is great!

Writer's Corner

Write a sentence that tells when your birthday is.

_____

Nouns • 47

Name _____

Practice the Months of the Year

Complete each sentence with the name of a month of the year. Remember that each month begins with a capital letter.

January	April	July	October
February	May	August	November
March	June	September	December

1. In N o vem b e r we celebrate Thanksgiving.

2. J anu a r y brings a new year.

3. Halloween is in O c t o b e r .

4. On the Fourth of J u l y, we see a lot of fireworks.

5. We give Valentine's Day cards in F e b ru a r y.

6. Labor Day is in S e p tem b e r .

7. In A p r i l there is a lot of rain.

8. The Easter Bunny will visit in M a rc h .

9. D e cem b e r is the last month.

10. Father's Day is in J u n e .

11. Flowers bloom during M a y .

12. A ugu s t is usually the hottest month of the year.

Name

Abbreviations

An **abbreviation** is a short form of a word. An abbreviation usually begins with a capital letter. Most abbreviations are followed by a period.

A Each day of the week has an abbreviation. Match each day to its abbreviation.

| Sunday | Monday | Tuesday | Wednesday | Thursday | Friday | Saturday |

| Wed. | Sat. | Mon. | Sun. | Tues. | Fri. | Thurs. |

B Some months of the year have abbreviations. Trace each one.

January Jan. February Feb. March Mar.

April Apr. August Aug. September Sept.

October Oct. November Nov. December Dec.

C Abbreviations are used for titles of people. Trace each title.

Dr. Brooks Mrs. Adams Mr. Conroy

D Write the abbreviation for each of these words.

October Oct. Doctor Dr. Monday Mon.

March Mar. Mister Mr. Thursday Thur.

Name

Initials

An **initial** takes the place of a person's name. An initial is the first letter in a name. An initial is always a capital letter. An initial is followed by a period.

Miles Lee Carr **M.L.C.**   Ella Ann Howe **E.A.H.**

A Underline the abbreviation or the initials in each sentence. Place a period after each abbreviation or after each initial.

1. <u>Mr.</u> Ward works in that skyscraper.

2. <u>Jan.</u> is the abbreviation for January.

3. <u>C.M.S.</u> are my initials.

4. <u>Dr.</u> Adams will arrive soon.

5. <u>Tues.</u> is the abbreviation for Tuesday.

B Write the initial for each name. Use a capital letter and a period.

Susan   S.   Mark Garcia   M.G.

Christopher   C.   Becca Wilson   B.W.

C Write your initials after your name at the top of this page.

Name _____

Common Nouns

A **common noun** can name any person. A common noun can name any place. A common noun can name any thing.

Ⓐ **Read the noun in each present. Color the present blue if the noun names a person. Make the present pink if the noun names a place. Color the present yellow if the noun names a thing.**

Ⓑ **Complete each sentence with a noun from the presents.**

1. We have many *pets* .

2. Who is that *boy* ?

3. We read books in the *library* .

4. I drink *milk* every day.

5. Please close the *door* .

6. My *mom* makes dinner for our family.

7. Kim and Matt went to play in the *park* .

8. The *city* has many cars and buses.

Name _____

Common Nouns and Proper Nouns

A **common noun** names any person, place, or thing.
A **proper noun** names a special person, place, or thing.

    girl   *Maggie*

Girl is a common noun. **Maggie** is a proper noun.

Complete each sentence with a noun from the
word bank. If the word is a proper noun, write **p**.
If the word is a common noun, write **c**.

Wood School	ladder	igloo	wind
Morris Library	smoke	Janice	breakfast

1. *Smoke* is coming from the chimney. **c**
2. *Morris Library* has story hour today. **p**
3. A strong *wind* blew the hat away. **c**
4. *Janice* rode a bus. **p**
5. We eat *breakfast* every morning. **c**
6. *Wood School* is closed today. **p**
7. Kevin's *igloo* melted. **c**
8. Firefighters climbed up the *ladder*. **c**

Name

Singular and Plural Nouns

When a noun names one, it is **singular**. When a noun names more than one, it is **plural**. Add the letter **s** to make most nouns plural.

A Look at the picture. Circle the nouns that are plural.

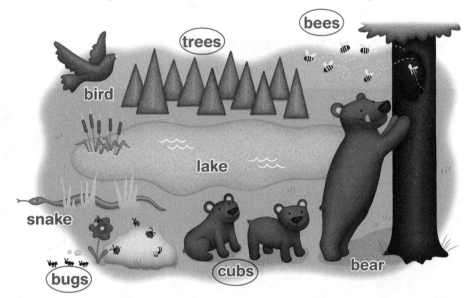

B Underline the correct noun and write it on the line.

1. Linda has two new _hats_ .   (hat <u>hats</u>)

2. Mom made a _salad_ for lunch. (salads <u>salad</u>)

3. All the _ducks_ are white.   (duck <u>ducks</u>)

4. Sandy drew a pretty _picture_ .   (<u>picture</u> pictures)

5. That is my favorite _song_ .   (<u>song</u> songs)

Nouns • 53

Name _____

More Singular and Plural Nouns

Read the sentences below. Then look at the underlined nouns. If the noun is singular, put an **X** in the first box. If the noun is plural, put an **X** in the second box.

	Singular	Plural
1. I have a basket of apples.		X
2. My sister has a cool bike.	X	
3. I hear a loud bell.	X	
4. Are the baseballs in the closet?		X
5. Sarah has three dogs.		X
6. I see two cars.		X
7. Mr. Wade wrote a book.	X	
8. We made a cake for the bake sale.	X	
9. Where are the girls?		X
10. Did you bring my CD?	X	

Writer's Corner

Write about some animals you like. Use a plural noun.

Possessives

A **possessive noun** shows ownership. Here is a way to show possession.

Claire has homework.   It is **Claire's** homework.
Aaron has a dog.   It is **Aaron's** dog.
The kitten has a tail.   It is the **kitten's** tail.

Add an apostrophe and s (**'s**) to show ownership.

A **Underline the word in each sentence that shows possession.**

1. The lion's paw had a thorn in it.

2. Is Ben's picture in the newspaper?

3. Marcy's gerbil won first prize.

4. Kim's crayons were brand new.

5. The bear's fur is dark brown.

B **Write the correct possessive noun.**

1. Anita has books. They are *Anita's* books.

2. The bull has horns. They are the *bull's* horns.

3. The nurse has a cap. It is the *nurse's* cap.

4. The bird has wings. They are the *bird's* wings.

5. The boy has an eraser. It is the *boy's* eraser.

Nouns • 55

Name _____

Singular Possessives

A singular noun names one person or animal.

> *girl*   *Tony*   *tiger*

An apostrophe and s (**'s**) are used to show possession when the noun is singular.

> *girl's*   *Tony's*   *tiger's*

● **Write the singular possessive of each word on the line. Remember to use an apostrophe and s ('s).**

spider	principal	Ryan	Linda
teacher	child	owl	

1. *Linda's* ponytail blew in the wind.

2. Are *Ryan's* gloves on the shelf?

3. Did anyone see the *teacher's* glue stick?

4. An *owl's* eyes are very large.

5. A *spider's* web is often sticky.

6. The *child's* toy was under the table.

7. The *principal's* message was loud and clear.

56 • Chapter 2

Name

Plural Possessives

A plural noun names more than one person or animal.

> boys   '   lions

To show that more than one person or animal
owns something, add only an apostrophe (')
to most plural nouns.

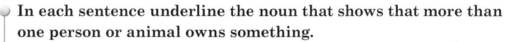

the girls have dolls	the **girls'** dolls
our dogs have food	our **dogs'** food
the teachers have a room	the **teachers'** room

○ **In each sentence underline the noun that shows that more than
one person or animal owns something.**

1. The rabbits' tails are short and stumpy.

2. My sisters' rooms are never in order.

3. The boys' voices echoed in the cave.

4. Can you find the foxes' tracks?

5. The students' papers hung on the bulletin board.

> To show belonging and ownership,
> a possessive is what to use.
> An apostrophe and the letter s
> will tell you whose is whose.

Writer's Corner

Write two sentences with plural possessives.

Name

Possessive Practice

Write the possessive for each sentence.

1. The monkeys have a cage. It is the *monkeys'* cage.

2. The birds have a nest. It is the *birds'* nest.

3. My brothers have cars. They are my *brothers'* cars.

4. The girls have sweaters. They are the *girls'* sweaters.

5. The cats have ears. They are the *cats'* ears.

6. The students have desks. They are the *students'* desks.

7. The teams have bats. They are the *teams'* bats.

8. The bears have a cave. It is the *bears'* cave.

9. The boys wear hats. They are the *boys'* hats.

10. My friends have books. They are my *friends'* books.

Name

Compound Words

A **compound word** is a word that is made by putting two words together.

bluebird   *raincoat*   *hairbrush*

The word **bluebird** is made by putting together the words **blue** and **bird**. What words are put together to make **raincoat** and **hairbrush**?

Underline the compound word in each sentence. Write the two words that make up the compound word. The first one is done for you.

1. We made <u>cupcakes</u>.   *cup* _____ *cakes*

2. Chris bought a <u>birdhouse</u>.   *bird* _____ *house*

3. My aunt is a <u>firefighter</u>.   *fire* _____ *fighter*

4. Look at that huge <u>waterfall</u>.   *water* _____ *fall*

5. My <u>birthday</u> is tomorrow!   *birth* _____ *day*

6. This is a big <u>airport</u>.   *air* _____ *port*

7. Did you see that <u>earthworm</u>?   *earth* _____ *worm*

Nouns • 59

Name

More Compound Words

Make a compound word by choosing the right word from each list. Then write the compound word on the line. The first one is done for you.

1. book **store** *bookstore*
   look
   store
   brush

2. door *mat* *doormat*
   hand
   hammer
   mat

3. camp *fire* *campfire*
   tree
   fire
   burger

4. mail *box* *mailbox*
   box
   card
   paper

5. shoe *lace* *shoelace*
   stone
   shirt
   lace

When you join two words together, you make a compound word. *Butterfly, snowball, and bluebird* are compound words that you have heard.

Name _____

Practice Compound Words

A Answer each riddle with a compound word. Use the words in the word bank to make compound words.

| guard | paper | hook | print |

1. I am at the end of a fishing line.
   What am I?   a fish *hook*

2. I bring news to people every day.
   What am I?   a news *paper*

3. I leave my mark on wet sand.
   What am I?   a foot *print*

4. I work at beaches and swimming pools.
   I save people's lives. Who am I?   a life *guard*

B Match each word in the first list with a word in the second list to make compound words.

1. bird *house*   ball

2. air *plane*   house

3. thunder *storm*   cloth

4. basket *ball*   storm

5. table *cloth*   plane

Nouns • 61

Name _____

Show What You Know

A Look at the underlined noun in each sentence. Write **p** on the line if the noun is a proper noun. Write **c** on the line if the noun is a common noun.

1. A <u>camel</u> does not need much water. **c**
2. It can travel through the <u>desert</u>. **c**
3. <u>Adam</u> can ride a camel. **p**
4. He rides it through the <u>Sahara</u>. **p**
5. His camel has two <u>humps</u>. **c**

B Write the day of the week or the month of the year.

1. What day of the week begins with **M**?   **Monday**
2. What day of the week begins with **F**?   **Friday**
3. Christmas comes during which month?   **December**
4. Which is a summer month?   **June, July, August**
5. What month of the year begins with **M**?   **March, May**

C Write the abbreviation for each word.

1. Doctor   *Dr.*   3. September   *Sept.*
2. Tuesday   *Tues.*   4. Monday   *Mon.*

Name

Show What You Know

A Write the initial for each underlined name.

1. Rose Waters *R.*   3. Brian Taylor *B.T.*

2. John Paul Jones *J.P.*   4. Zoe Mary Ward *Z.M.W.*

B Underline the plural noun in each group.

1. cat, dog, kittens, lion   3. paper, eraser, pencils, crayon

2. girls, boy, child, girl   4. tail, kite, string, trees

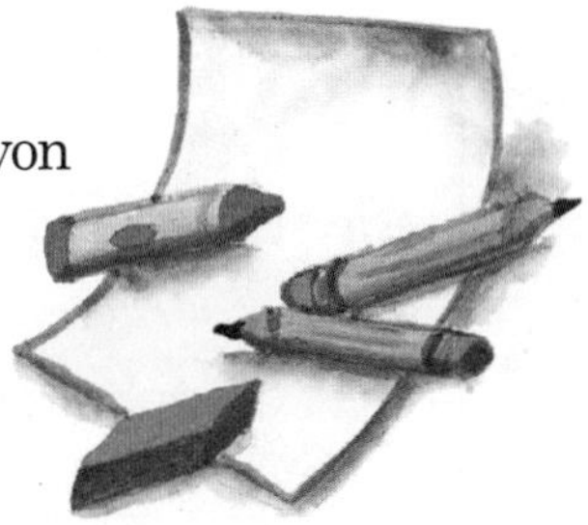

C Write a shorter way of showing possession for the underlined words.

1. The finger Maria has was cut.   *Maria's* finger

2. The shoe Brad has fell off.   *Brad's* shoe

3. The eyes the piglets have are shut.   *piglets'* eyes

4. The rolls the baker has are fresh.   *baker's* rolls

D Choose a word that best completes each compound word.

| where | berry | cut | dream |

1. blue *berry*   3. some *where*

2. day *dream*   4. hair *cut*

Nouns • 63

Nouns and Friendly Letters • 63

Get Ready to Write

What Is a Friendly Letter?

Everyone loves to get a letter. Friendly letters are letters to people we know. Here are some things you can write in a friendly letter.

Share a story or a message.

> I scored a goal today!

Say thank you.

> Thanks for taking me to the park.

Ask a favor.

> Can you teach me how to skate?

Imagine that you are going to write a letter. What are some things you might say? Write an example for each.

Share a story or a message.

_____

_____

Say thank you.

_____

_____

Ask a favor.

_____

_____

64 • Chapter 2

The Parts of a Friendly Letter

Friendly letters have five parts.

Date ——————————————————— March 28, 2007

Greeting ————— Dear Ms. Lee,

Body ————————— Thank you for making cupcakes for our class party. They were delicious. We had so much fun playing games and having snacks. Thank you for thinking of us.

Closing ——————————————— Your friend,

Signature ——————————————— Mr. Cooper

Look at the letter. Then answer the questions.

1. What is the date of the letter? *March 28, 2007*

2. Who wrote the letter? *Mr. Cooper*

3. What is the greeting? *Dear Ms. Lee,*

4. Which part of the letter says thank you? *the body*

5. What is the closing? *Your friend,*

The Five Parts

A friendly letter has five parts.

The **date** tells when the letter was written. The **greeting** tells who the letter is for. The **body** is the message of the letter. The **closing** says goodbye. The **signature** is the name of the person who wrote the letter.

A Match each part in the first list to its part in the second list.

1. date   Dear Luke,
2. greeting   Gavin
3. body   Your friend,
4. closing   August 9, 2007
5. signature   Can you come to my sleepover?

B Name each part of a letter by writing the correct number in the box.

1. body   2. **signature**   3. greeting
4. **closing**   5. **date**

> **5** January 21, 2007
>
> **3** Dear Gina,
>
> **1**   I am sorry you are not feeling well. Will you be back soon? We are doing some fun projects in school. We all miss you.
>
> **4** Your friend,
>
> **2** Rebecca

Putting the Letter Together

These parts of a letter are mixed up. Write the letter correctly. Then write in the boxes the names of the parts of a letter. One is done for you.

| body | signature | greeting | closing | date |

Brandon

Your cousin,

    That book you read sounds cool! May I borrow it? I promise to return it as soon as I am done.

Dear Kira,

August 10, 2008

| **date** | *August 10, 2008* |

Dear Kira, | **greeting**

body | *That book you read sounds cool! May I borrow it? I promise to return it as soon as I am done.*

closing | *Your cousin,*

Signature | Brandon

Writer's Workshop

PREWRITING

Pick a Topic

Friendly letters are letters to people we know. The letter can share a story or a message. It can say thank you. It can ask a favor.

Ava must think of to whom she will write. She also must think about the topic of her letter. Look at Ava's notes.

Friendly letters say different things. They can

share a story or a message.

say thank you.

ask a favor.

tell Grandma about our new puppy

thank Mr. Bernal for the book

ask Jayden to lend me her new video game

Write down as many ideas as you can. Write who your letter will be to. Then circle the idea you like best. This will be your topic.

PREWRITING

Plan Your Letter

Now Ava must plan her letter. She makes a chart to help. She makes sure that her chart has the five parts of a friendly letter.

Date: June 7, 2007
Greeting: Dear Grandma,
Body: got puppy soft yellow likes to swim
Closing: Love,
Signature: Ava

Make a plan in your notebook. Draw a chart like the one Ava made. Be sure to include a **date**, a **greeting**, a **body**, a **closing**, and a **signature**. Write your plan in the chart.

Writer's Workshop

DRAFTING

This is Ava's draft.

> *Dear Grandma,*
>
> *We have a new puppy. Her name is Buttercup. Buttercups fur is soft and yellow. She likes to swim in the lake. I cannot wait for you to meet her.*
>
> Love,
>
> Ava

Look at your chart. Make sure that you have all the parts of a friendly letter. If you think of other things to say, add them to your plan.

Write your draft in your notebook. Use your chart to help you. Remember to include all five parts of a friendly letter.

70 • Chapter 2

EDITING

Ava uses this Editing Checklist to check her draft.

> Dear Grandma, ∧*June 1, 2007*
>
> We have a new puppy. Her name is

I forgot to put the date in!

Look at the mistake Ava finds. How does she fix it?

Use the checklist to edit your letter. Check for one thing at a time. Think about ways to make your letter great. Remember, you can always make more changes later.

REVISING

Ava copies her letter. She adds changes that make it better.

Copy your letter. Make it better than it was before. Add anything from the checklist that you forgot. Add anything that will make your letter a great letter.

Writer's Workshop

PROOFREADING

Ava knows she can make her letter even better. She can make sure that her words and sentences are right. She uses this Proofreading Checklist to check her draft.

Look at the mistake that Ava finds. How does she fix it?

Proofreading Checklist

☐ Are all the words spelled correctly?

☐ Did I use capital letters?

☐ Did I use the right end marks?

☐ Did I use nouns correctly?

June 1, 2007

Dear Grandma,

We have a new puppy. Her name is Buttercup. Buttercup's fur is soft and

Read your story again. Is it better than it was before? Can you answer yes to the questions on the checklist? Put an **X** next to the questions you can answer yes to. If you cannot answer yes, change your draft until you can put an **X** next to the question.

PUBLISHING

When you share your work, you are publishing it. It is an exciting time. Your readers are seeing your very best work.

How will Ava publish her draft?

Copy your letter onto a sheet of paper. Write neatly. Copy everything exactly. Be sure you have all five parts of a letter.

You might draw a picture to go with your letter. Did you thank someone for a new toy? Draw a picture of the toy. Did you write a letter about your new home? Draw a picture of your new home.

The best part about writing a letter is sharing it. How will you share your letter?

I'm going to mail my letter to Grandma!

Deliver it to the person you wrote it to.

Send it to a friend in your class.

Put it on the bulletin board.

Give it to your parents.

Make a classroom mailbox.

Decide with your class how to share your letter. Come up with new and fun ways. And keep writing letters to people you know!

Verbs

In this chapter students will learn about

- action verbs
- verbs in the present tense
- irregular verbs *has* and *have*
- verbs in the past tense
- helping verbs
- verbs that tell what is happening now
- irregular verbs *saw* and *seen*
- irregular verbs *ate, eaten, gave,* and *given*
- irregular verbs *went, gone, did,* and *done*
- being verbs *am, is,* and *are*
- irregular verbs *was* and *were*
- adverbs

A Visual, Please

Interesting Irregular Verbs

Without Helper	With Helper
gave	given
went	gone
did	done
began	begun
broke	broken
knew	known

Grammar for Grown-ups

Meaningful Words

Verb comes from the Latin *verbum,* meaning "word." A verb is a word that is used to describe an action— *Arden jumps*—or a state of being—*I am tired.* Every sentence must have a verb; without a verb the words form an incomplete thought. The main verb in a sentence tells what the subject does or is. A helping verb helps the main verb show an action or state of being: *The girl has cut her hair.*

A verb has four principle parts: present *(run),* present participle *(running),* past *(ran),* and past participle *(run).*

A verb has tenses, including simple present *(send),* past *(sent),* and future *(will send);* present progressive *(am planning),* past progressive *(was planning),* and future progressive *(will be planning);* and present perfect *(have played),* past perfect *(had played),* and future perfect *(will have played).*

Regular verbs form the past and the past participle by adding *-d* or *-ed (boil, boiled, boiled).* The past and the past participle of irregular verbs do not follow any standard rules *(do, did, done).*

In a sentence the verb and the subject must agree. In the present tense *-s* or *-es* is added to the verb when the subject is a singular noun or the pronoun *he, she,* or *it*: *The girl talks. The girls talk.*

Daily Edits

The Daily Edits for this chapter provide students with daily practice editing sentences. Students should pay special attention to the use of verbs, including verb tenses, within each sentence.

Common Errors

Or "Double, Double, Can Cause Trouble"

Many young writers forget that when they add *-ed* to a verb that ends in a consonant preceded by a vowel, they must double the final consonant.

ERROR: The girls skiped down the driveway.
CORRECT: The girls skipped down the driveway.

ERROR: Gary beged for a bike.
CORRECT: Gary begged for a bike.

To help students avoid this common error, post the following rule at the top of a poster and display it in the classroom: *When a verb ends with a consonant that follows a vowel, double the consonant and then add the letters ed.* Invite students to list below the rule several verbs that follow the rule, such as *hopped, trimmed, clapped,* and *dipped.*

For Kids Who Are Ready

Also Known as "Drop It"

For students who are ready, introduce verbs that end in *y* preceded by a consonant, such as *marry, carry,* and *try.*

Explain that when a verb ends in *y* preceded by a consonant, the *y* is changed to *i* before adding *-ed.*

Matt **married** Tracie in Las Vegas.

Hope **carried** the picnic basket.

Lisa **tried** the eggplant.

To help students remember this rule, write the following at the top of a poster and display it for students: *When a verb ends in a consonant and the letter* y, *change the* y *to* i *when adding the letters* ed. Invite students to write on the poster other verbs that follow this rule, such as *fried, buried, studied, copied,* and *dried.*

Ask a Mentor

Real Situations, Real Solutions

Dear Grammar Geek,

Some of my students have trouble with irregular verbs used with helpers. Gave and given got us in trouble! Is there a way I can help my students identify common irregular verbs that use helpers?

Wanting to show some good examples,
Molly in Malibu

Dear Molly,

Display the visual on page 74a and review it with students. As students are exposed to other irregular verbs—such as chose, flown, lain, and mistaken—add them to the chart.

You are a good example,
Grammar Geek

Dear Grammar Geezer,

My students often tell or write stories that mix past and present tense verbs. How can I help them to be consistent?

In this tense, change isn't good,
Phil in Philadelphia

Dear Phil,

Revision is the key to eliminating the problem. Have students read their stories just for verb usage. Explain that if they begin a story in one tense, they should stick with it throughout. Be vigilant as students share stories orally, and help them to choose consistent tenses when they speak. Remember that the way students speak will often transfer to the way that they write.

Changing students' minds,
Grammar Geezer

Adey Bryant: www.CartoonStock.com

ACE GAMES AND PUZZLES
WE ARE HERE
YOU ARE HERE

How-to Articles

Genre Characteristics

At the end of this chapter, students will write a how-to article. They will be guided through the writing process in the Writer's Workshop. The completed how-to article will include the following:

- a topic that explains how to make or to do something
- a clear purpose in the beginning
- a list of needed materials
- a body that lists required steps
- steps listed in logical order
- order words, such as *first, next, then,* and *last*
- correct grammar, spelling, capitalization, and punctuation

Daily Story Starters

The Daily Story Starters for this chapter provide students with practice generating topics for how-to articles. This daily practice helps to prepare students for writing their how-to articles.

Allow time for students to complete the day's sentence. Then discuss the results with the class. Help students determine whether their topics are appropriate for a how-to article. Talk with students about what topics can be easily and clearly covered in a how-to article. Discuss with students who the audience for their how-to articles will be.

How Do You Do That?

How-to writing can offer guidance and direction for accomplishing a task or goal, such as childproofing your home. How-to writing can also provide step-by-step instructions for doing or making something, such as putting together an outdoor grill or making chili.

Effective how-to writing provides a comprehensive, yet concise, explanation of the topic. Ideas are detailed so the reader clearly understands each step of the process. Unimportant or unnecessary information is left out.

An effective how-to writer considers the audience. If the instructions are for children, for example, the language and ideas are appropriate for that age group. A how-to writer also considers the knowledge, background, and experience of the audience.

A how-to article includes an informative introduction, clearly stating the purpose of the piece and what is being taught. The body describes the materials needed and the steps required to accomplish the task or goal in logical order. Finally the piece presents a conclusion that summarizes what was taught, draws a conclusion, or makes a prediction.

Clear, concise steps are essential to effective how-to writing. The steps are presented in the order in which they should be completed. Information can be presented as numbered steps or as logical, sequential paragraphs, depending on the topic. It should be easy to follow from one step to the next through the use of numbers, letters, order words, or anything else that clarifies the order of the process. Throughout an effective how-to article, the writing is correct in grammar, punctuation, capitalization, and spelling.

Teacher's Toolbox

Try the following ideas to help your students get the most out of the Writer's Workshop:

- Guide students to find how-to articles in textbooks, such as science, reading, and social studies. Talk about how these textbooks use forms of how-to writing.

- Provide students with a variety of games that include directions. Help students go over the directions. Then allow groups to play the games. When they have finished, talk about whether the games could have been successfully played without reading the directions.

- Make a bulletin-board display of how-to pamphlets, brochures, recipe cards, and craft articles.

Reasons to Write

Discuss with students why it is important for the following people to become effective how-to writers:

- video game creators

- party planners

- bakers

Literature Links

You can add the following titles to your classroom library to offer your students examples of how-to articles:

The Kids' Multicultural Cookbook: Food & Fun Around the World   by Deanna F. Cook

Easy Art Fun: Do-It-Yourself Crafts for Beginning Readers by Jill Frankel Hauser

My First Book of How Things Are Made by George Jones

How-to Article

	Yes	No
My article tells how to make or do something.	☐	☐
My article has a What You Need list.	☐	☐
My article tells the steps in order.	☐	☐
My article uses order words.	☐	☐
I used verbs correctly.	☐	☐
I used complete sentences.	☐	☐
I spelled words correctly.	☐	☐
I used capital letters correctly.	☐	☐
I used end marks correctly.	☐	☐

Voyages in English 2

Student _____ Date _____

Teacher's Scoring Rubric

How-to Article

0 = not evident
1 = minimal evidence of comprehension
2 = evidence of development toward comprehension
3 = strong evidence of comprehension
4 = outstanding evidence of comprehension

	Points
Ideas	
has a topic that explains how to make or to do something	
Organization	
has a complete list of the necessary materials	
has logical steps organized in list form	
has instructions expressed in step-by-step order	
Voice	
is written in a natural voice	
Word Choice	
uses verbs correctly	
uses order words	
uses appropriate words	
words are recognizable	
Sentence Fluency	
has correct sentence structure	
Conventions	
grammar	
spelling	
punctuation and capitalization	

Voyages in English 2

Daily Voyages

Daily Edits

Monday	Tuesday	Wednesday	Thursday	Friday
Luanne flew to cuba for an Ønion.	Then she took a ~~baot~~ [boat] to belgium.	Luanne arrived in Belgium [in] january.	Belgium has ~~sweat~~ [sweet] raspberries.	~~Luannes~~ [Luanne's] raspberry and onion ~~soop~~ [soup] is yummy.
Sari is a ~~treassure~~ [treasure] Detective.	She ~~have~~ [has] a partner named sulu.	Sari and Sulu ~~rides~~ [ride] horses everywhere.	They ~~has~~ [have] many ~~advenchures~~ [adventures].	They ~~has~~ [have] not ~~fond~~ [found] any treasure yet.
Mr. Hive was ~~look~~ [looking] for a mummy.	The sad mummy was ~~traped~~ [trapped] in a pyramid.	Mr. Hive ~~wiggleed~~ [wiggled] through a crack.	The mummy [was] happy to have a ~~frend~~ [friend].	They ~~playd~~ [played] checkers all ~~nite~~ [night].
Did you see the Yellow spider.?	the spider ~~are~~ [is] as big as a bus.	This morning I ~~seed~~ [saw] it at the ~~libary~~ [library].	Jackie has ~~saw~~ [seen] it talking to ~~to~~ a man.	The spider is ~~try~~ [trying] to get to cleveland.
We ~~gone~~ [went] to the ~~cirkus~~ [circus] too late.	the bears quietly ~~eated~~ [ate] dinner.	The ~~klowns wipeed~~ [clowns wiped] off their makeup.	The circus owner ~~were~~ [was] sad for ~~use~~ [us].	He ~~gived~~ [gave] us ~~tikets~~ [tickets] for tomorrow.

Daily Story Starters

Monday	Tuesday	Wednesday	Thursday	Friday
A relative taught me to	At school I made	My hobby is	A strange thing I made was	In the winter I like to make
Once I planted	I taught someone how to	One time I baked a	It was fun when I built	I learned how to make
My favorite snack to make is	The prettiest thing I made was	My favorite game is	My friends want to know how I	My friend taught me to
I often like to	It was fun to make	I can do	Last summer I learned how to	I know how to cook
One chore I have is	I can draw a	I know how to decorate	Outside I like to play	I can take care of

Chapter Adaptors

SPEAKING & LISTENING

Ask students to write action verbs on the board. Then read aloud a story that uses several action verbs, substituting in order the verbs on the board for the action verbs in the story. Pause before reading each verb and ask students which ending the verb should have. *(s, ed, or no ending)* Repeat to create more nonsense stories.

ENGLISH-LANGUAGE LEARNERS

Write several simple sentences on the board, using the different verb forms taught in this chapter. *(Examples: Tim kicks the ball. The students ride the bus. Ellie and Clare are singing. Joseph played baseball yesterday.)* Then draw two columns on the board. Label the first column *Noun* and the second *Verb*. Invite volunteers to come to the board, choose one sentence, and write the noun from the naming part of the sentence and the verb from the action part in the appropriate column. Remind students why a verb has a particular ending. *(Example: Played ends in ed because it tells about what Joseph did yesterday.)* Then guide students to come up with their own sentences.

SILLY RECIPES

Ask students to imagine that a strange creature has arrived at their home for dinner. *(Examples: unicorn, creature from outer space)* Tell students that the creature eats unusual foods. Have students write what they might make for the creature to eat and how to cook it, using order words. *(Examples: grasshopper slime pie, worm and walnut stew)* Then have students draw a picture of their dinner guest and what it is having for dinner. Invite volunteers to share their recipes and drawings.

RETEACHING

Give students a simple game or task, such as tick-tack-toe or planting a seed. Guide students to write step-by-step instructions for completing the action. Suggest that students act out each step. When students have finished, invite volunteers to share their instructions. Have the rest of the class play the game or pantomime the action. Discuss whether any steps need to be revised and why.

WRITING & EDITING

Tell students that one way to be sure that all the steps of a how-to article are included is to have a friend or family member act out the steps, one by one. Tell students to take notes about any steps that were difficult to follow. Encourage students to add details wherever necessary to make their how-to articles clearer and more complete.

RETEACHING

Write on separate note cards the steps needed to complete simple tasks. *(Examples: making a sandwich, building a snowman)* Shuffle each set of cards and have small groups work together to arrange in the correct order the cards for each task. Have students write out the complete task, using order words. Then ask students to draw each step. When they have finished, invite students to share their work.

CHAPTER 3

Verbs and How-to Articles

How to Make an Ice-Cream Sundae

Ice-cream sundaes are fun to make and to eat.

What You Need

bowl   whipped cream

ice cream   cherry   chocolate sauce

Steps

1. First put a scoop of ice cream in a bowl.

2. Next cover the ice cream with chocolate sauce.

3. Then put on some whipped cream.

4. Last top with a big cherry.

Is your mouth watering yet? Go ahead and eat!

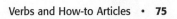

Name

Action Verbs

A **verb** is a word that shows action. You cannot have a sentence without a verb.

You do many actions during the day. You walk, talk, play, and read. *Walk, talk, play,* and *read* are action verbs.

Underline the verb in each sentence. Then write the verb on the line.

1. The bell rings. *rings*

2. The duck waddles. *waddles*

3. Birds fly. *fly*

4. Rabbits hop. *hop*

5. Dogs bark. *bark*

6. The horse gallops. *gallops*

7. Our canary sings. *sings*

8. Babies laugh. *laugh*

Run and *jump* and *play* and *sing*— these are action words. When you want to show what happens, use an action verb.

Writer's Corner

Write a sentence about an action you like to do. Use one of the verbs above if you need help.

Name _____

More Action Verbs

Many verbs are action words. In speaking and writing, you use many different action words.

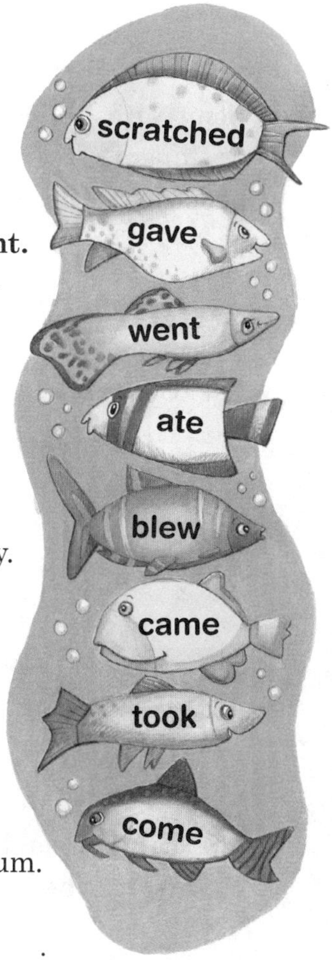

A **Complete each sentence with a verb on the right.**

1. At the ball game, we *ate* hot dogs.

2. Did he *come* with you?

3. The farmer *gave* the horses some hay.

4. Our dog *scratched* his nose.

5. Jack *came* here to see us.

6. Yesterday our club *went* to the museum.

7. Our teacher *took* us to see the aquarium.

8. The fan *blew* the papers across the room.

scratched

gave

went

ate

blew

came

took

come

B **Write two sentences. Use a verb from the fish in each sentence.**

1. _____

2. _____

Name _____

Verbs in the Present Tense

Some verbs tell what happens often. When a verb tells what **one** person or thing does often, add the letter **s**. When a verb tells what **two or more** people or things do often, do not add the letter **s**.

one:

Devin **reads** every day.

more than one:

Rene and Ana **read** after dinner.

Ⓐ Complete each sentence with the correct verb on the right.

1. Dave *listens* to the teacher.

2. The men *paint* houses.

3. Gerry *jumps* rope.

4. The door *opens* wide.

open	opens
jump	jumps
paint	paints
listen	listens

Ⓑ Find in each sentence the verb in the present tense. Write the verb on the line. If it ends in s, circle the s.

1. Casper barks every night. *bark(s)*

2. Beth and I hear him in our bedroom. *hear*

3. Casper covers his eyes with his paws. *cover(s)*

4. He sees the moon in the sky. *see(s)*

Name _____

Has and *Have*

Has and **have** are verbs in the present tense.

Has is used when you speak about **one** person, place, or thing.

*Tommy **has** a guitar.*

Have is used when you speak about **more than one** person, place, or thing.

*Sato and Mari **have** a new kitten.*

Have is also used with the words **I** and **you**.

*I **have** a toothache.*   *You **have** a funny mask.*

A Underline the correct verb to complete each sentence. The first one is done for you.

1. Chuck (has have) a kite.
2. Plants (has have) roots.
3. The castle (has have) a tower.
4. A dog (has have) four legs.
5. You (has have) blue eyes.
6. An orange (has have) vitamin C.

B Write **has** or **have** to complete each sentence.

1. Do you *have* any pets?

2. I *have* a funny poem.

3. The salad *has* tomatoes in it.

4. This cow *has* a calf.

5. I *have* a purple skateboard.

Verbs • 79

Name _____

Verbs in the Past Tense

Some verbs tell what happened in the past. Add the letters **ed** to most verbs to make them tell action in the past.

present:

*The girls **walk** the dog every morning.*

past:

*The girls **walked** the dog yesterday.*

If a verb ends in a silent **e**, drop the **e** before adding the letters **ed**.

*dance   danc**ed***

Complete each sentence with a verb from the word bank.

> leaked   wiggled   filled
> climbed   laughed

1. Water *leaked* out of the pipe.

2. Alex *filled* the water jug.

3. The boys *laughed* at the clowns.

4. A worm *wiggled* on the beach.

5. The tiger *climbed* the tree.

Name

More Verbs in the Past Tense

Some verbs tell what happened in the past. If a verb ends with a consonant following a vowel, the consonant is usually doubled before adding the letters **ed**.

skip   *skip**ed***

A **Drop the silent e and add the letters ed to each verb. Write the verb on the line.**

1. smile *smiled*   3. like *liked*

2. tape *taped*   4. hope *hoped*

B **Double the final consonant and add the letters ed to each verb. Write the verb on the line.**

1. mop *mopped*   4. step *stepped*

2. hop *hopped*   5. beg *begged*

3. jog *jogged*   6. trim *trimmed*

Writer's Corner

Write a sentence about something you did yesterday.
Use a verb in the past tense.

Verbs • 81

Name _____

Working with Verbs

A The first sentence tells about something that happens often. Complete the second sentence with a verb that tells what happened in the past. Use the word bank.

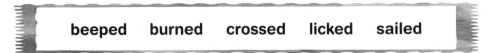

| beeped | burned | crossed | licked | sailed |

1. The boat <u>sails</u> on the water.   The boat *sailed* on the water.

2. The children <u>cross</u> the street.   The children *crossed* the street.

3. The cat <u>licks</u> her paws.   The cat *licked* her paws.

4. The driver <u>beeps</u> his horn.   The driver *beeped* his horn.

5. The candle <u>burns</u> slowly.   The candle *burned* slowly.

B Write **has** or **have** to complete each sentence.

1. Josh *has* a new backpack.

2. You *have* never seen a whale?

3. I *have* a pet turtle.

4. The American flag *has* 50 stars.

Name

More Work with Verbs

A **Add the letters ed to make the verb past tense.**

1. Yesterday I *talked* on the phone. **talk**

2. Sarah *picked* berries. **pick**

3. I *walked* the dog yesterday. **walk**

4. Last week I *climbed* a tree. **climb**

B **Drop the silent e and add the letters ed.**

1. The baby *smiled* at me. **smile**

2. My uncle *lived* in France. **live**

3. Sue *baked* oatmeal cookies. **bake**

4. Allison *tickled* her brother. **tickle**

C **Double the final consonant and add the letters ed.**

1. Scott *stopped* to see you after school. **stop**

2. Everyone *clapped* after the band played. **clap**

3. Min *dropped* a penny into the well. **drop**

4. I *dipped* the banana in chocolate. **dip**

Verbs • 83

Name _____

Hurrah for Helping Verbs

A **helping verb** helps another verb tell the action in the sentence.

*Jamie **will catch** some big fish.*

The verb is **catch**. The helping verb is **will**.

A Circle the helping verb in each sentence. The verb it helps is underlined.

1. A beaver (can) <u>make</u> the most interesting hideout.
2. Its home (is) <u>made</u> of sticks and stones.
3. You (will) <u>find</u> the beaver's home in a stream.
4. A beaver (will) <u>repair</u> its home at night.
5. This beaver (was) <u>building</u> a home.

B Complete each sentence with a helping verb from the word bank.

may	am	are	will	have

1. The fish *are* swimming.

2. I *am* running in the track race.

3. It *may* rain on our picnic tomorrow.

4. Pogo *will* hide in his doghouse during storms.

5. The cows *have* stood for an hour under the tree.

Is and *was* and *will* and *can*— these verbs help other verbs. When the action in a sentence needs a hand, you use a helping verb.

Name _____

Verbs That Tell What Is Happening Now

Some verbs show an action that is happening now. Add the letters **ing** to show an action that is happening now. Use the helping verbs **am, is,** or **are.**

jump   *jump**ing***

*The dolphins **are jumping** in the water.*

Show that these actions are happening now. Add the letters ing to each verb.

1. Who is *answering* the door? **answer**

2. We are *sailing* the boat. **sail**

3. I am *listening* to the radio. **listen**

4. May I ask who is *calling* ? **call**

5. The girls are *painting* pictures. **paint**

6. Who are you *pointing* to? **point**

7. Hallie and Ashley are *talking* . **talk**

8. Heather is *playing* the piano. **play**

Writer's Corner

Write a sentence about something you see now. Use a verb with the letters *ing.*

Name

More Things That Are Happening Now

When a verb ends in a silent **e**, drop the **e** before adding the letters **ing**. Remember to use the helping verbs **is, am,** and **are.**

> *We dance.*   *We are danc**ing.***

When a verb ends with a consonant following a vowel, the consonant is usually doubled before adding the letters **ing**.

> *She skips.*   *She is skipp**ing.***

A Drop the silent **e** and add the letters **ing** to each verb.

1. My aunt is *baking* cookies.   **bake**

2. Alex and Eli are *making* a sandcastle.   **make**

3. I am *moving* away.   **move**

4. Brad is *hoping* to borrow that book.   **hope**

B Double the final consonant and add the letters **ing** to each verb.

1. The dogs are *begging* for a bone.   **beg**

2. My brother is *jogging* in the rain.   **jog**

3. Corn is *popping* in the kitchen.   **pop**

4. I am *flipping* pancakes.   **flip**

Name

Verbs Review

Remember that adding the letters **ing** shows that an action is happening now. If a verb ends in a silent **e**, drop the **e** and add the letters **ing**.

Ⓐ **Add the letters ing to each verb.**

1. I am *joining* the Nature Club. **join**

2. An acorn is *falling* from the tree. **fall**

3. The teacher is *talking* to the class. **talk**

4. Dan is *milking* the cow. **milk**

5. What is Daryl *pointing* to? **point**

Ⓑ **Drop the silent e and add the letters ing to each verb.**

1. The children are *raking* the leaves. **rake**

2. Celia is *hoping* we will visit Gram. **hope**

3. Uncle Al is *taping* the show for us. **tape**

4. My friends are *skating* in the park. **skate**

5. I think that dog is *smiling* ! **smile**

Verbs • 87

Name _____

More Verbs Review

If a verb ends with a consonant following a vowel, double the consonant before adding the letters **ing**.

A **Double the consonant and add the letters ing to each verb.**

1. The fish are *flipping* in their bowl.   **flip**

2. My dad was *chatting* with his friends.   **chat**

3. James and Lee are *mopping* the floor.   **mop**

4. The frogs are *hopping* really high!   **hop**

5. Why are we *stopping* ?   **stop**

B **Write a sentence about each picture. Use the verb under each picture. The verb should end in ing.**

comb

_____
_____

clap

_____
_____

Name _____

Saw and Seen

Some verbs are not strong. They need help doing their job.

Saw is a strong verb. **Saw** never needs a helper. **Seen** is not a strong verb. **Seen** always needs a helper. Some helpers are **has, have, am, is, are, was,** and **were.**

*Alexis **has seen** the stars every night.*

Ⓐ Underline the correct verb in each sentence. Watch for helpers.

1. Who has (saw <u>seen</u>) the planet Venus?

2. I (<u>saw</u> seen) it through a telescope.

3. The red glow around Venus was (saw <u>seen</u>) by Emily.

4. Jacob and Madison (<u>saw</u> seen) the planet Mercury.

5. Mike and Hannah have (saw <u>seen</u>) the rings around Saturn.

Ⓑ Write saw or seen to complete each sentence. Remember to look for helpers.

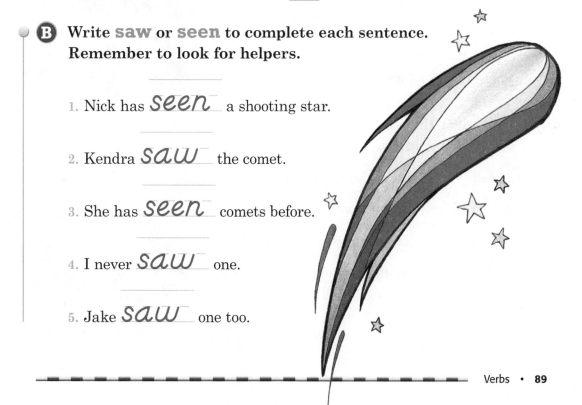

1. Nick has *seen* a shooting star.

2. Kendra *saw* the comet.

3. She has *seen* comets before.

4. I never *saw* one.

5. Jake *saw* one too.

Verbs • 89

Name

Ate and *Eaten, Gave* and *Given*

Remember that some verbs need help doing their job. Some helpers are
has, have, am, is, are, was, and **were**.

Ate is a strong verb. **Eaten** is not a strong verb. **Eaten** always needs a helper.

*The cat **has eaten** the cheese.*

Gave is a strong verb. **Given** is not a strong verb. **Given** always needs a helper.

*Abby **has given** Jessica a talking pencil.*

A **Underline the correct verb in each sentence.
Watch for helpers.**

1. Andy (<u>ate</u> eaten) cereal for breakfast.

2. He has (ate <u>eaten</u>) all the grapes.

3. Laura (<u>ate</u> eaten) the bread.

4. The crust was (ate <u>eaten</u>) by the robins.

5. A gray squirrel (<u>ate</u> eaten) the acorn.

B **Underline the correct verb in each sentence.
Watch for helpers.**

1. Julio has (gave <u>given</u>) the boys a piece of apple pie.

2. I (<u>gave</u> given) my parakeet some water.

3. A birthday gift was (gave <u>given</u>) by Paul.

4. Some flies were (gave <u>given</u>) to the spider.

5. Olivia (<u>gave</u> given) a loud shout.

Name _____

Went and Gone, Did and Done

Remember that some verbs need helpers. Some helpers are **has, have, am, is, are, was,** and **were.**

Went is a strong verb. **Gone** is not a strong verb. **Gone** always needs a helper.
*The mice **have gone** down the hole.*

Did is a strong verb. **Done** is not a strong verb. **Done** always needs a helper.
*The dishes **were done** before Luis went outside.*

Ⓐ Write **went** or **gone** to complete each sentence.

1. Danny has *gone* to Cartoon World.

2. Julie *went* to New York City.

3. We *went* to the beach.

4. Will has *gone* to soccer camp.

5. Tyler was *gone* in a flash.

Ⓑ Underline **did** or **done** to complete each sentence.

1. Beth has (did <u>done</u>) well.

2. We have (did <u>done</u>) the first page.

3. Billy (<u>did</u> done) the painting.

4. The project was (did <u>done</u>) by Regina.

5. Brandon (<u>did</u> done) his work at school.

Verbs • 91

Name _____

Am and Is

Some verbs do not show action. These verbs are called **being verbs**. **Am** and **is** express being.

Use the being verb **am** with the word **I**.

   I am *six years old.*

Use the being verb **is** when you tell about **one** person, place, or thing.

   Lisa is *six years old.*

A **Underline the correct verb in each sentence.**

1. The bag of popcorn (<u>is</u> am) on the counter.
2. I (is <u>am</u>) in a new school.
3. The earth (<u>is</u> am) home for many insects.
4. She (<u>is</u> am) the winner of the contest!

B **Complete each sentence with the correct being verb.**

1. I *am* learning about animals.
2. A fox *is* is a sly animal.
3. A lion *is* a large cat.
4. I *am* not a fish.
5. An elephant *is* a huge animal.
6. I *am* a mammal.

Name _____

Are

Verbs that do not show action are called being verbs. Some being verbs are **am** and **is**. **Are** is another being verb.

Use the being verb **are** when you tell about **more than one** person, place, or thing.

> *Jon and Anne **are** seven years old.*

Also use **are** with the word **you**.

> *You **are** a funny person.*
> *You **are** good singers.*

A **Underline the correct verb in each sentence.**

1. You (is <u>are</u>) my best friend.
2. Candace (am <u>is</u>) the tallest girl in class.
3. They (<u>are</u> am) going to the park.
4. Dean and Adam (<u>are</u> is) twins.
5. I (<u>am</u> are) a fast reader.

B **Write your own sentences. Use each being verb below.**

1. **am** _____
   _____

2. **is** _____
   _____

3. **are** _____
   _____

Verbs • 93

Name _____

Was and Were

Was and **were** are being verbs.

When you write about **one** person, place, or thing, use **was**.

> *Dave **was** outside.*

When you write about **more than one** person, place, or thing, use **were**.

> ***Jorge and Matt** **were** outside.*

Also use **were** with the word **you**.

> *You **were** late for the game.*

Ⓐ Underline the correct verb in each sentence.

1. Cole (<u>was</u> were) with me.

2. Dawn and Shelby (was <u>were</u>) at the party.

3. The girls (was <u>were</u>) in the pool.

4. The plumber (<u>was</u> were) in the basement.

Ⓑ Complete each sentence with was or were.

1. Many grapes _were_ on the vine.

2. Gold _was_ in the stream.

3. A million earthworms _were_ in the soil.

4. This raisin _was_ a grape.

5. A pot of gold _was_ at the end of the rainbow.

Am, is, are, was, and were—
these are being words.
When you do not show action,
you use a being verb.

Name _____

Watching for Helping Verbs

Remember, some verbs are strong. Some verbs need helping verbs.
Remember to look for **has, have, am, is, are, was,** and **were.**

A Underline **saw** or **seen** to complete each sentence.
Look for helpers.

1. Susan (<u>saw</u> seen) that movie.

2. Jeff has (saw <u>seen</u>) that movie too.

3. Tessa and Amy (<u>saw</u> seen) a play instead.

4. Gretchen has (saw <u>seen</u>) both.

B Underline the correct verb to complete each sentence.
Look for helpers.

1. We have (ate <u>eaten</u>) hot dogs.

2. They (<u>did</u> done) that many times.

3. Jonah (<u>ate</u> eaten) the orange.

4. The men (<u>went</u> gone) to the party.

5. We were (went <u>gone</u>) by five o'clock.

6. Tony (<u>gave</u> give) Tasha the game.

7. The cookies were (did <u>done</u>) in 20 minutes.

8. Will you (gave <u>give</u>) me the basketball?

Verbs • 95

Name _____

Watching for Being Verbs

Remember, some verbs can express being. Look for **am, is, are, was,** and **were.**

A Underline the correct verb to complete each sentence.

1. The teacher (<u>was</u> were) glad we won the prize.

2. I (<u>am</u> is) a good swimmer.

3. Many books (is <u>are</u>) in the library.

4. Three boys (was <u>were</u>) in the wagon.

5. The sun (<u>is</u> are) a star.

6. You (is <u>are</u>) always on time.

B Complete each sentence. Use a word from the word bank. Use each word only once.

are	is	was	were	am

1. Kim and Ken *are* twins.

2. Randy *was* happy.

3. Cindy *is* a soccer star.

4. Celia and Aaron *were* at their grandma's house.

5. I *am* taller than my sister.

Name _____

Adverbs

An **adverb** is a word that tells more about a verb.

Some adverbs tell **how** something happens. These words often end in **ly**.

The sun shone brightly.   *The rabbit ran quickly.*

How did the sun shine?   *How did the rabbit run?*

      brightly   **quickly**

Complete each sentence with an adverb from the word bank.

> **gently loudly neatly slowly proudly carefully**

1. Billy *neatly* arranged the books on the shelf.

2. Our class yelled *loudly* at the game.

3. The turtle moved *slowly* down the road.

4. The team *proudly* showed their trophy.

5. The breeze blew *gently*.

6. Mom let me *carefully* hold my baby brother.

Writer's Corner

Write your own sentence. Use the adverb *quietly*.

Name _____

Show What You Know

A Underline the verb in each sentence. If the verb is in the present tense, write **present** on the line. If the verb is in the past tense, write **past** on the line.

1. The boats <u>sailed</u> from the harbor.   *past*

2. Carol <u>returned</u> her books to the library.   *past*

3. Milla <u>paints</u> a pretty picture.   *present*

4. The rain always <u>fills</u> the bucket.   *present*

5. We <u>traveled</u> by train across the United States.   *past*

B Complete each sentence. Show that something is happening now by adding the letters **ing** to the verb.

1. The children are *clapping* for the singers.   **clap**

2. Tonya is *skating* on the lake.   **skate**

3. Patty Rabbit is *hopping* home.   **hop**

4. Brian is *chatting* with my sister.   **chat**

5. The water is *dripping* in the sink.   **drip**

Name _____

Show What You Know

A **Underline the two verbs in each sentence. Then circle the verb that is the helper.**

1. Shannon (has) gone to the computer lab.
2. The alligators (have) eaten a tasty dinner.
3. The class (is) planning a Halloween party.
4. They (are) going to school.
5. An apple (was) given to Joely.

B **Underline the correct verb to complete each sentence.**

1. Last week I (see saw) an aardvark.
2. Our class (ate eaten) three pizzas.
3. You (was were) the first one to answer.
4. Martin (has have) a new piano.
5. He (went gone) to the zoo.
6. Andy and Sam (has have) caught many fish.
7. Kristy and Tim (is are) leaving tomorrow.

C **Underline the adverb that tells how in each sentence.**

1. The paper wasps' nest is made perfectly.
2. They make a nest carefully.
3. The wasps patiently make the cells of paper.
4. Each row of cells is neatly arranged.
5. I slowly walked away from the nest.

Get Ready to Write

What Is a How-to Article?

You can share how to do things in a how-to article. A how-to article teaches others how to make something or do something.

Title — | HOW TO MAKE A PAPER SNOWFLAKE

Beginning — | It's simple to make a paper snowflake.

What You Need list —

What You Need

white paper   glitter   scissors   glue

Steps to complete the activity —

Steps
1. First fold your paper two times.
2. Next cut a few shapes around the edge of the paper.
3. Then carefully unfold your paper.
4. Last add glue and a little glitter.

Answer these questions about the how-to article.

1. What is the how-to article about?

making a paper snowflake

2. Where do you learn what the topic is?

in the Beginning

3. Where do you find out what you will need?

in the What You Need list

4. Where do you learn about the steps you need to follow?

under Steps

Order in a How-to Article

When you give directions, it is important to think about the right order. The words **first**, **next**, **then**, and **last** tell the correct order.

● **The steps below are not in order. Write the order words First, Next, Then, and Last to tell the correct order.**

Ⓐ *First* — stay calm during the fire drill.

Last — go outside.

Then — walk down the hall in a line.

Next — leave the classroom quietly.

Ⓑ *Then* — open your eyes.

Next — count to 10.

Last — tag the first person you see.

First — close your eyes.

First
Next
Then
Last

Steps in a How-to Article

Where does each step belong? Write it on the correct line.

freeze for an hour.	pour juice into the tray.

eat them!	put a craft stick in each cube.

Have you ever made frozen pops? All you need is juice, an ice-cube tray, and craft sticks.

1. **First** *pour juice into the tray.*

2. **Next** *put a craft stick in each cube.*

3. **Then** *freeze for an hour.*

4. **Last** *eat them!*

put the soil into the cup.	cover the seed with soil.

water it.	press the seed into the soil.

Start your own garden. You need a seed, a cup, some soil, and water.

1. **First** *put the soil into the cup.*

2. **Next** *press the seed into the soil.*

3. **Then** *cover the seed with soil.*

4. **Last** *water it.*

Plan a How-to Article

Think about something you know how to make.
Fill in the blanks. Write what you need. Draw a
picture of each step.

How to _____

Making _____ is easy and fun.

What You Need

Steps

1. **First**

3. **Then**

2. **Next**

4. **Last**

Writer's Workshop

PREWRITING

Pick a Topic

A how-to article tells how to do something or make something. The topic can be anything you know how to make or do.

how to play kickball

how to make peanut butter surprise

how to make a bank

how to make an ice-cream sundae

Ben is writing a how-to article. Look at Ben's topic ideas.

List or draw your topic ideas in your notebook. Then think about each idea. Is it something you are an expert at making? Is it something you are a star at doing? Is it something others would like to learn?

Circle the topic you like best. Then write it below.

My topic is:

How to _____

PREWRITING

Plan Your How-to Article

Now Ben must plan his how-to article. First he writes a What You Need list. Then he writes his steps on separate sentence strips.

WHAT YOU NEED

bowl   whipped cream

ice cream   cherry

chocolate sauce

Steps

put ice cream in bowl

cover with chocolate sauce

put on whipped cream

top with a cherry

Now plan your how-to article. Write a What You Need list in your notebook. Then think about the steps. Think about what your reader needs to know. Write your steps on separate sentence strips or sheets of paper. Then put your steps in the right order.

Writer's Workshop

DRAFTING

This is Ben's draft.

How to Make an Ice-Cream Sundae

Ice-cream sundaes are fun to make and to eat.

What You Need

bowl   whipped cream

ice cream   cherry   chocolate sauce

Steps

1. First put a scoop of ice cream in a bowl.

2. Next covered the ice cream with chocolate sauce.

3. Put on some whipped cream.

4. Last top with a cherry.

Is your mouth watering yet? Go ahead and eat!

Look at your plan. Be sure your sentence strips are in the right order. Add anything that will make your draft clear.

Write your how-to article in your notebook. Use your plan as you write. Include everything you listed in your plan.

To show when something happens, use the words **first**, **next**, **then**, and **last**.

EDITING

Ben uses this Editing Checklist to check his draft.

Editing Checklist
- ☐ Do I tell how to make or do something?
- ☐ Do I have a beginning?
- ☐ Do I tell readers what they will need?
- ☐ Do I list the steps in order?
- ☐ Do I use order words?

1. First put a scoop of ice cream in a bowl.
2. Next covered the ice cream with chocolate sauce.
   Then
3. ʌPut on some whipped cream.

I forgot an order word!

Look at the mistake Ben finds. How does he fix it?

Now is the time to make your paper great. Use the Editing Checklist. Try reading your draft aloud. When you find a spot that could be better, mark it on your paper.

REVISING

Ben revises his draft. He writes a new copy. He includes his changes from editing.

Copy your draft. Add anything that will make your draft better. Take out anything that is not helpful.

Writer's Workshop

PROOFREADING

Ben uses this Proofreading Checklist to check his draft.

Proofreading Checklist

☐ Are all the words spelled correctly?

☐ Did I use capital letters?

☐ Did I use the right end marks?

☐ Are all the verbs used correctly?

1. First put a scoop of ice cream in a bowl.

2. Next ~~covered~~ cover the ice cream with chocolate sauce.

3. Then put on some whipped cream.

Look at the mistake that Ben finds. How does he fix it?

Read your how-to article again. Use the checklist to check your draft. Check for one thing at a time. Use the proofreading marks chart at the back of this book. Remember, you can also ask a friend to proofread your draft.

PUBLISHING

Look at how Ben publishes his how-to article. Remember, when you share your work, you are publishing.

Are you ready to share your work? Copy it onto a sheet of paper. Copy your words exactly. Publish the best copy of your work.

You might draw a picture to go with your how-to article. You can draw a picture of the things your reader needs. You can draw a picture of the steps. Or you can draw a picture of what the thing they are doing or making looks like.

Sharing your writing is a great way to show what you know. How will you publish your writing? Decide with your class. Use one of these ideas or one of your own.

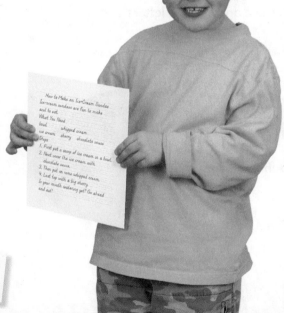

Make a poster.

Do a demonstration.

Put in a class How-to Book.

Read it to the class.

Give it to a friend who wants to learn something new.

Pronouns and Adjectives

In this chapter students will learn about

- pronouns
- using *I* and *me*
- adjectives
- sensory words
- adjectives that compare

A Visual, Please

Spelling Adjectives That Compare

When an adjective ends in e,

drop the e and add the letters *er* or *est*.

nic~~e~~ + est = nicest

When an adjective has a single vowel before a final consonant,

double the final consonant and add the letters *er* or *est*.

thin + n + est = thinnest

Grammar for Grown-ups

Standing In

Pronoun comes from the Latin prefix *pro-*, meaning "for," and the Latin root *nomen*, meaning "name." Pronouns are words used in place of nouns. Some pronouns have the qualities of person, gender, number, and case.

Pronouns indicate person. Pronouns in the first person identify the speaker. Pronouns in the second person identify the person spoken to. Pronouns in the third person identify the person or thing spoken about. Third person singular pronouns reflect gender.

The three cases of personal pronouns are subject *(I, you, he, she, it, we, they)*, possessive *(mine, yours, his, hers, its, ours, theirs)*, and object *(me, you, him, her, it, us, them)*. A subject pronoun must always agree with its verb: *She cries, they cry.*

Tell Me All About It

Adjective comes from the Latin word *adjectivum*, meaning "something that is added." An adjective modifies the meaning of a noun or a pronoun.

Adjectives can be used to count *(three, sixty, fourth)* or to describe *(sandy, clear, red)*. They can come before the words they modify *(bright sun, salty tears)*, or they can come after linking verbs as subject complements: *She is smart. The roses are red.*

Daily Edits

The Daily Edits for this chapter provide students with daily practice editing sentences. Students should pay special attention to their use of pronouns and adjectives in each sentence.

Common Errors

Otherwise Known as "Am I I *or am I* me?"

Many speakers and writers make the common error of placing *I* and *me* in the wrong part of a sentence.

ERROR: Hannah and me went to school.
CORRECT: Hannah and I went to school.

ERROR: Leo gave the cookies to Carly and I.
CORRECT: Leo gave the cookies to Carly and me.

To help students avoid this common error, write on the board the following sentence: *I like me.* Guide students to identify *like* as the verb of the sentence. Explain that in sentences *I* usually comes before the verb and *me* usually comes after the verb.

For Kids Who Are Ready

Or "Did Him *Do It?"*

Many students will distinguish between subject and object pronouns based on an intuitive understanding of spoken language. The student book offers practice with the subject pronoun *I* and the object pronoun *me.* If students are ready to learn other subject pronouns and object pronouns, discuss the following concepts with them:

The subject pronouns *I, you, he, she, it, we,* and *they* are used in the naming part of a sentence, before the action verb. The object pronouns *me, you, him, her, it, us* and *them* are used in the action part of a sentence, after the action verb.

ERROR: They gave the medal to he.
CORRECT: They gave the medal to him.

ERROR: Her stopped at the store.
CORRECT: She stopped at the store.

Share the above examples with students. Expand on the concept with additional examples.

Ask a Mentor

Real Situations, Real Solutions

Dear Grammar Geek,

Is there a good way to help my students correctly spell adjectives that compare when there are spelling changes in the base word?

Hoping for help,
Helen in Hartford

Dear Helen,

Display the visual on page 110a and invite students to refer to it when writing adjectives that compare. Leave the visual on display during tests, even spelling tests, as a reminder for students.

Hoping that helps, Helen,
Grammar Geek

Dear Grammar Geezer,

Some of my students have gone overboard adding -er and -est to adjectives! What do I do when Ann tells me she saw "the boringest movie last night?"

Grateful (not Gratefuller) for your help,
Mr. G

Dear Mr. G,

Gently explain that for some adjectives that have more than two syllables and for adjectives of three or more syllables, they should use more to compare two things and most to compare more than two things. Thus, I saw the boringest movie last night becomes I saw the most boring movie last night. Consistently correct these errors in students' speech and remind them to check for this error in their writing.

The most grateful grammarian,
Grammar Geezer

Descriptions

"When you described it as a remote house in the country…….."

Adey Bryant: www.CartoonStock.com

Genre Characteristics

At the end of this chapter, students will write a description. They will then be guided through the writing process in the Writer's Workshop. The completed description will include the following:

- a beginning that names the topic
- a middle that describes a person, a place, a thing, or an event
- vivid adjectives
- sensory words
- correct grammar, spelling, capitalization, and punctuation

Daily Story Starters

Some Daily Story Starters for this chapter provide students with practice brainstorming topics for descriptions, real or imaginary. Other Daily Story Starters provide students with practice writing sentences that describe the familiar or imaginary. This daily practice helps students understand how to choose topics and also broadens students' understanding of how descriptions are useful in all kinds of writing.

Begin each day by writing on the board the Daily Story Starter. Allow time for students to complete the sentence. Then discuss the results as a class.

Talk with students about what topic is suggested by the completed sentence. Help students determine when a topic is a good topic for a description. Allow students to compare sentences in order to demonstrate the varied ways the same topic can be described.

Describe It for Me

An effective description is like a photograph—an image that seems almost real. Whether it is part of a longer piece of writing or complete in itself, its focus on the topic is sharp and distinct, so the reader always knows exactly what is being described. Its content is illustrative, developing and printing a picture in the reader's mind.

The writer of an effective description captures the reader's attention with an informative beginning, keeps the reader engaged in a middle with logical connections, and crafts a summarizing ending that leaves a lingering impression. Rich sensory details make the piece both satisfying and informative. The language is always appropriate for the audience.

The description may be organized using time order, spatial order, or order of importance. A description is well constructed, and the sentences flow from one to the other in a logical progressive order. These sentences are correct in grammar, spelling, capitalization, and punctuation.

Teacher's Toolbox

Try the following ideas to help your students get the most out of the Writer's Workshop:

- Encourage students to keep a journal or picture journal to write or draw their impressions of interesting people, places, things, or events.

- Add to your classroom library literature rich in descriptive language.

- Create a bulletin-board display of descriptive marketing materials, such as descriptions of appealing vacation spots, toys, or food.

Reasons to Write

Share with students the following list of people who write descriptions. Discuss why it is important to become a good writer of descriptions.

- video game creators

- movie or book reviewers

- scientists who study volcanoes

Literature Links

You can add to your classroom library the following titles to offer your students examples of descriptions:

Alice Ramsey's Grand Adventure by Don Brown

Frog and Toad All Year by Arnold Lobel

Abuela by Arthur Dorros

Description

	Yes	No
My description tells about a person, a place, a thing, or an event.		
My description has a topic sentence that grabs the reader.		
My description uses sensory words.		
I used pronouns and adjectives correctly.		
I used complete sentences.		
I spelled words correctly.		
I used capital letters correctly.		
I used end marks correctly.		

Voyages in English 2

© Loyola Press

Teacher's Scoring Rubric

Description

- 0 = not evident
- 1 = minimal evidence of comprehension
- 2 = evidence of development toward comprehension
- 3 = strong evidence of comprehension
- 4 = outstanding evidence of comprehension

Ideas	Points
is about a person, a place, a thing, or an event	
Organization	
has a beginning that includes a topic sentence	
has a logical sequence	
Voice	
is written in a natural voice	
Word Choice	
uses pronouns and adjectives correctly	
uses sensory words	
words are recognizable	
Sentence Fluency	
has correct sentence structure	
Conventions	
grammar	
spelling	
punctuation and capitalization	

Voyages in English 2

Daily Voyages

Daily Edits

Monday	Tuesday	Wednesday	Thursday	Friday
greg planted seeds around a round his his house.	The seeds grew greew into pretty prety Purple plants.	watered Greg water his plants evary every day.	One On day he forgot to turn off the water watter.	jungle A purple jungl swallowed his House.
rusty The car rusty was brokin broken.	A Family of squirrels lived in the old car.	Trey came along and ficksed fixed the Car.	nice he was nise to let the squirrels staye stay.	him They helped he clean cleen the car.
and I I and Fred found a crab on the beech beach.	me The crab pinched I on the Ear!	dance I did a funny danse because my ear hert hurt.	to then the crab ran to quickly the water.	leave l alone Fred and me will leev crabs a lone.
makes My Uncle make soft pretzels.	has He have pretzel parties on sundays.	uncle's My uncles pretzels and are salty tasty.	to He wants build a pretzel factory factry.	he builds I hope him build factory the factry soon!
like catch My brothers likes to katch Butterflies.	They biggest Them caught the bigest butterfly in the world wirld.	butterfly bigger the butter fly was bigest than a Bowling ball.	pulled It pull my brothers across a field feild.	They decided the Thay decide to let go of big butterfly.

Daily Story Starters

Monday	Tuesday	Wednesday	Thursday	Friday
The jungle is	I like the smell of	Snowflakes are	Space creatures are	On the moon, everything is
I like to visit	My racecar would be	My favorite drink is	I like to build	An animal I like is
On sunny days I go to	The bottom of the ocean is	My favorite thing is	I like it when I hear	I took a trip to
I have an interesting	My favorite room is	Pirates wear	The inside of a submarine is	If I were six inches tall, I would
Rainy days are	I like to pretend I live	The desert is	My favorite food is	My cave would be

Chapter Adaptors

SPEAKING & LISTENING

Invite volunteers to describe their favorite food without saying what it is. Ask students to use sensory words. Encourage students to include what they know about how the dish is made. Have volunteers guess what food is being described.

RETEACHING

Ask students to draw a picture that shows their favorite season of the year. Then have students write below their drawings a topic sentence that could begin a description of their season. Remind students that a topic sentence grabs the reader's attention. Display students' work around the room.

USE YOUR SENSES

Collect in a bag several items that can be described by using the senses. *(Examples: a candle, an orange, a pen, tape, a bell)* Have students take turns wearing blindfolds and choosing one item from the bag out of sight of the rest of the class. Tell the blindfolded students to use their senses to describe the item. Then have the rest of the class guess the item.

RETEACHING

Choose a brief story that is appropriate for students' reading level and that uses pronouns. Photocopy and distribute the story to the class. Read aloud the story and have students follow along. Then have students go on a pronoun scavenger hunt, circling all the pronouns they can find in the story. When students have finished, invite volunteers to read aloud one of the sentences with a pronoun. Then help students use the story to determine what noun or nouns the pronoun is replacing.

SPEAKING & LISTENING

Write sentences on the board about a field trip or other activity the class has recently enjoyed. Include sentences that use adjectives that compare. Leave a space on the board where the adjective should go. As you read aloud each sentence, have students suggest adjectives that describe the noun in that sentence. Write the suggested adjectives underneath each sentence in list form. Have students read the sentence several times, using a different adjective each time.

WRITING & EDITING

After students finish their five-senses charts in the Writer's Workshop, have them exchange their charts with partners. Encourage students to look over their partner's chart and to suggest additional sensory words that are appropriate for the topic. Remind students that they do not have to use their partner's suggestions in their drafts.

ENGLISH-LANGUAGE LEARNERS

In many languages adjectives follow nouns. Some English-language learners may need extra practice using adjectives in English correctly. Guide students to understand that the adjective is usually placed before the noun. *(Example: the rusty car)* Ask students to say nouns that name things and adjectives that describe them. *(Examples: dog, ball; little, red)* Write on the board the nouns and adjectives in list form. Have students come up with sentences that use the nouns and adjectives from the lists. *(Example: The little dog barked.)*

CHAPTER 4

Pronouns, Adjectives, and Descriptions

Nothing is better than the pond next to my house. All around it are big rocks. I like to dip my feet in the cool water. I love the sweet smell of lilacs. Sometimes Liam and I visit the pond together. We nibble the tangy huckleberries that grow nearby. The frogs and the crickets sound like a crowd of people talking.

Name _____

Pronouns

A **pronoun** is a word that takes the place of a noun or a group of nouns. Some pronouns you might know are **I**, **you**, **they**, **her**, **me**, **he**, **him**, **it**, and **us**.

it   he   they   you   we   her

Circle the pronoun in the second sentence that takes the place of the underlined noun or nouns.

1. Ann has <u>the present</u>.   Ann has (it.)
2. <u>The book</u> is on the shelf.   (It) is on the shelf.
3. <u>Sue and Rob</u> came to my house.   (They) came to my house.
4. <u>Tom</u>, saddle the horse.   (You) saddle the horse.
5. <u>John and I</u> went to the park.   (We) went to the park.
6. Peggy gave <u>Lynn</u> a gift.   Peggy gave (her) a gift.
7. <u>Ryan</u> has a small robot.   (He) has a small robot.
8. <u>Meg's cousins</u> played outside.   (They) played outside.
9. <u>Brad</u> saw Mike.   (He) saw Mike.
10. Kim found <u>her trumpet</u>.   Kim found (it.)

> *I, me, she, he, it, we, you,* and *they*—
> these pronouns just might come your way.
> They stand in for nouns; they take their place,
> like *he* for Jim or *it* for vase.

Name

More Pronouns

Complete each sentence with the correct pronoun. The pronoun should take the place of the underlined noun or nouns.

1. Abby will carry that box.

   She will put it on the table.

2. Karen and I are not home.

   We are in the pool.

3. Where is my ticket?

   Do you have *it* ?

4. Let's watch Joe practice.

   Do you see *him* ?

5. Jack pitched the ball.

   Did you see how far *he* threw it?

6. Aunt Celine gave Jesse and me the basket.

   She also gave *us* the blanket.

he
She
it
We
us
him

Writer's Corner

Write a sentence about doing something with your best friend.
Use the pronoun *we.*

Pronouns and Adjectives • 113

Name _____

Practice with Pronouns

A pronoun is a word that takes the place of a noun.

● **Write the correct pronouns to complete these stories.**

they She It

GOLDILOCKS

Goldilocks went to visit the three bears.

She liked the little bear's cereal.

It tasted delicious. When

the three bears came home, *they*

were surprised to see Goldilocks.

He him you it

THE STUMPY TAIL

Bear wanted to catch some fish. *He* was

very hungry. "I will put my tail in the icy pond,"

he said. When he pulled out his tail, *it*

snapped off. What a surprise to *him* !

Were *you* surprised too?

Name _____

Pronouns Review

A **Write the correct pronoun to complete each sentence.**

1. The book belongs to Caden and Tim.

   Please give it to *them* .

2. Kate is going to the mall.

   May I go with *her* ?

3. Chloe and I like dinosaurs.

   We read books about them.

4. Connor and Bailey can sing.

   They sang a duet for the show.

5. Kara showed Jacob her computer.

   She let *him* use it.

B **Underline the correct pronoun to complete each sentence.**

1. (She Her) reads adventure books.

2. Ryan bought (she her) a new pencil.

3. Did you put (they them) in the closet?

4. (They Them) are my friends.

5. (He Him) threw the ball.

6. Maggie took (he him) to the zoo.

7. (We Them) are doing our math problems.

8. (Me You) have a sweater like mine.

Pronouns and Adjectives • 115

Name _____

Pronouns *I* and *Me*

I and **me** are pronouns. Use **I** and **me** when you talk about yourself. Use **I** in the naming part of a sentence. Use **me** in the action part of a sentence.

John and **I** *are friendly.*
I *am friendly.*

The pony is for **me.**
Andy bought tickets for Jeff and **me.**

● **Read these sentences aloud. Listen for the pronouns I and me. Underline I or me in each sentence. Notice that I is always a capital letter.**

1. <u>I</u> want to row the boat.

2. Ally let <u>me</u> try.

3. She watched <u>me</u> row across the lake.

4. My sister and <u>I</u> had a picnic on the shore.

5. Ally let <u>me</u> roast the marshmallows.

Name _____

More Work with *I* and *Me*

A Write **I** or **me** to complete each sentence.

1. Noah and *I* walked through the forest.

2. *I* found a fossil.

3. He told *me* he'd never seen one.

4. *I* told him it is a print in a stone.

5. Ava and *I* wrote a funny poem.

6. The teacher gave Ava and *me* a prize.

7. Miss Lane told *me* to read it to the class.

8. *I* like to write poems.

B Write your own sentence using the pronoun **I**.

_____

C Write your own sentence using the pronoun **me**.

_____

Pronouns and Adjectives • **117**

Name _____

Using *I* in Sentences

Sometimes **I** can be used in the middle of a sentence. This makes a sentence more interesting.

Here is a different way to begin a sentence.

1. Think of a place.

2. Think of what you do there.

3. Make a sentence.

*At home **I** do the dishes.*

A **Make a sentence. Match each group of words in the first list with a group of words from the second list.**

a place	what I do there
1. At the circus __d__	a. I play soccer.
2. In school __c__	b. I feed the chickens.
3. On the farm __b__	c. I learn to read.
4. On the playground __a__	d. I watch the funny clowns.

B **Follow the same directions as above to make more sentences.**

1. At the movies __b__	a. I meet many people.
2. At camp __a__	b. I eat popcorn.
3. Under the oak tree __d__	c. I buy food.
4. In the store __c__	d. I rest.

Name

Practice Using *I* in Sentences

Write your own sentences. First think of a place. Use the pictures for help. Then think of what you do there.

1. *In the car*

2. *At the zoo*

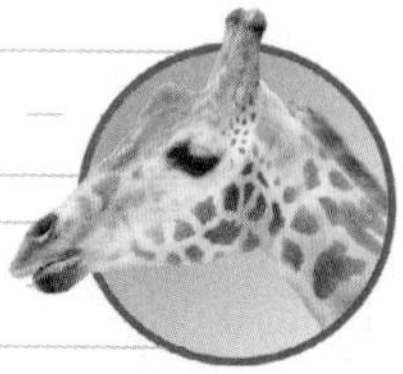

3.

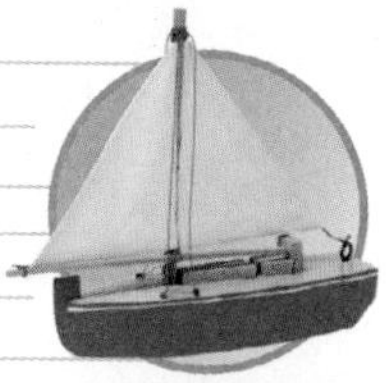

4.

5.

Writer's Corner

Write a sentence about a place you go to and what you do there. Use *I* in the middle of the sentence.

Pronouns and Adjectives • 119

Name _____

Pronoun Review

Pronouns are words that take the place of nouns. Some pronouns are about you. Some pronouns are about other people, animals, or things.

A **Write I or me to complete each sentence.**

1. The coach picked _me_ for the team.

2. Is the present for _me_ ?

3. Brody and _I_ met at the door.

4. Ryan, Olivia, and _I_ went to the store.

5. Josh lent _me_ his bike.

6. May Amelie and _I_ go with you?

B **Circle the correct pronoun for the underlined word or words.**

1. Dave and I travel together.   They   (We)
2. Yue Wan and Jenny are in the pool.   (They)   We
3. The pencil should be sharpened.   She   (It)
4. Jacy, ride your bike home.   (You)   Him
5. I gave Adia a birthday present.   (her)   she
6. Did Emily give that to Tyler and me? we   (us)
7. Where is Justin going?   (he)   him
8. I went with Jose and Maria.   they   (them)

Name _____

More Pronoun Review

A Complete each sentence with a pronoun from the word bank. Use each pronoun once.

| We | he | him | It | I | me |

1. *We* are getting Oscar ready for a race.

2. Sara and *I* gave Oscar some turtle food.

3. *It* is Oscar's favorite snack.

4. Sara takes good care of *him*.

5. She asked *me* to fill his water dish.

6. Sara and I hope *he* is the winner.

B Underline the correct pronoun to complete each sentence.

1. (<u>He</u> Him) got a new watch for his birthday.
2. I wrote (she <u>her</u>) a long letter.
3. Damon watched (they <u>them</u>) play ball.
4. (<u>She</u> Her) plays the radio softly.
5. (<u>It</u> Him) was a sunny afternoon.
6. A spaceship carried (<u>them</u> they) to the moon.
7. Mr. Kovach told (they <u>us</u>) about the eclipse.
8. (<u>We</u> Us) take ballet lessons.

Pronouns and Adjectives • 121

Name

Adjectives

An **adjective** tells about a noun. Adjectives describe nouns.
They can tell how something looks, feels, sounds, tastes, or smells.

*Ann has **brown** hair.*   *The baby has **little** toes.*

*Joe lives in a **big** house.*

**Use an adjective from the word bank to
complete each sentence.**

chilly	slow	funny	Red	six	soft

1. The *funny* clown made me laugh.

2. *Red* leaves fell from the trees.

3. My rabbit has *soft* fur.

4. Peter caught *six* fish.

5. It is a *chilly* day.

6. The *slow* turtle lost the race.

An adjective's
a special word
that tells about a noun.
Some adjectives
to describe a shoe
are *big*, *smelly*, or *brown*.

Name _____

More Adjectives

Look at the underlined noun in each sentence. Circle the adjective that tells about the noun. The first one is done for you.

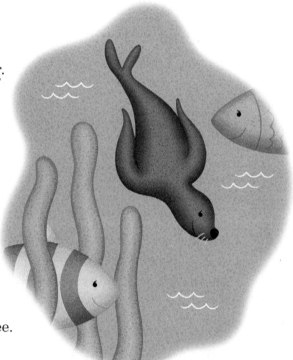

1. The (tiny) seal drank milk.

2. The (white) milk tasted good.

3. The seal fell into the (blue) water.

4. The (little) seal swam around.

5. His (brown) body was a blur.

6. A (gray) squirrel builds a house.

7. The house is a (big) nest.

8. The nest is in a (small) tree.

9. (Tasty) nuts are hidden in the tree.

10. Don't disturb this (busy) animal.

Writer's Corner

Write a sentence about your school. Use an adjective that describes *school*.

Name _____

Practice with Adjectives

A Circle the adjective in each sentence. Underline the noun that the adjective describes.

1. Our town has a (shady) <u>park</u>.

2. There are (old) <u>statues</u> in the park.

3. There is a statue of a man with a (long) <u>beard</u>.

4. The man holds a (large) <u>book</u>.

5. Another statue is of a (giant) <u>horse</u>.

6. There are (new) <u>benches</u> by the horse.

7. The club has (long) <u>meetings</u>.

8. We will have our (spring) <u>picnic</u> there.

B Complete each sentence with the correct adjective. Use the adjectives in the bell. Then underline the noun that the adjective describes. **Possible answers shown.**

cracked
curious
helpful
historic
important

1. Kate saw the *historic* <u>Liberty Bell</u>.

2. The *helpful* <u>guide</u> told the bell's history.

3. The *curious* <u>visitors</u> asked questions.

4. When it was new, this *important* <u>bell</u> hung in Independence Hall.

5. The *cracked* <u>bell</u> does not ring anymore.

Name

Sensory Words

People have five senses. They are **sight, sound, smell, taste,** and **touch**. Some adjectives tell about how things look, sound, smell, taste, or feel. These adjectives are called **sensory words**.

*We watch the **bright** sunrise.*   *I love **buttery** popcorn.*

*I listen to the **loud** cars.*   *The puppy has **soft** fur.*

*She wears **sweet** perfume.*

A **Match the sensory words to the thing being described.**

1. sour smoke, orange flame   a. a teakettle
2. bumpy walnuts, sweet chocolate   b. a window
3. sharp thorns, soft petals   c. a campfire
4. whistling noise, white steam   d. a rose
5. dusty curtains, smooth glass   e. a brownie

B **Read the story. Write a sensory word that tells about the underlined noun. Use the words in the word bank.**

sweet	Loud	bright	sour	gritty

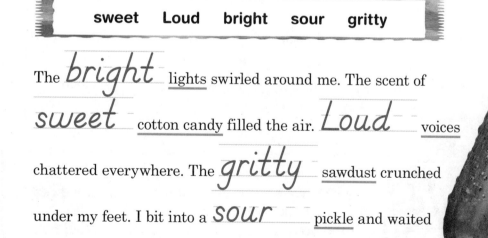

The *bright* lights swirled around me. The scent of *sweet* cotton candy filled the air. *Loud* voices chattered everywhere. The *gritty* sawdust crunched under my feet. I bit into a *sour* pickle and waited for the show to start.

Name

More Sensory Words

A Circle the sensory word that describes each underlined noun.

1. Deserts are (dry) areas.
2. Deserts have (hot) days.
3. Animals in deserts are usually (small) creatures.
4. (Colorful) flowers bloom in the desert.
5. That cactus has (red) flowers.

B Write the adjective that best describes each noun.
Use an adjective from the word bank. **Answers will vary.**

broken	silly	heavy	loud
pretty	soft	spicy	warm

1. the _____ girl

2. a _____ clown

3. a _____ backpack

4. the _____ window

5. a _____ blanket

6. a _____ coat

7. the _____ music

8. the _____ food

Five senses help us describe the world
we see, we smell, we taste, we touch, we hear.
Use sensory words when you write,
and your description will be loud and clear.

Name _____

Adjectives That Compare

To compare two people, places, or things, add the letters **er** to an adjective. To compare three or more people, places, or things, add the letters **est** to an adjective.

long   *long**er***   *long**est***

A **Underline the adjective in each sentence that ends in er or est.**

1. The sky is <u>brighter</u> today than yesterday.
2. This is the <u>newest</u> flower in the garden.
3. The <u>coolest</u> spot is under the tree.
4. The kitten was <u>slower</u> than the rabbit.
5. Megan is <u>taller</u> than Brent.

B **Practice adding the letters er and est to these adjectives. Write the new words on the lines.**

	er	est
1. fast	*faster*	*fastest*
2. cold	*colder*	*coldest*
3. hard	*harder*	*hardest*
4. short	*shorter*	*shortest*
5. strong	*stronger*	*strongest*

Pronouns and Adjectives • 127

Name _____

More Adjectives That Compare

Some adjectives end in a consonant and have a short vowel sound before the consonant. To make these adjectives compare, double the consonant before adding the letters **er** or **est**.

 hot   *hot**ter***   *hot**test***

Some adjectives end in silent **e**. To make these adjectives compare, drop the silent **e** before adding the letters **er** or **est**.

 cute   *cut**er***   *cut**est***

A **Make these adjectives compare by doubling the consonant and adding the letters er or est.**

	er	est
1. sad	*sadder*	*saddest*
2. thin	*thinner*	*thinnest*
3. big	*bigger*	*biggest*

B **Make these adjectives compare by dropping the e and adding the letters er or est.**

How do you make adjectives that compare? Add -er or -est. These letters help you write about more than two or three.

	er	est
1. large	*larger*	*largest*
2. simple	*simpler*	*simplest*
3. gentle	*gentler*	*gentlest*

Name _____

Adjective Review

A **Underline the adjective in each sentence.**

1. A <u>giant</u> tree is near the house.

2. It has <u>rough</u> bark.

3. In autumn it has <u>colorful</u> leaves.

4. The leaves fall on a <u>windy</u> day.

5. It is fun to jump into the <u>biggest</u> pile of leaves.

B **Complete each sentence with a sensory word from the popcorn box.**

1. I ran across the *smooth* marble floor to the snack stand.

2. The *buttery* scent of popcorn filled my nose.

3. We got popcorn and *sour* candy.

4. We found seats in the *dark* theater and waited for the movie to start.

5. When the *loud* music began to play, I sat back to enjoy the show!

buttery
smooth
sour
dark
loud

Writer's Corner

Write a sentence with the adjective *softest*. Then write a sentence with the adjective *safer*.

Name

More Adjective Review

A Add the letters **er** and **est** to each adjective. If an adjective ends in a consonant and has a short vowel, double the consonant before adding the letters **er** or **est**. If an adjective ends in silent **e**, drop the silent **e** before adding the letters **er** or **est**.

	er	est
1. thin	*thinner*	*thinnest*
2. great	*greater*	*greatest*
3. nice	*nicer*	*nicest*
4. dark	*darker*	*darkest*
5. short	*shorter*	*shortest*

B Complete each sentence with the correct adjective from the word bank. You will not use all of the adjectives.

| tiny | careful | loud | cold | old | bright |

1. The *bright* moon shone in the sky.

2. Dawn licked a *cold* ice-cream cone.

3. The truck made a *loud* noise as it stopped.

4. A *tiny* mouse slid into the hole in the floor.

Name _____

Colorful Poems

You can write your own poems about colors. Here is a poem about the color white.

*White is the color of
a fluffy cloud,
a wet snowball,
and a scoop of vanilla ice cream.*

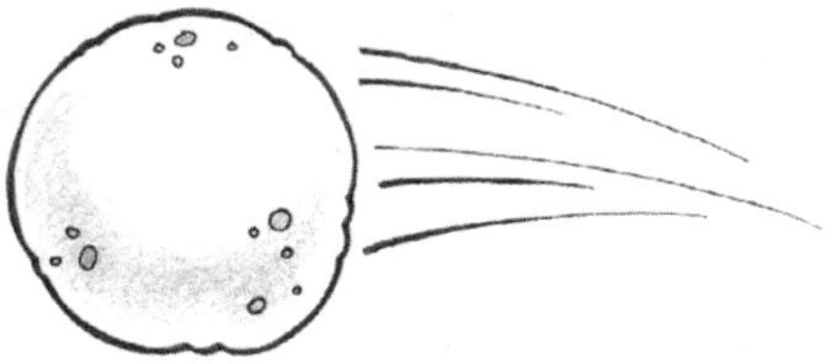

A **Finish these poems. Think of things that are each color. The poems do not have to rhyme.** Answers will vary.

Yellow is the color of
a shiny ring,
a spoonful of honey,
_____

and _____ .

Red is the color of
a pretty valentine,
_____
a _____ ,
and a screeching fire engine.

B **Write a poem about colors. On the first line, write the name of a color you like. On the next three lines, write three things the color makes you think of. Use adjectives to describe the things.**

_____

_____ is the color of

_____ ,

_____ ,

and _____ .

Name _____

Show What You Know

Ⓐ Read the words in the pictures. Color the nouns **red**, the adjectives **blue**, and the pronouns yellow.

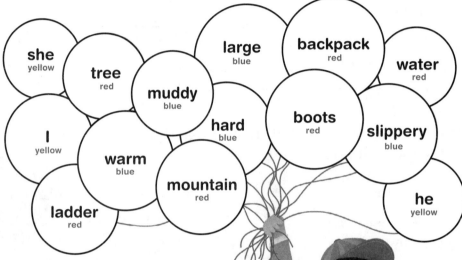

she
yellow

tree
red

large
blue

backpack
red

water
red

muddy
blue

I
yellow

hard
blue

boots
red

slippery
blue

warm
blue

mountain
red

ladder
red

he
yellow

Ⓑ Underline the pronoun in each sentence.

1. <u>They</u> went to the zoo.

2. The baseball player caught <u>it</u>!

3. Jon saw <u>him</u> climb the ladder.

4. <u>We</u> work hard every day.

5. Dorothy and <u>I</u> are friends.

6. <u>She</u> will be nine years old soon.

7. Please feed <u>them</u> every morning.

8. <u>He</u> wrote a funny story.

9. <u>You</u> climbed over the wall.

10. Joe gave the bats to Susie and <u>me</u>.

Name _____

Show What You Know

Use a word from the word bank to complete each sentence. Use each word once. Write **a** on the line if the answer is an adjective. Write **p** on the line if the answer is a pronoun.

you	bright	stormy	Her	smaller
five	they	He	biggest	She

1. *Her* name is Jennifer. __p__

2. It will be a *stormy* day. __a__

3. *She* is Sean's mother. __p__

4. Are *you* coming with me? __p__

5. Steve has *five* brothers. __a__

6. Joey rode the *bright*, shiny bike. __a__

7. Park School is the *biggest* school in town. __a__

8. *He* went to the store to get milk. __p__

9. Did Billy and Julie say where *they* were going? __p__

10. Rachel walked with the *smaller* children. __a__

Get Ready to Write

What Is a Description?

Did you ever tell a friend about a new toy? Have you ever told your parents about your day at school? If you did, you gave a description. A **description** tells about a person, a place, a thing, or an event.

I love going to the fair! I visit the mooing cows and clucking chickens. The air smells like piney sawdust. Games and rides light up the night. Sweet cotton candy fills my mouth. My fingers are sticky and pink from my tasty treat.

Answer these questions about the description.

1. What is the description about?

going to the fair

2. Where do you learn what the topic is?

in the first sentence

3. What words tell about sight, sound, smell, touch, and taste?

sight *pink*

sound *mooing, clucking*

smell *piney*

taste *sweet, tasty*

touch *sticky*

Topic Sentences

A description begins with a topic sentence. The **topic sentence** tells what you are describing. A topic sentence grabs a reader's attention.

Topic Sentence

I love to wake up to the sounds and smells of breakfast.
The smell of bacon tickles my nose. I hear the pop of the toaster and the hiss of spattering butter. Soon I hear eggs cracking against a bowl. I am up before the eggs hit the pan.

Which is a better topic sentence? Write an X next to the better sentence in each pair.

1. I like lemonade. ☐

   Cold lemonade is perfect on a hot day. ☒

2. My bedroom is nice. ☐

   My bedroom is my favorite place to be. ☒

3. My sister is the cutest baby ever. ☒

   This is what my sister looks like. ☐

4. We have Movie Night every week. ☒

   We watch movies. ☐

Sensory Words

Sensory words paint a picture in a reader's mind. They help the reader imagine the description.

shiny coin **sight**   *sour* apple **taste**

barking dogs **sound**   *hot* sand **touch**

flowery candle **smell**

A Circle the sensory words in each description. Then draw a line to the sense it uses.

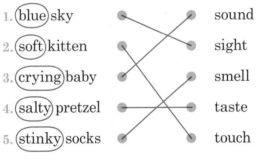

1. (blue) sky — sound
2. (soft) kitten — sight
3. (crying) baby — smell
4. (salty) pretzel — taste
5. (stinky) socks — touch

B Fill in each blank with a sensory word from the word bank.

1. a *fuzzy* caterpillar
2. big *green* eyes
3. a *cold* winter night
4. my *shady* hideout
5. a *screaming* siren

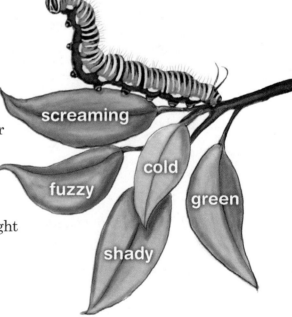

screaming · cold · fuzzy · green · shady

Sensory Words in a Description

A Look at each topic. List three sensory words for each.

recess	a thunderstorm	pizza

B Write one sentence that describes each thing. Use the sense next to each thing.

1. a fireworks show (**sight**)

2. a farm (**sound**)

3. a campfire (**smell**)

4. hot cocoa (**taste**)

5. tree bark (**touch**)

Writer's Workshop

PREWRITING

Pick a Topic

A description tells about a person, a place, a thing, or an event.

my new fish

my friend Liam

the pond near my house

my mom's chicken soup

Maya is writing a description. She lists her topic ideas in her notebook. Then she circles the topic she likes best.

List or draw your topic ideas in your notebook. Your topic can be about a person, a place, a thing, or an event.

Now think about each topic. Is it something you can describe well? Would others like to read about it? Can you think of a good topic sentence? Choose the topic you like best.

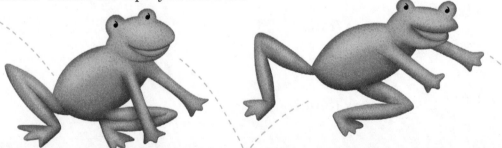

PREWRITING

Plan Your Description

Maya must plan her description. She wants to be sure to add sensory words. She uses a five-senses chart to help her think of ideas. Here is her five-senses chart.

Topic: the pond near my house	
sight	big rocks
sound	frogs and crickets sound like people
smell	lilacs
taste	tangy huckleberries
touch	cool water

Draw in your notebook a five-senses chart like the one Maya used. What sensory words can you think of? Try to write about each of your senses.

Writer's Workshop

DRAFTING

Maya has a lot of sensory words in her five-senses chart. She uses her chart to write her draft. This is Maya's draft.

> Nothing is better than the pond next to my house. All around it are big rocks. I like to dip my feet in the cool water. I love the smell of lilacs. Sometimes Liam and me visit the pond together. We nibble the tangy huckleberries that grow nearby. The frogs and the crickets sound like a crowd of people talking.

Look at the chart you made. Can you think of anything to add? Add any words that will make a better description.

Write your description in your notebook. Begin with a topic sentence that will grab your reader's attention. Use your five-senses chart as you write. Help your readers see, smell, hear, taste, and feel what you describe.

EDITING

Maya wants to make her draft great.
She reads her draft. She uses this
Editing Checklist for help.

sweet
I love the⁁smell of lilacs. Sometimes

Liam and me visit the pond together.

We nibble the tangy huckleberries that

Look at the mistake that Maya finds. How does she fix it?

Read your draft. See if you can answer yes to the questions
on the Editing Checklist. Mark any parts that could
be better. Help your readers see, smell, hear, taste,
and feel what you describe.

I forgot a sensory word!

REVISING

After Maya edits her draft, she revises it.
She fixes the mistake she marked. She
copies her draft on a sheet of paper.

Copy your draft. Make your description
better than it was before. Fix any
mistakes you marked.

Descriptions • 141

Writer's Workshop

PROOFREADING

Maya proofreads her description. She looks at this Proofreading Checklist as she reads. She marks her paper where she wants it to be better.

Proofreading Checklist

☐ Are all the words spelled correctly?

☐ Did I use capital letters?

☐ Did I use the right end marks?

☐ Are pronouns and adjectives used correctly?

I love the sweet smell of lilacs. Sometimes

                I

Liam and ⌃me visit the pond together.

We nibble the tangy huckleberries that

Look at the mistake Maya finds. How does she fix it?

Read your description again. Check the Proofreading Checklist as you read. Put an **X** next to the question if you can answer yes. You might ask a partner to proofread your paper. Have your partner use the checklist.

Fix any mistakes you see. Use the proofreading marks chart on the inside back cover of your book. Mark your corrections on your paper.

PUBLISHING

When you publish, you share your work with others. Maya is almost ready to publish. She carefully copies her description onto a sheet of paper. Maya wants to share her very best work. She publishes by putting her description on a bulletin board.

Copy your description. Write as neatly as you can. You might type it on a computer instead.

How will you publish your description? Decide with your class. Use one of these ideas or one of your own.

Frame it.

Hang it up.

Put it on a bulletin board.

Read it to the class.

Make a class book of Descriptions.

Descriptions • 143

Contractions

In this chapter students will learn about

- contractions
- contractions with *not*
- contractions with *am, is,* and *are*
- contractions with *have* and *has*
- contractions with *had*

A Visual, Please

Contraction Equations

you're = you + are

BUT

your = your
(not a contraction)

they're = they + are

BUT

there = there
(not a contraction)

Grammar for Grown-ups

Contractions That Care

A contraction is formed when two words are combined and one or more letters are omitted. An apostrophe is used to represent the missing letter or letters. In writing, contractions are a way of representing oral language. They help improve the flow of writing and keep it from becoming stilted.

It is a commonly accepted practice to use contractions in informal writing, such as personal narratives or friendly letters. It is better, however, not to use them in more formal expository pieces. Avoiding contractions when writing research reports, for example, may help students distinguish between a formal and an informal tone.

Among the most commonly seen contractions are those formed with *not*. In these cases the contraction is formed with a verb and *not (can't, don't, aren't)*. Some contractions are formed using a subject pronoun and a form of *be*. These include contractions with *am, is,* and *are (I'm, she's, he's, we're, you're)*. Contractions may also use a form of *have*, which include contractions with *has* and *had (she's, he's, we've, they've, he'd, she'd, we'd)*.

Daily Edits

The Daily Edits for this chapter provide students with daily practice editing sentences. Students should pay special attention to their use of contractions.

Common Errors

Or "Apostrophes Have Feelings Too"

Some developing writers, when joining words to make a contraction, mistakenly leave out the apostrophe.

ERROR: Tamera cant swim.
CORRECT: Tamera can't swim.

ERROR: Peter hasnt seen the ocean.
CORRECT: Peter hasn't seen the ocean.

To help students avoid this common error, remind them of the purpose and importance of an apostrophe. Point out that in a contraction, an apostrophe replaces a letter or letters that are left out. As students revise their writing, remind them to check for missing apostrophes.

For Kids Who Are Ready

Otherwise Known as "Will You Join Us?"

For students who are already comfortable with the contractions taught in this chapter, introduce contractions with *will*.

Tell students that contractions with *will* are formed in the same way as other contractions they have learned. In contractions with *will*, the apostrophe replaces the *wi*.

EXAMPLES: we + will = we'll
she + will = she'll
he + will = he'll
I + will = I'll
they + will = they'll

Share the above examples with students. Encourage them to practice using contractions with *will* in sentences.

Ask a Mentor

Real Situations, Real Solutions

Dear Grammar Geek,

My students frequently misuse your and you're in their writing. How can I help them?

Yours truly,
Eleanor

Dear Eleanor,

Display the visual on page 144a. When they are unsure about using a contraction, have students ask themselves whether the two words that make up the contraction can be substituted in the sentence. If they can, the contraction is being used correctly.

You're on your way,
Grammar Geek

Dear Grammar Geezer,

Some of my students use the contraction ain't in their writing and speech. How can I make them see that ain't isn't a word?

Ain't this a pickle,
Kenny from Kansas

Dear Kenny,

This is a pickle! But it's nothing a simple explanation can't solve. Remind students that contractions are made up of two words, and write on the board the following examples: didn't = did + not, isn't = is + not, aren't = are + not, ain't = ? Then ask students to name the two words that make up the contraction ain't. The silence should prove your point! Tell students that because ain't can't be separated into two words, it isn't a real contraction. Work with the class to come up with contractions that should be used instead of ain't, such as isn't and aren't.

Let's make ain't extinct,
Grammar Geezer

Andrew Toos: www.CartoonStock.com

Book Reports

Genre Characteristics

At the end of this chapter, students will write a book report. They will be guided through the writing process in the Writer's Workshop. The completed book report will include the following:

- a beginning that names the book's title, author, and main characters
- a middle that describes what happens in the book
- an ending that gives the writer's opinion
- correct grammar, spelling, capitalization, and punctuation

Daily Story Starters

The Daily Story Starters for this chapter provide students with practice brainstorming topics for book reports. This daily practice will help to get students thinking and writing about books they have read.

Begin each day by writing on the board the Daily Story Starter. Allow time for students to complete the sentence. Then discuss the results as a class. Because the purpose of this activity is to help students think of book types and topic ideas, talk to students about their ideas and whether the ideas are appropriate for their book reports.

Read and Report

Expository writing is writing that informs. One of the most common forms of expository writing is the report. For students, perhaps the most common report is the book report. An effective book report begins with a thought-provoking book and an enthusiastic reader. Fiction works are often the best subjects for classroom book reports. A well-written book report goes beyond recalling character, setting, plot, and theme—it also shows the conclusions that the reader has drawn and judgments the reader has made.

Effective book reports are logically organized. The writer provides general information about the story in the beginning, often describing the main characters and the setting. The middle briefly summarizes main events in time order. The ending discusses the report writer's opinion of the book, often sharing insights or recommendations to potential readers.

Effective book reports are written in a confident, lively voice. They use exact words that make a book's plot understandable. Sentences that express the writer's opinion are strategically placed for impact. Effective book reports are correct in grammar, spelling, capitalization, and punctuation.

Teacher's Toolbox

Try the following ideas to help your students get the most out of the Writer's Workshop:

- Add to your classroom library a variety of quality fiction.

- Before writing begins, meet individually with each student about the book he or she has chosen. Guide the student to recall important information *(characters, setting, plot, conclusion)*. Invite the student to express his or her opinion and to cite parts of the book that support the opinion.

- Remind students not to watch videos or DVDs of their books because important parts of the story are often changed.

Reasons to Write

Share with students the following list of people who write reports. Discuss why it is important to become a good report writer.

- teachers
- movie or book reviewers
- doctors

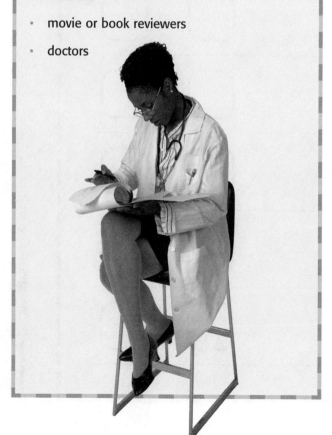

Literature Links

You can add to your classroom library the following titles to offer your students good topics for book reports:

Days With Frog and Toad by Arnold Lobel

Babe: The Gallant Pig by Dick King-Smith

Chang's Paper Pony by Eleanor Coerr

Book Report

	Yes	No
My report is about a book I have read.	☐	☐
My beginning tells the title, author, and characters.	☐	☐
My middle tells what happens.	☐	☐
My ending tells my opinion.	☐	☐
I used contractions correctly.	☐	☐
I used complete sentences.	☐	☐
I spelled words correctly.	☐	☐
I used capital letters correctly.	☐	☐
I used end marks correctly.	☐	☐

Voyages in English 2

Teacher's Scoring Rubric

Book Report

0 = not evident
1 = minimal evidence of comprehension
2 = evidence of development toward comprehension
3 = strong evidence of comprehension
4 = outstanding evidence of comprehension

Ideas	Points
is about a book that the student has read	

Organization	
has a beginning that tells the title, author, and characters	
has a middle that tells what happens	
has an ending that expresses the student's opinion of the book	

Voice	
is written in a natural voice	

Word Choice	
uses contractions correctly	
words are recognizable	

Sentence Fluency	
has correct sentence structure	

Conventions	
grammar	
spelling	
punctuation and capitalization	

Voyages in English 2

Daily Voyages

Daily Edits

Monday	Tuesday	Wednesday	Thursday	Friday
A Police car moveed (moved) slowly in the dark park.	A rober (robber) was loose in the neighbor-hood (neighborhood).	Officer diaz heard a loud noise.	He jump (jumped) out of his car.	He found the Robber hideing (hiding) in a trash can.
get the kids out of the the (the) water!	I sees (see) hundreds of Jellyfish in the water.	Thay (They) look like pretty balloons.	look at that big jelly fish (jellyfish)!	Stay a way (away) because jellyfish sting.
have you ever seened (seen) a rainbow?	There is a pot of Gold at the end.	I can'nt (can't) find the end of the rain-bow (rainbow).	Elves knows (know) where the rianbow (rainbow) ends.	I havent (haven't) seen an elf befor (before).
Joshua drew a pichure (picture) of a Peacock.	He color (colored) it green and blu (blue).	He did'nt (didn't) know what other collor (color) to use.	the peacock lookeed (looked) at itself.	The Peacock asked joshua to ad (add) purple.
I's (I'm) running in a rase (race) today.	Dirk jackson is runing (running) in the same race.	Hes (He's) the faster (fastest) kid at school.	Iv'e (I've) been practicing bye (by) running up the stairs.	Im goin (I'm going) to win this race.

Daily Story Starters

Monday	Tuesday	Wednesday	Thursday	Friday
The funniest book is	The best book about outer space is	The smartest character in a book is	A strange book I read was	A book with good pictures is
A book about the past is	A book I didn't like is	The scariest book is	The best fairy tale is	The last book I read was
The best mystery book is	The best boy character is	The best book about kids is	A good book with monsters is	A sad book is
My favorite girl character is	The best hero in a book is	The best adventure book is	A book I've read many times is	The best book someone read to me is
My favorite animal character is	If I could be any character, I would be	I like books about	My favorite author is	A book that taught me something was

Chapter Adaptors

SPEAKING & LISTENING

Ask students to choose a character from the book they are writing about. Have students orally present their book reports dressed as the character. Encourage students to use accents and props.

RETEACHING

Write the contractions from this chapter on separate note cards. Then write the corresponding two words that make up each contraction on other note cards. Shuffle the cards and have students play a game of concentration, matching each contraction to its corresponding words.

THINK, WRITE, PUBLISH!

Ask students to draw three pictures of important things that happen in their favorite book. Have students put the events in the order in which they happened. Then have students write sentences about each picture. Invite students to illustrate a cover and to include the book's title and author. Display the finished books in the classroom for everyone to read.

RETEACHING

Have students each choose a book for a book report. Allow time for students to free write about their books. Encourage students to write about their feelings about the book as well as about the characters and what happens in the book. When they have finished, talk with students about words they wrote that indicate their opinion of the book. Remind students to save their free-writing notes to help them write their drafts.

ENGLISH-LANGUAGE LEARNERS

Invite English-language learners to discuss books written in their primary language. Ask students to talk about the characters, what happens, and their opinions of the books. Tell students that by talking about these books, they are giving an informal book report. Have students write in English one or two sentences about what they have discussed. Have students refer to their notes when they write their book reports about a book written in English.

WRITING & EDITING

Explain to students that one way to check writing for misspelled words is to read backward from right to left, one word at a time. Help students begin by pointing at and checking the last word in their book reports. Tell students that they should point at each word and check the spelling, moving backward through the report.

CONTRACTION ICE-CREAM CONES

Photocopy outlines of ice-cream cones and scoops of ice cream. Distribute one scoop and one cone to each student. Assign each student a word that that can be used to make a contraction. *(Examples: have, she, not)* Have students write their word on their scoops and color them. Allow students to decorate and write their names on the cones. Collect the scoops and put them in a box. Invite a volunteer to pick one scoop from the box and to give a contraction using the word on the scoop. Allow the student to attach the scoop to his or her cone if the correct answer is given. Repeat until every student has had a turn and made an ice-cream cone.

CHAPTER

5

Quotation Station

Reading is to the mind what exercise is to the body.

–Joseph Addison
author

Contractions and Book Reports

Lion

Zebras →

Elephants

A Great Book!

by Julio Arroyo Covas

Louise Fatio wrote the book <u>The Happy Lion</u>. The Happy Lion lives at a zoo in France. Every day friends come by to visit him. His friends are Francois, Monsieur Dupont, and Madame Pinson. One day the lion sees that his cage is open. So the lion decides to return his friends' visits. When his friends see him, they run away. The Happy Lion can't figure out why. I think this book is great because of the lion. No matter what happens, he's a happy lion!

Contractions and Book Reports • 145

Name

Contractions

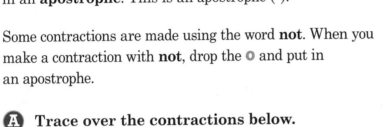

A **contraction** is a short way of writing two words. When you write a contraction, you leave out a letter or letters and put in an **apostrophe**. This is an apostrophe (').

Some contractions are made using the word **not**. When you make a contraction with **not**, drop the **o** and put in an apostrophe.

A **Trace over the contractions below.**

do not	have not	has not	did not
don't	*haven't*	*hasn't*	*didn't*

B **Write the contraction for the two underlined words.**

1. I <u>do not</u> have a hole in my pocket.   *don't*

2. Matt <u>has not</u> put the puzzle together.   *hasn't*

3. The birds <u>have not</u> flown south yet.   *haven't*

4. Leslie <u>did not</u> plant the seeds correctly.   *didn't*

5. Tomas <u>has not</u> made his bed today.   *hasn't*

6. They <u>have not</u> been to the museum.   *haven't*

7. I <u>do not</u> want to go to the mall.   *don't*

8. We <u>did not</u> have time to fly the kites.   *didn't*

Name _____

Contractions Practice

A Underline the contraction that is spelled correctly to complete each sentence.

1. Jorge (<u>didn't</u> did'nt) find his skates.

2. My brother and I (do'nt <u>don't</u>) stay up late.

3. Chris (<u>hasn't</u> has'nt) read that book.

4. The rabbits (<u>haven't</u> have'nt) eaten the carrots and lettuce.

5. Paul (<u>didn't</u> did'nt) finish the math problems.

B Complete each sentence with a contraction on the right. You will use some contractions twice. **Sample answers shown.**

1. Deshan *hasn't* done his homework.

2. I *don't* want to play in the snow.

3. My sister *didn't* pack my lunch.

4. The trees *haven't* shed their leaves yet.

5. This apple *hasn't* been eaten.

don't

hasn't

haven't

didn't

Writer's Corner

Write a sentence about a food you do not like.
Use the contraction *don't*.

Contractions • 147

Name _____

More Contractions with *Not*

Remember that some contractions are made with the word **not**.
Here are more contractions that are made with the word **not**.

Ⓐ Trace over the contractions below.

could not   are not   does not   is not

couldn't   *aren't*   *doesn't*   *isn't*

Ⓑ Write the contraction for the two underlined words.

1. Molly <u>does not</u> take piano lessons.
2. Those explorers <u>are not</u> giving up.
3. The sun <u>is not</u> seen at night.
4. A worm <u>does not</u> have bones.
5. The birds <u>are not</u> flying too close.
6. Bryan <u>could not</u> tie his shoes.
7. The river <u>is not</u> very deep.
8. The train <u>could not</u> move on the track.

doesn't

aren't

isn't

doesn't

aren't

couldn't

isn't

couldn't

Name _____

Writing Contractions with *Not*

Complete each sentence with a contraction. Use a word from the lily pads. You will use some contractions twice.
Sample answers shown.

1. The lions **aren't** in the cage.

2. A toad **doesn't** have smooth skin.

3. An egg **isn't** square.

4. The fox **couldn't** catch the rabbits.

5. This cow **doesn't** have horns.

6. Wild animals **aren't** friendly.

7. I **couldn't** pet the lion at the zoo.

8. That pickle **isn't** sweet.

9. The bell **didn't** ring on time.

10. The fish **haven't** been fed today.

couldn't
didn't
aren't
haven't
isn't
doesn't

Name _____

Working with Contractions

Some contractions are made using the word **not**. Here are more contractions made using the word **not**.

A Trace over the contractions below.

was not *wasn't*

were not *weren't*

cannot *can't*

will not *won't*

B Write the contraction for the underlined words.

1. The gorillas <u>were not</u> fed yet.   *weren't*

2. Rory <u>was not</u> in the three-legged race.   *wasn't*

3. Jason <u>cannot</u> keep the squirrel as a pet.   *can't*

4. A scout <u>will not</u> play with matches.   *won't*

5. The horses <u>were not</u> wild.   *weren't*

6. It <u>was not</u> too cold to play outside.   *wasn't*

7. I <u>will not</u> eat peanut butter and pickles.   *won't*

8. She <u>cannot</u> mix the paint.   *can't*

Name

More Working with Contractions

Underline the contraction that is spelled correctly in each sentence.

1. The train (<u>wasn't</u> was'nt) at the station.

2. Kerry (wo'nt <u>won't</u>) skip rope with me.

3. Dogs (<u>can't</u> ca'nt) climb trees.

4. The deer (<u>won't</u> wo'nt) eat the leaves.

5. The birds (were'nt <u>weren't</u>) flying today.

6. (<u>Wasn't</u> Was'nt) your birthday last week?

7. I (ca'nt <u>can't</u>) catch the butterfly.

8. Flowers (<u>won't</u> wo'nt) grow without water.

9. (<u>Can't</u> Ca'nt) Terry play the game?

10. It (was'nt <u>wasn't</u>) a good day for a picnic.

A contraction is a way
to write two words as one.
Replace a letter or letters with an apostrophe,
and it's already done.

Writer's Corner

Write a sentence about a place you will not go.
Use the contraction *won't*.

Name

Contractions with *Not* Review

A contraction is a short way of writing two words. When you write a contraction, you leave out a letter or letters and put in an apostrophe.

A Write the correct contraction for each set of words.

do not	*don't*	will not	*won't*
cannot	*can't*	did not	*didn't*
has not	*hasn't*	have not	*haven't*
were not	*weren't*	are not	*aren't*
could not	*couldn't*	does not	*doesn't*
is not	*isn't*	was not	*wasn't*

B Write the two words that make up each underlined contraction.

1. The boys <u>don't</u> have a game today. — *do not*

2. This window <u>won't</u> open. — *will not*

3. A queen bee <u>doesn't</u> do any work. — *does not*

4. The rooster <u>didn't</u> crow on time. — *did not*

5. Her goldfish <u>weren't</u> in the pond. — *were not*

6. We <u>haven't</u> opened the presents yet. — *have not*

Name

More Contractions with *Not* Review

A Write the contraction for the two words in blue.

1. I *couldn't* write a poem about trees.   **could not**

2. Sue *hasn't* given Dad the mail.   **has not**

3. A fir tree *doesn't* have leaves.   **does not**

4. Emil *won't* search for frogs.   **will not**

5. Turtles *aren't* very fast.   **are not**

6. The apples *haven't* ripened.   **have not**

7. Pepper *isn't* wearing a collar.   **is not**

8. Our old house *wasn't* very big.   **was not**

B Write a sentence using the contraction **doesn't**.

C Write a sentence using the contraction **isn't**.

Name _____

Contractions with *Am* and *Is*

Some contractions are made with the word **am**. When you make a contraction with **am**, use an apostrophe in place of the **a**.

A Trace over the contraction below.

I am   *I'm*

Some contractions are made with the word **is**. When you make a contraction with **is**, use an apostrophe in place of the **i**.

B Trace over the contractions below.

he is   she is   it is

he's   *she's*   *it's*

C Write the contraction for the two underlined words.

1. <u>I am</u> going to New York City.   *I'm*

2. <u>He is</u> my favorite author.   *He's*

3. <u>It is</u> time to walk the dog.   *It's*

4. <u>She is</u> running in a race.   *She's*

5. <u>I am</u> seven years old today.   *I'm*

Name _____

Contractions with *Are*

Some contractions are made with the word **are**. When you make a contraction with **are**, use an apostrophe in place of the **a**.

Ⓐ Trace over the contractions below.

you are	we are	they are
you're	*we're*	*they're*

Ⓑ Write the two words that make up each contraction.

we're	you're	they're
we are	*you are*	*they are*

Ⓒ Underline the contraction that is spelled correctly in each sentence.

1. I know (you're yo'ure) going to camp.
2. (Wer'e We're) going to camp too.
3. (They're The'yre) not going with us.
4. (Yo'ure You're) going to be in Cabin A?
5. (We're Wer'e) in Cabin B!

Name _____

Contractions with *Am*, *Is*, and *Are*

A Look at the words below. Put the words together to make contractions. You will use some words more than once. Write the contractions on the lines.

he's   I'm

you're

she's   it's

we're   they're

B Write the contraction for the two underlined words.

1. You are going to make a cake.   You're

2. Do you think he is coming to town?   he's

3. They are going with Emily.   They're

4. Grace thinks it is a hard song.   it's

5. I know we are going to like the play. we're

6. She is not coming home.   She's

Name _____

Contractions with *Have*

Some contractions are made with the word **have**. When you make a contraction with **have**, use an apostrophe in place of the **ha**.

A Trace over the contractions below.

I have	you have	we have	they have
I've	*you've*	*we've*	*they've*

B Write the contraction for the two underlined words.

1. I have been at the swimming pool.   *I've*

2. Do you think we have bought too many cookies?   *we've*

3. You have got mustard on your shirt.   *You've*

4. I think they have got enough balloons.   *they've*

5. We have done a lot of painting today.   *We've*

6. Did you hear about what I have won?   *I've*

7. They have told us to bring cake.   *They've*

8. I think we have put up too many streamers.   *we've*

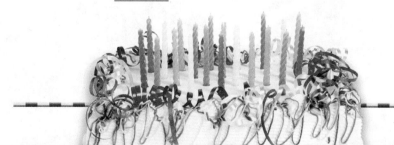

Contractions • 157

Name _____

Contractions with *Has*

Some contractions are made with the word **has**. When you make a contraction with **has**, use an apostrophe in place of the **ha**.

A **Trace over the contractions below.**

he has	she has	it has
he's	*she's*	*it's*

B **Write in each sentence the contraction for the blue words.**

1. I think *he's* gone to the store.   **he has**

2. *It's* been a long day.   **It has**

3. Petra says *she's* forgotten the letter.   **she has**

4. I think *she's* got a swimming pool.   **she has**

5. *It's* never been broken.   **It has**

6. *He's* stopped at Marc's house.   **He has**

158

Name

Contractions with *Have* and *Has*

A **Draw a line from the words in the first list to their contractions in the second list.**

1. I have
2. he has
3. it has
4. they have
5. you have
6. she has
7. we have

they've
it's
we've
she's
he's
you've
I've

B **Write each sentence. Write a contraction for the underlined words in each sentence.**

1. <u>I have</u> got a parakeet.

   I've got a parakeet.

2. Do you know where <u>they have</u> been?

   Do you know where they've been?

3. I think <u>she has</u> gone home.

   I think she's gone home.

4. <u>He has</u> been at Cary's house.

   He's been at Cary's house.

5. I think <u>you have</u> stayed up too late.

   I think you've stayed up too late.

Contractions • 159

Name _____

Reviewing Contractions

A Write the contraction for each set of words.

it is *it's*

they have *they've*

I am *I'm*

we have *we've*

you are *you're*

she is *she's*

he has *he's*

you have *you've*

it has *it's*

we are *we're*

he is *he's*

they are *they're*

she has *she's*

I have *I've*

B Underline the contraction in each sentence. Then write the two words that make up the contraction.

1. <u>It's</u> for my teacher. *it is*

2. I think <u>I've</u> got a dollar. *I have*

3. Cara thinks <u>she's</u> a good pitcher. *she is*

4. <u>We're</u> going to ride the Zapper. *We are*

5. <u>I'm</u> tall enough to ride it. *I am*

Name

More Reviewing Contractions

Write in each sentence the contraction for the two blue words.

1. *It's* ____ a pretty day.   **It is**

2. Dad said that *he's* ____ going to work.   **he is**

3. Rachel said *she's* ____ going swimming.   **she is**

4. *I'm* ____ making a sandcastle.   **I am**

5. *They're* ____ going to watch me.   **They are**

6. I think *it's* ____ stopped raining.   **it has**

7. *They've* ____ lived here for 20 years.   **They have**

8. I think *I've* ____ met your sister.   **I have**

9. *We've* ____ flown to Egypt twice.   **We have**

10. *You've* ____ been to the zoo?   **You have**

11. *We're* ____ having a party.   **We are**

12. *You're* ____ joking!   **You are**

161

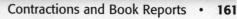

Name _____

Contractions with *Had*

Some contractions are made with the word **had.** When you make a contraction with **had**, use an apostrophe in place of the **ha**.

Ⓐ Draw a line from the words in the first list to their contractions in the second list.

1. he had   she'd
2. I had   I'd
3. she had   he'd

Ⓑ Write the contraction for the blue words.

1. *She'd* better get here on time.   **She had**

2. I knew *he'd* gotten a new bike.   **he had**

3. *I'd* eaten two apples.   **I had**

4. I think *she'd* shut off the light.   **she had**

5. Mom said *I'd* slept too long.   **I had**

6. *He'd* given me the garden hose.   **He had**

Writer's Corner

Write a sentence about a member of your family. Use the contraction *he'd* or *she'd.*

Name _____

More Contractions with *Had*

Some contractions are made with the word **had**. When you make a contraction with **had**, an apostrophe takes the place of the **ha**.

A Trace over the contractions below.

you had   we had   they had

you'd   *we'd*   *they'd*

B Write the two words that make up the underlined contraction in each sentence.

1. Alena said they'd been to the movie theater.   *they had*

2. Jared wondered where you'd been.   *you had*

3. I wish we'd taken a blanket.   *we had*

4. You'd better do your homework.   *You had*

5. They'd been on a long plane ride.   *They had*

6. We'd won a prize.   *We had*

Name

Show What You Know

A Draw a line from each contraction to the word or words that make up the contraction.

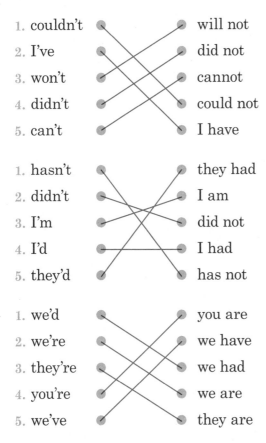

1. couldn't — will not
2. I've — did not
3. won't — cannot
4. didn't — could not
5. can't — I have

1. hasn't — they had
2. didn't — I am
3. I'm — did not
4. I'd — I had
5. they'd — has not

1. we'd — you are
2. we're — we have
3. they're — we had
4. you're — we are
5. we've — they are

B Underline the correct contraction to complete each sentence.

1. Brady (haven't <u>couldn't</u>) find his gloves.

2. Melody (<u>wasn't</u> weren't) playing in the sun.

3. (<u>I've</u> I'm) gotten a new raincoat.

4. During the thunderstorm, the team (hasn't <u>didn't</u>) play ball.

Name _____

Show What You Know

A Underline the contraction in each sentence. Then write the word or words that make up the contraction.

1. The peanuts <u>weren't</u> for the elephants. *were not*

2. I think <u>I've</u> discovered a new planet! *I have*

3. The octopus <u>won't</u> come out of its home. *will not*

4. <u>I'm</u> ready to put the bait on my hook. *I am*

5. We <u>can't</u> see the moon tonight. *cannot*

B Write each sentence. Write a contraction for the underlined words.

1. The whale watchers <u>have not</u> seen a whale.

The whale watchers haven't seen a whale.

2. You <u>do not</u> have the right time.

You don't have the right time.

3. <u>I am</u> ready to enter the spaceship.

I'm ready to enter the spaceship.

Get Ready to Write

What Is a Book Report?

Have you ever read a book that you really liked? Have you ever read a book that wasn't very good? In a book report you tell about a book you have read. You share

the **title**—the name of the book. Underline the title of the book.

the **author**—the person who wrote the book.

the **characters**—the people or things in the book.

your **opinion**—how you felt or what you thought about the book.

Title ——— Aunt Eater's Mystery Vacation is by Doug Cushman. ——— Author

The book is about Aunt Eater. Aunt Eater takes a ——— Character

vacation to rest and read mystery books. But she

ends up in a real mystery! I like this book because

Opinion ——— Aunt Eater is smart and she likes mysteries.

● **Answer these questions about the book report.**

1. What is the title of the book?

Aunt Eater's Mystery Vacation

2. Who is the author of the book?

Doug Cushman

3. Who are the characters?

Aunt Eater

4. How does the writer feel about this book?

The writer likes this book.

Parts of a Book Report

A good book report has a **beginning**, a middle, and an **ending**.

The **beginning** tells the title and the author's name. It also tells who the characters are. Remember to underline the title.

The middle tells what happens in the book.

The **ending** tells how you feel or what you thought about the book.

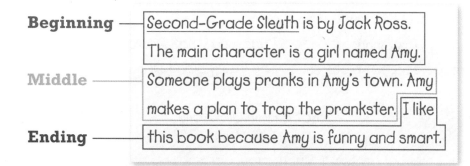

Beginning — Second-Grade Sleuth is by Jack Ross. The main character is a girl named Amy.

Middle — Someone plays pranks in Amy's town. Amy makes a plan to trap the prankster. I like

Ending — this book because Amy is funny and smart.

The parts of a book report are all mixed up. Write the correct number in each box to put the report in order.

1. beginning   2. middle   3.ending

3 This book is great because it shows that we are all special.

1 Why Can't I Fly? is by Ken Brown. It's about Cecil the Ostrich.

2 Cecil can't fly like other birds. But he finds out he has his own special talent.

167

Opinions in Book Reports

Your **opinion** is how you feel or what you think about a book. Tell your opinion of the book in the ending. Explain why you feel the way you do.

First tell your opinion. Here are some opinions you might have about a book.

I like this book.   I thought the book would be better.

I didn't like this book.   Everyone should read this book.

Then tell why you have the opinion you do. Here are some reasons why you might feel the way you do.

The story was funny.   I guessed what would happen right away.

The book has great pictures.   The story didn't make sense.

> **Not a Plain Old Story**
> **by Lee Martin**
>
> Just a Plain Old Tree is by Beth Chung. It is a story about Zena and Rudi. On a walk they hear a noise coming from a hole in a tree. They crawl inside to investigate. Zena and Rudi find themselves in a magical place full of flying animals that act like people. This book is great! The pictures are good. The story makes you laugh.

1. What is Lee's opinion of this book?

   Lee thinks the book is great.

2. Why does Lee feel the way he does?

   Lee thinks the pictures are good and the story is funny.

Organize a Book Report

A chart can help you organize a book report. A chart can help make sure you don't forget any parts.

○ **Pick a book you have read. Fill in the chart below. The first, last, and important words in a book title should begin with capital letters. Remember to underline the title.**

Beginning	Title	
	Author	
	Characters	
Middle	What happens	
Ending	How I felt about the book and why	

Writer's Workshop

PREWRITING

Pick a Topic

Julio is writing a book report. First he needs to pick a topic. Julio thinks about the books that he's read. He lists them in his notebook. Then he circles The Happy Lion. He thinks his classmates would enjoy hearing about this book the most.

Diary of a Worm

The Giving Tree

Henry and Mudge in the Sparkle Days

If You Give a Pig a Party

The Happy Lion

Make a list of books you have read. Then think about each book. Do you remember the book well? Would you enjoy writing about it? Would others enjoy reading it? Pick the book you will write about. Circle the title.

PREWRITING

Plan Your Book Report

Julio needs to plan his book report. He knows that if he makes a plan first, his report will be easier to write. Here is the plan Julio makes.

Beginning	Title	<u>The Happy Lion</u>
	Author	Louise Fatio
	Characters	The Happy Lion, Francois, Monsieur Dupont, Madame Pinson
Middle	What happens	The Happy Lion's friends visit him. The lion goes out to visit friends. People are scared of the lion.
Ending	How I felt about the book and why	I liked this book. No matter what, the lion is always happy.

Make a plan for your book report. Draw a chart like Julio's in your notebook. Make sure you include the **beginning**, the **middle**, and the **ending**. Fill in all the information. Read the book again if you need to.

Writer's Workshop

DRAFTING

Julio has a lot of information in his chart. He uses his chart to write his draft. Julio is careful to follow his plan.

> *A Great Book!*
>
> *by Julio Arroyo Covas*
>
> *Louise Fatio wrote the book <u>The Happy Lion</u>. The Happy Lion lives at a zoo in France. Every day friends come by to visit him. His friends are Francois, Monsieur Dupont, and Madame Pinson. One day the lion sees that his cage is open. So the lion decides to return his friends' visits. When his friends see him, they run away. The Happy Lion ca'nt figure out why. I think this book is great because of the lion.*

Write your draft in your notebook. Use your plan as you write. Read your book again if you need to. Add anything to your book report that will make it great. Remember that you'll have time to make changes later.

EDITING

Julio edits his report to make it better. He uses this checklist. He checks for one question at a time.

Editing Checklist

☐ Does my book report have a beginning, a middle, and an ending?

☐ Does the beginning tell the title, the author, and the characters?

☐ Does the middle tell about what happens in the book?

☐ Does the ending tell my opinion?

☐ Does the ending tell why I have the opinion I do?

they run away. The Happy Lion ca'nt figure out why. I think this book is great because of the lion. ∧*No matter what happens, he's a happy lion!*

Look at the mistake Julio finds. How does he fix it?

Edit your book report. Use the checklist that Julio used. Make any changes that will make your draft better.

Read aloud your book report. How does it sound? How can you make it better?

My ending doesn't tell why I have my opinion.

REVISING

Julio revises his draft. He fixes the mistake he marked. He copies it onto a sheet of paper.

Copy your draft. Fix any mistakes you marked. Make sure you can answer yes to all the questions on the checklist.

Writer's Workshop

PROOFREADING

Julio proofreads his book report. By proofreading he will catch even more mistakes.

Julio uses a proofreading checklist. He reads his paper carefully. He looks at one question at a time.

Proofreading Checklist

☐ Are all the words spelled correctly?

☐ Did I use capital letters?

☐ Did I use the right end marks?

☐ Are contractions used correctly?

return his friends' visits. When his friends see him,
                           can't
they run away. The Happy Lion ca'nt figure out why.

Look at the mistake Julio finds. How does he fix it?

Proofread your paper. Use the Proofreading Checklist. If you have trouble checking a mistake, ask a friend or your teacher for help. Make your book report one that others will enjoy reading.

PUBLISHING

When you publish you share your book report with others. Julio is excited to publish his book report. He wants other people to read <u>The Happy Lion</u>. Julio makes a clean copy of his book report. Then he makes a poster for the book and puts it with his report.

Copy your book report onto a sheet of paper. Add a title for your book report. Maybe someone will read your book report and want to read the book you chose!

Decide how to publish your book report. Here are some ways you might publish. Can you think of other ways?

Put your book report on the class bulletin board.

Pretend you are selling the book on TV.

Put all the book reports in a class magazine.

Draw an ad for your book. Attach it to your book report.

Word Study

In this chapter students will learn about

- synonyms
- antonyms
- homophones

A Visual, Please

Using See *and* Sea

> A sailor went to **sea**
> to **see** the fish below,
> but all that he could **see**
> was the bottom of the
> deep blue **sea**.

Grammar for Grown-ups

Synonym Study

The word *synonym* comes from the Greek *syn* ("plus") and *onoma* ("name"). Synonyms are words with nearly the same meanings. Examples of synonyms include *quiet, silent; talk, speak; begin, start;* and *find, discover.* Students should take care when replacing a word with its synonym. Often a word may have a more exact meaning in the context of a sentence. For example, *long* and *extended* are synonyms, but a *long arm* and an *extended arm* mean two different things.

Antonym Analysis

The word *antonym* comes from the Greek *anti* ("against") and *onoma* ("name"). Antonyms are words that have opposite meanings. Words that have multiple meanings may have several antonyms, depending on the word's usage. Examples of antonyms include *strong, weak; light, heavy; always, never;* and *bright, dark.*

Regarding Homophones

The word *homophone* comes from the Greek *homoios* ("identical") and *phone* ("sound"). Homophones are words that sound the same, but have different spellings and meanings, such as *to, two,* and *too.* The word *homophone* is often confused with *homonym* or *homograph. Homograph,* which comes from the Greek *homoios* ("identical") and *graph* ("to write"), can more literally be interpreted as "the same letters." Homographs are words that are spelled the same but have different pronunciations and meanings, such as *tear* (a verb) and *tear* (a noun). Homonyms are words that have the same spelling and pronunciation but different meanings, such as *bark* (the sharp sound a dog makes) and *bark* (the tough covering of a tree). Homophones are sometimes called *homonyms.*

Daily Edits

The Daily Edits for this chapter provide students with daily practice editing sentences. Students should pay special attention to their use of homophones.

Common Errors

Or "There Is Too Much to Do in Two Days"

Some developing writers misuse the homophones *too, to,* and *two.* To help students avoid this common error, write on the board the sentence *There is too much to do in two days.* Help students use the sentence to understand the usage of *too, to,* and *two.* Tell students to use the sentence to check *too, to,* and *two* in their own writing.

For Kids Who Are Ready

Also Known as "The More, the Merrier"

For students who are already comfortable with synonym pairs, introduce the concept of words with more than one synonym.

EXAMPLES: quiet: silent, hushed, mute, noiseless

pretty: beautiful, attractive, lovely

happy: glad, cheerful, delighted, joyful

Share the above examples with students. Emphasize that because synonyms have varied meanings, students should check a dictionary to make sure they are using the word that best suits their purpose.

Ask a Mentor

Real Situations, Real Solutions

Dear Grammar Geek,

Homophones habitually hinder my students. How can I help without hindering their headway? Help!

Mr. Gilbert

Dear Mr. Gilbert,

Display the visual on page 176a. Because the differences between homophones cannot be heard when read aloud, students will benefit most from seeing homophones written in sentences. This will help students learn the definition of each homophone and pair it with its correct spelling. The more often students see a homophone in context, the more likely they will be able to use it correctly in their own writing.

Write and they'll get it right,
Grammar Geek

Dear Grammar Geezer,

My students frequently use the same words over and over. How can I help them add variety to their vocabulary?

Beyond the basics,
Christina

Dear Christina,

One of the easiest ways to expand students' vocabulary is by encouraging them to use synonyms in place of words they repeatedly use. Review common synonym pairs often and remind students that replacing words with synonyms can add variety to their speech and writing.

A synonym supporter,
Grammar Geezer

Research Reports

"Miss Travers, bring me that report on absenteeism.... Miss Travers?...Miss Travers?..."

Adey Bryant: www.CartoonStock.com

Genre Characteristics

At the end of this chapter, students will write a research report. They will be guided through the writing process in the Writer's Workshop. The completed research report will include the following:

- a beginning that states the topic
- a middle that includes important facts
- facts presented without opinions
- an ending that summarizes
- correct grammar, spelling, capitalization, and punctuation

Daily Story Starters

The Daily Story Starters for this chapter provide students with practice brainstorming topics for research reports. This daily practice helps students understand the variety of topics they can research.

Begin each day by writing on the board the Daily Story Starter. Allow time for students to complete the sentence. Then discuss the results as a class. Because the purpose of this activity is to generate topics for research reports, talk to students about their ideas and whether the ideas interest them and whether the topics are narrow enough for a research report.

Show What You Know

A research report is an expository piece that provides information about a specific topic. The information is derived from a variety of sources found by the writer. The writer then interprets, analyzes, and draws conclusions from the information to develop a topic sentence and supporting ideas.

The writer of a research report often completes a process such as the following: choose a topic, form a preliminary topic sentence, locate sources, take notes on note cards, draft, revise, edit, and publish.

Effective research reports include a beginning that states the topic, a middle that supports the topic, and an ending that summarizes the report. Throughout the piece, the writer uses formal language, a variety of sentence styles and lengths, and correct grammar, spelling, capitalization, and punctuation.

Chapter 7 of the student book provides lessons and activities that teach students how to use reference tools. You may find it helpful to teach Chapter 7 prior to·or concurrently with Chapter 6 in order to prepare students to write their research reports.

Teacher's Toolbox

Try the following ideas to help your students get the most out of the Writer's Workshop:

* Add to your classroom library a variety of nonfiction works to spark topic ideas.

* Invite a guest speaker, such as a doctor, to explain to the class why he or she writes research reports and how they are used.

* Encourage students to look for topic ideas in age-appropriate news, science, or nature magazines.

* Meet with students as they are considering topics. Discuss students' possible topics and guide them to pick an appropriate topic that isn't too broad.

Reasons to Write

Share with students the following list of people who write research reports. Discuss why it is important to become a good research report writer.

* scientist
* teacher
* nurse

Literature Links

You can add to your classroom library the following titles to offer your students examples of well-crafted expository writing:

What's It Like to Be a Fish? by Wendy Pfeffer

Cheetahs (Zoobooks Series) by Linda C. Wood

Beacons of Light: Lighthouses by Gail Gibbons

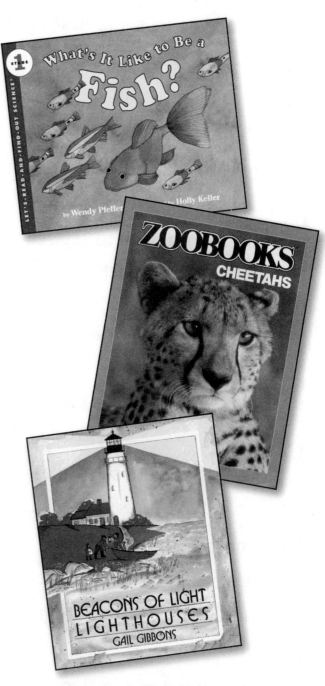

Name _____ Date _____

Research Report

	Yes	No
My beginning has a topic sentence.	☐	☐
My middle tells important facts.	☐	☐
My ending sums up the report.	☐	☐
My report leaves out my opinion.	☐	☐
I used synonyms to replace words used over and over.	☐	☐
I used antonyms correctly.	☐	☐
I used homophones correctly.	☐	☐
I used complete sentences.	☐	☐
I spelled words correctly.	☐	☐
I used capital letters and end marks correctly.	☐	☐

Voyages in English 2

© Loyola Press

Student _____   Date _____

Teacher's Scoring Rubric

Research Report

0 = not evident
1 = minimal evidence of comprehension
2 = evidence of development toward comprehension
3 = strong evidence of comprehension
4 = outstanding evidence of comprehension

Ideas	Points
is about a topic that can be researched	
Organization	
has a beginning that includes a topic sentence	
has a middle that tells relevant facts	
has an ending that sums up the report	
Voice	
is written in a natural voice	
does not include the writer's opinion	
Word Choice	
replaces overused words with synonyms	
uses homophones correctly	
uses antonyms correctly	
words are recognizable	
Sentence Fluency	
has correct sentence structure	
Conventions	
grammar	
spelling	
punctuation and capitalization	

Daily Voyages

Daily Edits

Monday	Tuesday	Wednesday	Thursday	Friday
Mr. Parker rides his bike to the beech [beach].	The waves krash [crash] on the sand.	Mr. parker runs and jump [jumps] into the waves.	the day gets hoter [hotter] and hoter [hotter].	Mstr. [Mr.] Parker stay's [stays] in the cold water.
Have you herd [heard] of a dog eating pancakes?	tell [Tell] me all about it?	Jack and me [I] waked [walked] to Gary's house.	Garys [Gary's] mom made buttermilk pan cakes [pancakes].	Rex jumpped [jumped] on the table and eight [ate] them!
Sasha maded [made] a swiming [swimming] pool for her doll.	See [She] filled a soup boll [bowl] with water.	She useed [used] a ruler for a diveing [diving] board.	A napkin! maded [made] a good towel.	I tink [think] her doll had a great time.
Maren rights [writes] spy stories.	Maren's spy sales [sails] the seven sees [seas].	Her spy croses [crosses] the hott [hot] deserts.	He is smartest [smarter] than the bad guy.	He save [saves] the world every weak [week].
You are allmost [almost] done with daily edits.	Witch [Which] story did you like best?	We [we] hopp [hope] you liked editing.	You dided [did] a terrific job!	Keep on writing and sharing your werk [work].

Daily Story Starters

Monday	Tuesday	Wednesday	Thursday	Friday
I want to know more about	I've always wondered how	An interesting animal is	What is it like in	How do they make
I want to know why	What is it like to be	A place I'd like to explore is	Who discovered	Something useful is
I don't know a lot about	An amazing thing is	I've always wondered where	Why is it called	Something in nature I like is
I took an interesting trip to	A fact I'd like to share is	I've always wondered why	Who invented the	I like reading about
Who was the first person to	I know a lot about	A country I want to visit is	Why do we celebrate	Someone in history I like is

Chapter Adaptors

MAKE A SENTENCE SANDWICH

Distribute to students cut-out drawings of bread slices, lunchmeat slices, cheese slices, and tomato slices. Then write on the board *The brown dog runs.* Explain that in the sentence the verb is the "meat," the noun is the "cheese," and the adjective is the "tomato." Tell students that the top piece of bread is the capital letter of the first word, and that the bottom piece of bread is the end mark. Guide students to write on each cutout the correct part of the sentence and to assemble their sentence sandwiches. Repeat the activity with other sentences.

RETEACHING

Draw on the board a chart with the headings *What I Know, What I Want to Know,* and *What I Have Learned.* Guide students to choose a topic and to complete the **K** column of the chart. Instruct students to write in the **W** column questions that they have about the topic. Then have students use research materials to answer their questions, and write the answers in the **L** column. Explain that KWL charts can help guide students' research whenever they write research reports.

ENGLISH-LANGUAGE LEARNERS

Provide English-language learners with letter tiles from a word game. Give each student two piles, each with the letters necessary to spell out the words in a homophone pair. Say the word and help each student correctly spell the word one way and then the other. Talk about the meaning of each word. Say additional sentences that use each homophone and have students indicate which spelling of the word is correct. Repeat with additional homophones.

SPEAKING & LISTENING

Have partners make a TV commercial for a product. *(Examples: toothpaste, spaghetti sauce, car)* Tell students that they should include facts and opinions in their commercials. *(Examples: This spaghetti sauce is made with tomatoes. This sauce is delicious!)* Have partners make a poster of their product. Invite volunteers to share their commercials and posters. After each commercial is presented, help the class identify the facts and the opinions used. Remind students that research reports should not contain opinions.

WRITING & EDITING

Have students write or edit their drafts in the school library. Point out that as they write their research reports, they may find that they are missing an important fact. Tell students that if they are not sure whether a fact is true, they can use references to double-check the fact.

DINOSAUR FACT HUNTERS

Have small groups of students research different kinds of dinosaurs. Encourage each student in each group to provide two facts. Have students write the facts in their own words. Then ask each group to make a dinosaur poster recording their facts and sources. Display the posters in the classroom.

RETEACHING

Write on the board the lyrics to a popular nursery rhyme or song. Then have students take turns offering synonyms for specific words. *(Example: Paddle, Paddle, Paddle Your Ship)* When students have finished, read or sing the new rhyme or song as a class.

CHAPTER

6

Word Study and Research Reports

An Enormous Animal

The blue whale is the largest animal on Earth. It lives in the sea. Some blue whales weigh 200 tons. A blue whale's tongue can weigh as much as an elephant. A blue whale's food is called krill. Krill are very tiny animals that are like shrimp. Blue whales can eat 12,000 pounds of krill a day. The blue whale is the largest animal, but it eats some of the smallest food.

Word Study and Research Reports • 177

Name _____

Synonyms

Synonyms are words that have the same or almost the same meaning.
Use a synonym instead of using the same word over and over.

Be **quiet**.
Be **silent**.

Did you **talk** to me about that?
Did you **speak** to me about that?

Andy is **afraid** of the elephant.
Andy is **scared** of the elephant.

The squirrel will **find** the nut.
The squirrel will **discover** the nut.

Did the cat **hurt** the mouse?
Did the cat **harm** the mouse?

James started to **pull** the wagon.
James started to **tug** the wagon.

When can you **begin**?
When can you **start**?

It's **hard** to turn this doorknob.
It's **difficult** to turn this doorknob.

Write a synonym for each word. Use the examples above.

1. discover *find*

2. talk *speak*

3. start *begin*

4. silent *quiet*

5. tug *pull*

6. hard *difficult*

7. harm *hurt*

8. afraid *scared*

Synonyms, synonyms, we know quite a few.
Quick and *fast*, *shout* and *yell*, *glad* and *happy* too.
Synonyms, synonyms, how our list will grow.
Words that we call synonyms are jolly friends to know.

Name _____

Synonym Practice

Read each sentence. Write a synonym for the underlined word. Use the words on the right for help.

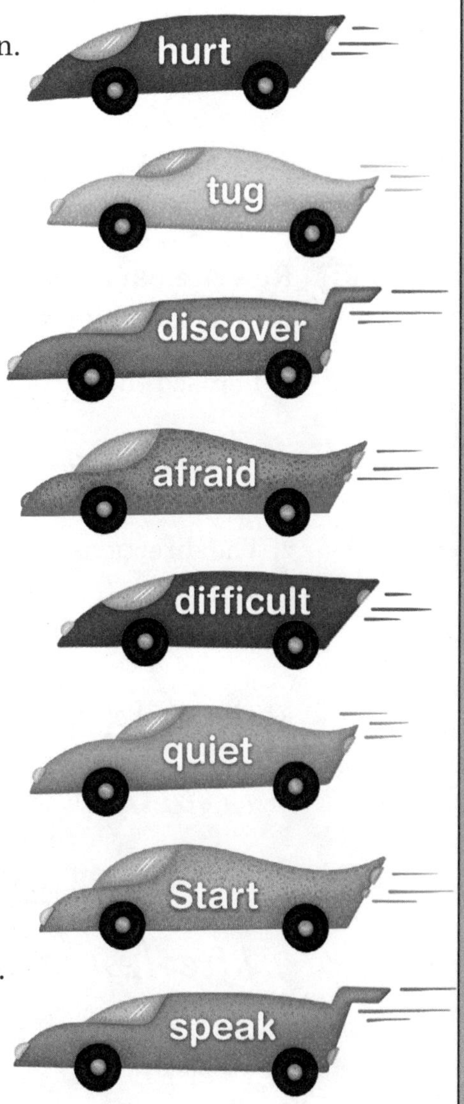

1. Justin will <u>pull</u> the heavy wagon.

   Justin will *tug* the heavy wagon.

2. Are you <u>scared</u> of storms?

   Are you *afraid* of storms?

3. The audience was <u>silent</u>.

   The audience was *quiet*.

4. <u>Begin</u> the race now.

   Start the race now.

5. Please <u>talk</u> about your trip.

   Please *speak* about your trip.

6. Did Logan <u>find</u> the diamond?

   Did Logan *discover* the diamond?

7. Be sure you don't <u>harm</u> the grass.

   Be sure you don't *hurt* the grass.

8. The math problem was <u>hard</u>.

   The math problem was *difficult*.

hurt
tug
discover
afraid
difficult
quiet
Start
speak

Word Study • 179

Name _____

More Synonyms

A Read the words in the balls. Color each pair of synonyms the same color.

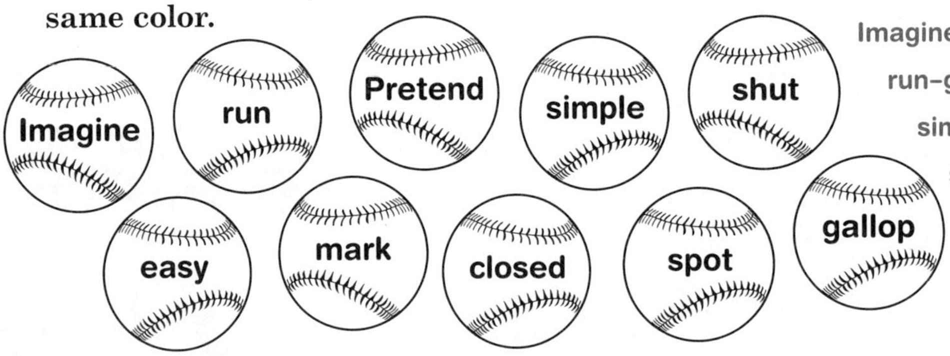

Imagine   run   Pretend   simple   shut

easy   mark   closed   spot   gallop

Imagine–Pretend
run–gallop
simple–easy
shut–closed
mark–spot

B Rewrite each sentence using a synonym in place of the underlined word.

1. I erased the <u>mark</u> on my paper.

   I erased the spot on my paper.

2. The directions were <u>easy</u> to follow.

   The directions were simple to follow.

3. The wind <u>closed</u> the door.

   The wind shut the door.

4. The horse will <u>run</u> across the field.

   The horse will gallop across the field.

5. <u>Pretend</u> that you have three wishes.

   Imagine that you have three wishes.

Name _____

More Synonym Practice

A Look at the words. Write on the line a synonym for each word.

easy *simple*

imagine *pretend*

shut *closed*

spot *mark*

run *gallop*

B Read each sentence. Circle the correct synonym for the underlined word.

1. This recipe is simple. (hard (easy))

2. Did you clean that mark off of the floor? ((spot) paper)

3. I like to imagine that I am an actor. (worry (pretend))

4. We might gallop like horses in gym today. ((run) hop)

5. Leah closed the cupboard. ((shut) opened)

Writer's Corner

Write two sentences about two things you do well.
Use *easy* in one sentence. Use *simple* in the other sentence.

Name

Working with Synonyms

A Read the words in the hearts. Color each pair of synonyms the same color.

happy   small   big   little

pal   large   friend   glad

happy–glad
small–little
big–large
pal–friend

B Rewrite each sentence. Use a synonym in place of the underlined word.

1. My pal and I work together.

   My friend and I work together.

2. We fold a large sheet of paper.

   We fold a big sheet of paper.

3. Then we glue on small yellow stars.

   Then we glue on little yellow stars.

4. Our teacher will be glad to see the card we made.

   Our teacher will be happy to see the card we made.

Name _____

Synonyms Review

A **Read the pairs of words. Write yes if the pairs are synonyms. Write no if the pairs are not synonyms.**

1. find   discover   *yes*   4. closed   shut   *yes*

2. easy   big   *no*   5. pull   little   *no*

3. talk   simple   *no*   6. hurt   harm   *yes*

B **Draw a line from each word in the first list to its synonym in the second list.**

1. quiet   imagine

2. mark   friend

3. pal   happy

4. hard   spot

5. pretend   silent

6. glad   difficult

Writer's Corner

Write two sentences about two things in your bedroom.
Use *large* in one sentence. Use *big* in the other sentence.

Name

Antonyms

Antonyms are words that have opposite meanings.

always never	strong weak	right wrong	light heavy
inside outside	open close	night day	come go

🔘 **Read each sentence aloud. Write the antonym of the underlined word. Use the words in the bricks for help.**

1. The answer is <u>right</u>.   *wrong*

2. Please take the cat <u>outside</u>.   *inside*

3. I <u>always</u> eat peanut butter.   *never*

4. My bookbag is <u>heavy</u>.   *light*

5. That was a <u>strong</u> rope.   *weak*

Name _____

More Antonyms

Write each sentence. Replace the underlined word with its antonym. Use the word bank if you need help.

| heavy | go | open | day | never |

1. Please <u>close</u> the door.

   Please open the door.

2. The party lasted all <u>night</u>.

   The party lasted all day.

3. This book is <u>light</u>.

   This book is heavy.

4. I <u>always</u> clean my room.

   I never clean my room.

5. Can Belle <u>come</u> too?

   Can Belle go too?

Writer's Corner

Write two sentences about things you have to do. Use the antonyms *night* and *day*.

Word Study • 185

Name

Antonym Practice

Here are some more antonyms.

up down	sad happy	over under	small large

short tall	high low	far near	thick thin

Complete each sentence with the antonym of the underlined word. Use the words above if you need help.

1. Tara lives <u>near</u> us, but Cole lives *far* from us.

2. A kitten is <u>small</u>, but a lion is *large* .

3. Chloe sings <u>high</u>, but Hope sings *low* .

4. This pole is <u>thin</u>, but that one is *thick* .

5. Lee is <u>happy</u> today, but his sister is *sad* .

6. Julie is going <u>up</u> the stairs, but Daniel is going *down* .

7. My cousin is <u>tall</u>, but I am *short* .

8. The rabbit hopped <u>under</u> the bush, but the bird flew *over* it.

Name _____

Working with Antonyms

Look at each set of pictures. Write the correct word for each picture. Use the antonym pairs below for help.

full	fast	stop	dry	cold	first
empty	slow	go	wet	hot	last

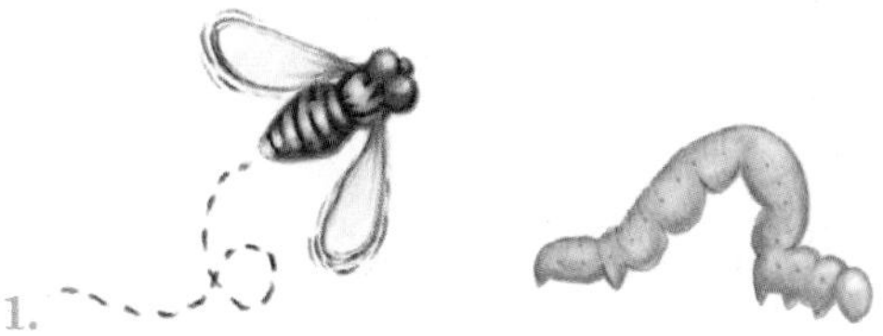

1. *fast*   *slow*

4. *dry*   *wet*

2. *last*   *first*

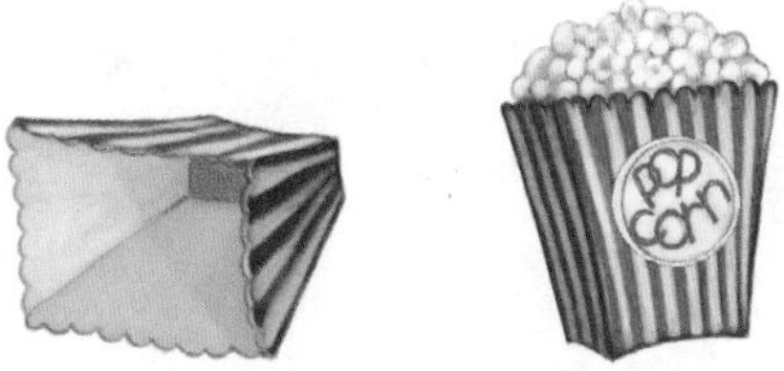

5. *empty*   *full*

3. *cold*   *hot*

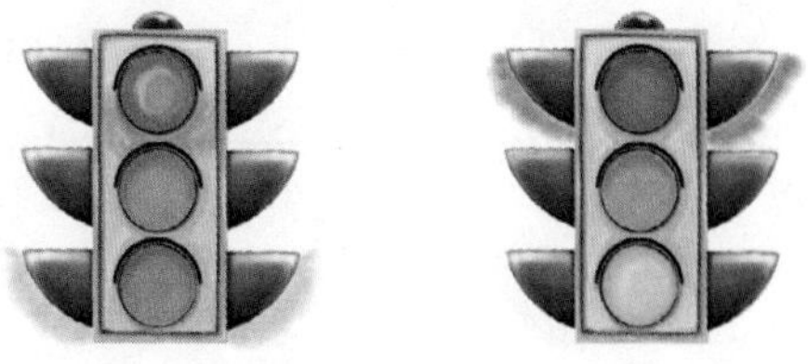

6. *stop*   *go*

Name _____

Antonyms Review

A **Match each question with the correct answer. Then underline the antonyms in each question and answer.**

1. Is a turtle <u>fast</u>?   No, he is <u>last</u> in line.

2. Was the jar <u>full</u>?   No, it is <u>slow</u>.

3. Is Peter <u>first</u> in line?   No, it is <u>cold</u>.

4. Is the dog's nose <u>hot</u>?   No, it was <u>empty</u>

5. Does a green light mean <u>stop</u>?   No, it is <u>dry</u>.

6. Is the sidewalk <u>wet</u>?   No, it means <u>go</u>.

B **Match each word in the first list to its antonym in the second list.**

1. light   empty

2. sad   never

3. full   under

4. always   heavy

5. over   happy

1. inside   thin

2. thick   last

3. fast   outside

4. come   go

5. first   slow

Name

Synonyms and Antonyms Review

A **Read each sentence. Circle the correct synonym for the underlined word.**

1. Andy is <u>afraid</u> of alligators. ((scared) glad)

2. Jeff is a <u>silent</u> boy. ((quiet) loud)

3. Leslie is my best <u>pal</u>. (enemy (friend))

4. That math problem is <u>simple</u>. ((easy) hard)

5. Sam likes to <u>imagine</u> that he is a basketball player. (start (pretend))

6. Eric <u>closed</u> the comic book. (opened (shut))

B **Read each sentence. Write an antonym for the underlined word.**

1. My brother thinks he is always <u>right</u>. *wrong*

2. Your uncle is <u>short</u>. *tall*

3. It is <u>cold</u> today. *hot*

4. I <u>always</u> wear my hair this way. *never*

Name

Homophones

Homophones are words that sound alike but are spelled differently and have different meanings. Look at these homophones.

*I thought I **knew** the answer.*   *Our car is in the driveway.*
*This shirt is **new**.*   *The clock is an **hour** fast.*

*Do you want to **buy** it?*   *Did you **meet** my cousin?*
*Did the train pass **by**?*   *There is **meat** on this sandwich.*

Underline the correct homophone in each sentence.

1. The bus is one (our hour) late.

2. Is your bike (knew new)?

3. Dad drove (by buy) the parade.

4. Do lions eat (meet meat)?

5. Anita will (buy by) the lemons.

6. Carlos (new knew) his street address.

7. I got to (meet meat) my favorite actor!

8. (Hour Our) science experiment was fun.

Writer's Corner

Write two sentences about the grocery store. Use *buy* in one sentence. Use *by* in the other sentence.

Name _____

Homophone Practice

A **Write the correct word in each blank.**

meat

hour   buy

by   new

meet   Our

knew

1. Jacob *knew* he would get a *new* bike.

2. *Our* party starts in one *hour* .

3. Stop *by* the store and *buy* some milk.

4. Did you *meet* the man who doesn't eat *meat* ?

B **Read each sentence. If the underlined homophone is correct, put an X on the line. If the homophone is not correct, write the correct homophone on the line.**

1. Did Shelby <u>meat</u> Josh? *meet*

2. Can Marissa come to <u>our</u> house? *X*

3. Anthony wants to <u>buy</u> that game. *X*

4. Is that the <u>knew</u> book? *new*

5. Did Melanie come <u>buy</u> the house? *by*

6. Your watch is one <u>hour</u> slow. *X*

7. I <u>knew</u> that you had my book! *X*

Name

More Homophones

Here are some more homophones.

Lily is reading a fairy **tale**.   It is **eight** o'clock.
The squirrel has a bushy **tail**.   Ryan **ate** his breakfast.

Here is your birthday cake.   Will you **be** at Ethan's party?
Did you **hear** the bird?   Erin was stung by a **bee**.

A Underline the correct homophone in each sentence.

1. Did you (hear here) the jet roar?

2. Jada told us a fairy (tail tale).

3. Tyler (ate eight) Chinese food.

4. (Hear Here) is the hidden treasure!

5. The bear's (tail tale) is short.

6. (Ate Eight) pencils rolled off the desk.

B Underline the homophone pair in each sentence.

1. Stand here until you hear the bell ring.

2. Dylan ate eight pieces of candy.

3. We listened to a tale about a peacock's colorful tail.

4. That bee will be going back to its hive.

Name

Working with Homophones

You will probably use these homophones when you write.

*Can you **see** the board?*   *Look at the baby **deer**!*

*This ship sails the **sea**.*   *Kara is a **dear** little girl.*

*What did you **write** about?*   *My arm was **weak** after I broke it.*

*Is this the **right** house?*   *Halloween is next **week**.*

Underline the correct homophone in each sentence.

1. Make a (write right) turn on Clark Street.

2. Alexa is a (deer dear) friend.

3. The (see sea) is very rough today.

4. There was a (deer dear) in our yard.

5. The branch fell because it was (week weak).

6. I should (write right) to my grandma.

7. May I (see sea) the dinosaur bone?

8. I have piano lessons every (week weak).

Writer's Corner

Write two sentences about yourself. Use the homophones *write* and *right.*

Name _____

Practice Working with Homophones

Complete each sentence. Use a homophone of a word on the right.

1. The story tells how the elephant got its *tail*.

   dear

2. Isabel could *hear* the robins singing.

   tale

3. Caleb *ate* at a Mexican restaurant.

   our

4. We spent an *hour* in the dinosaur museum.

   here

5. A strange animal passed *by*.

   buy

6. I saw a *deer* in the woods.

   sea

7. I can *see* Venus through this telescope.

   knew

8. Katelyn got a *new* bike for Christmas.

   eight

Homophones, homophones,
we know quite a few.
Dear and *deer*, *here* and *hear*,
to and *two* and *too*.
Homophones, homophones,
how our list will grow.
Words that we call homophones
are jolly friends to know.

Name

Homophones Review

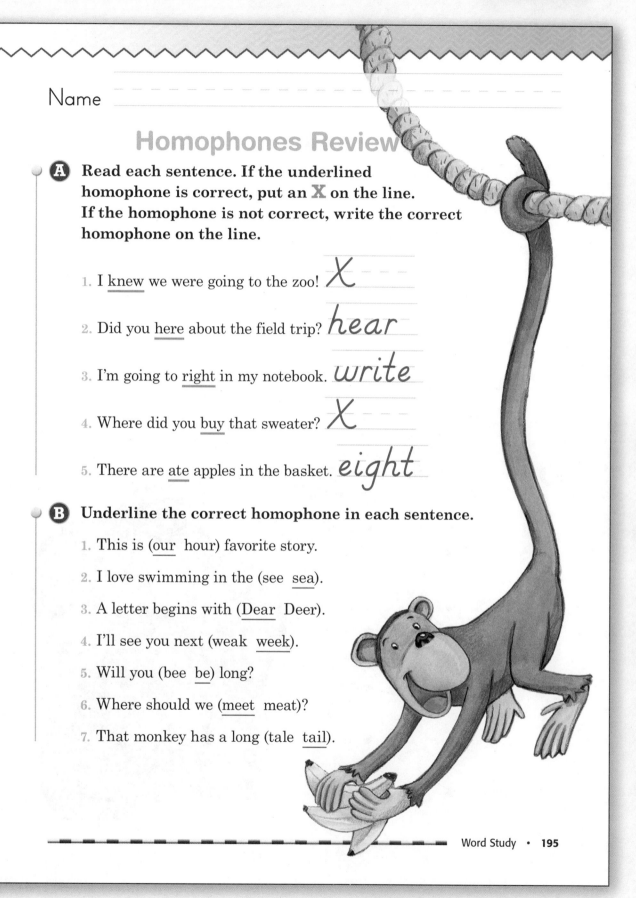

A Read each sentence. If the underlined homophone is correct, put an **X** on the line. If the homophone is not correct, write the correct homophone on the line.

1. I <u>knew</u> we were going to the zoo! *X*

2. Did you <u>here</u> about the field trip? *hear*

3. I'm going to <u>right</u> in my notebook. *write*

4. Where did you <u>buy</u> that sweater? *X*

5. There are <u>ate</u> apples in the basket. *eight*

B Underline the correct homophone in each sentence.

1. This is (<u>our</u> hour) favorite story.

2. I love swimming in the (see <u>sea</u>).

3. A letter begins with (<u>Dear</u> Deer).

4. I'll see you next (weak <u>week</u>).

5. Will you (bee <u>be</u>) long?

6. Where should we (<u>meet</u> meat)?

7. That monkey has a long (tale <u>tail</u>).

Word Study • 195

Name _____

Show What You Know

Ⓐ Find a synonym in the list for each underlined word. Write the letter on the line.

1. Riley is <u>afraid</u> of the dark. *e* ___

2. Did Dad <u>discover</u> the beavers' home? *b* ___

3. Be <u>quiet</u>. *d* ___

4. Can lightning <u>harm</u> you? *c* ___

5. Jamie started to <u>tug</u> at his mother's skirt. *a* ___

a. pull

b. find

c. hurt

d. silent

e. scared

Ⓑ For each set, draw a line from each word in the first list to its antonym in the second list.

1. dry — weak
2. full — last
3. strong — empty
4. small — wet
5. first — large

1. tall — low
2. high — light
3. inside — never
4. heavy — outside
5. always — short

Name _____

Show What You Know

A **Underline the antonyms in each sentence.**

1. Does Chad live <u>near</u> the lake or <u>far</u> from the lake?

2. Did the dog go <u>over</u> or <u>under</u> the fence?

3. Is the pizza crust <u>thick</u> or <u>thin</u>?

4. Was your answer <u>right</u> or <u>wrong</u>?

5. Shall I <u>open</u> or <u>close</u> the window?

6. Is your sister <u>happy</u> today, or is she <u>sad</u>?

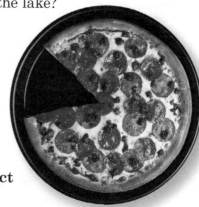

B **Complete each sentence with the correct homophone.**

eight
ate

sea
see

hear
here

Write
Right

tale
tail

new
knew

1. Look at the dolphin swimming in the *sea* .

2. Our school has a *new* computer.

3. Can you *hear* the hoot of the owl?

4. Henry wore the number *eight* on his shirt.

5. A monkey can swing by its *tail* .

6. *Write* your name at the top of your paper.

Word Study • 197

What Is a Research Report?

Get Ready to Write

A **research report** tells facts about one topic. A research report can tell about a person, a place, a thing, or an event.

The **beginning** of a research report names the topic.

The **middle** of a research report tells more about the topic. Information about the topic comes from different sources.

The **ending** of a research report sums up the report.

Beginning ——— A brachiosaurus is a kind of dinosaur. It was 40 feet tall and 80 feet long. It weighed 60 tons.

Middle ——— The brachiosaurus ate plants. Bones of the brachiosaurus have been found in Colorado. A brachiosaurus skeleton is on display in Chicago.

Ending ——— The brachiosaurus was a huge, gentle dinosaur.

○ **Answer these questions about the research report.**

1. What is the topic of the research report?

  the brachiosaurus

2. What fact told what the brachiosaurus ate?

  The brachiosaurus ate plants.

3. What does the ending say about the topic?

  The brachiosaurus was a huge, gentle dinosaur.

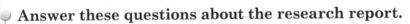

The Topic of a Research Report

A research report is about one **topic**. The topic is something you want to know more about. It can be about a person, a place, a thing, or an event.

The **beginning** of a research report has a **topic sentence**. A topic sentence tells what your research report is about. A topic sentence should grab the reader's attention. It should make the reader want to learn more.

Look at these topic sentences. Each one tells about a topic. But some sentences are more interesting than others.

I have a goldfish.

Goldfish are one of the most popular pets.

My report is about walking sticks.

A walking stick is an insect that looks like a stick.

The Statue of Liberty is cool.

The Statue of Liberty is a huge statue in New York.

Look at each topic. Write your own topic sentence. Try to grab the reader's attention. Answers will vary.

1. **zebras**

   _____

   _____

2. **firefighters**

   _____

   _____

Fact and Opinion

The **middle** of your research report gives **facts**. A fact is something that is true. You can get facts from books, encyclopedias, or on the Internet.

Be sure your report doesn't give your **opinion**. An opinion tells what you think or feel.

FACT: *Polar bears have black skin under their fur.*

OPINION: *I like polar bears.*

A Read each sentence. Underline **F** if the sentence is a fact. Underline **O** if the sentence is an opinion.

Polar bears are not really white.	**F** O
I'd like to see a polar bear.	F **O**
Polar bears eat meat.	**F** O
I think it would be fun to have a polar bear.	F **O**
Polar bears are my favorite animal.	F **O**
Black skin helps the polar bear stay warm.	**F** O

B Circle one of these topics. Write three facts about it. Find facts in books, in encyclopedias, or on the Internet.

dinosaurs   Thanksgiving   pirates

FACT: _____

FACT: _____

FACT: _____

Finding Facts

You can find facts in the library. You look for facts in **sources**. Some sources you can look in are encyclopedias, nonfiction books, and the Internet. Write the facts in your own words.

You find facts by answering questions. Here are some questions you might answer with facts.

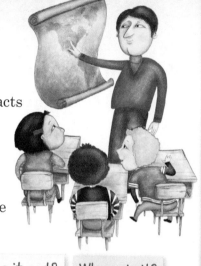

| What does he, she, or it look like? | What does it eat? | Where is it? |

| Where does he, she, or it live? | How big is it? | What did he or she do? |

○ **Choose one of these topics. Find three facts about the topic. Find one fact in each kind of source.**

spiders   tigers   George Washington   Alaska

Fact 1: _____

nonfiction book _____

_____

Fact 2: _____

encyclopedia _____

_____

Fact 3: _____

the Internet _____

_____

Writing and Organizing Notes

As you find facts, write them down. Write them in your own words on note cards.

Write the fact at the top of the note card. Write where you found the fact at the bottom of the note card.

If the fact is from	Write
a book	the title, the author, and the page number
an encyclopedia	the article title, the encyclopedia name, the volume number, and the page number
the Internet	the web address

After you have taken notes, put the cards into piles. Make a pile for each kind of information that you have. Note cards might look like this.

Red pandas live in Nepal, Burma, and central China.

"Red Pandas." Encyclopedia Britannica. Vol. 2, p. 245

Red pandas weigh less than 20 pounds.

www.tigerhomes.org/animal/redpanda.cfm

Look at the facts that you wrote on page 201. Write each fact at the top of a separate note card. Write where you found the fact at the bottom. Then find three more facts. Write a note card for each fact. Put your cards into piles. Put facts that go together in the same pile.

Writing an Ending

In the **ending** you sum up your research report.

Look at these endings. Which endings do you think are better?

Some goldfish are orange.

Goldfish are good pets because they are easy to take care of.

I'm glad I chose this topic.

Walking sticks are bugs with clever costumes.

So now you know what I know about the Statue of Liberty.

The Statue of Liberty is one of the most visited places in New York.

Read the research reports below. Add an ending sentence to each.

Abraham Lincoln worked his whole life to end slavery. Many people did not agree with him. Southern states wanted to keep slavery. Lincoln's army fought the Southern armies. Finally Lincoln made the Emancipation Proclamation. It freed the slaves.

The crew of Apollo 11 made the first mission to the moon. Neil Armstrong, Michael Collins, and Edwin "Buzz" Aldrin were the crew. The trip from Earth to the moon took four days. Neil Armstrong took the first step on the moon.

Writer's Workshop

PREWRITING

Pick a Topic

Cady is writing a research report. A research report has facts. First Cady must pick a topic. Cady thinks about things she would like to know more about. She lists them in her notebook.

skateboarding

the Pilgrims

blue whales

Florence Nightingale

Cady circles the topic she likes best. This is the topic she will write about.

Make a list of topics. Think about people, places, things, and events. Is the topic something you want to know more about? Is it something you can find a lot of information about? Is it something others might want to know more about? Circle the topic you want to write about.

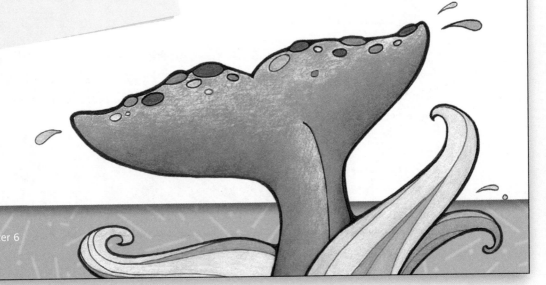

PREWRITING

Plan Your Research Report

Cady plans her research report. First she goes to the library. She finds facts in an encyclopedia. She finds more facts on the Internet. The librarian helps her find Web sites that have good information.

Then Cady writes each fact on a separate note card. She puts the note cards into piles. One pile is about what blue whales eat. The other pile is about the size of blue whales.

Blue whales eat krill.

Learn All About Whales

by Kath Buffington, p.16

Blue whales can weigh

200 tons.

yahooligans.yahoo.com/

content/animals.html

Do research in the library. Find facts about your topic. Write each fact on a separate note card. Write the facts in your own words. Remember to write where you found each fact.

When you have finished, put the note cards into piles. Did you write about an animal, like Cady did? Make one pile with facts about what the animal looks like. Make another pile about what the animal eats. Make a third pile about where the animal lives.

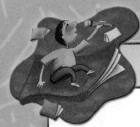

Writer's Workshop

DRAFTING

Cady wrote a lot of note cards. She uses her cards to write her report. Here is Cady's draft.

An Enormous Animal

The blue whale is the largest animal on Earth. It lives in the see. Some blue whales weigh 200 tons. A blue whale's tongue can weigh as much as an elephant. A blue whale's food is called krill. Krill are very tiny animals that are like shrimp. Blue whales can eat 12,000 pounds of krill a day. I think blue whales are really cool.

Write your draft in your notebook. Remember to write a topic sentence that grabs the reader's attention. Write in the middle of your report the facts that you found. Include facts that your reader might want to know. Write an ending that sums up the topic. Remember that you can make changes to your draft later.

EDITING

Cady must edit her research report. She wants to make sure it makes sense and has all its parts.

Cady uses this Editing Checklist. She checks one question at a time.

like shrimp. Blue whales can eat 12,000 pounds of krill a day. ~~I think blue whales are really cool.~~ The blue whale is the largest animal, but it eats some of the smallest food.

Look at the mistake Cady finds. How does she fix it?

Use the Editing Checklist to edit your report. Check for one question at a time. When you have finished, read aloud your research report. Can you add anything to make your report better? Mark your changes on your draft.

> I didn't leave out my opinion!

REVISING

Cady fixes the mistakes she marked. Then she makes a new copy of her draft.

Copy your draft. Fix any mistakes you marked. Make sure you can answer yes to all the questions on the checklist.

Writer's Workshop

PROOFREADING

Cady wants to proofread her research report. By proofreading she will catch even more mistakes. She uses this Proofreading Checklist. She carefully checks one question at a time.

Proofreading Checklist

☐ Are all the words spelled correctly?

☐ Did I use capital letters?

☐ Did I use the right end marks?

☐ Can I replace any words with synonyms?

☐ Are antonyms used correctly?

☐ Are all homophones used correctly?

An Enormous Animal

The blue whale is the largest animal on Earth.

It lives in the ~~see.~~ sea. Some blue whales weigh 200

tons. A blue whale's tongue can weigh as much as

Look at the mistake Cady finds. How does she fix it?

Use the Proofreading Checklist to check your draft. Look for one kind of mistake at a time. Make your words and sentences as clear as you can. Remember to read over your draft to make sure that you did not add any new mistakes.

PUBLISHING

After all her hard work, Cady is excited to publish her report. She writes the final copy. Then she draws a picture of a blue whale on the cover of her report. Cady publishes her report by reading it to her class.

Recopy your research report. Write as neatly as you can. Make sure that you did not add any new mistakes. Remember to add a title.

Now decide how to publish our research report. Here are some ways you might publish it. Can you think of other ways?

Read your report to your class.

Make a class magazine.

Make a classroom encyclopedia. Include everyone's research reports.

Hang your report on a classroom bulletin board.

Research Tools

In this chapter students will learn about

- alphabetical order
- dictionary skills
- encyclopedia skills
- fiction and nonfiction books
- parts of a book
- the Internet

A Visual, Please

Parts of a Dictionary

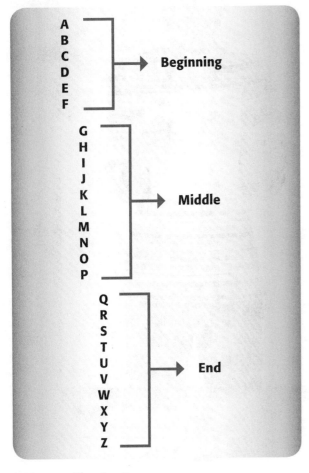

Tools of the Trade

Long Live the Library

Research tools provide students with an all-access pass to the world of knowledge and information. The library is a hub of research materials. Dictionaries, encyclopedias, fiction books, nonfiction books, and computers are all gathered under one roof for the purpose of discovering and sharing information. Teaching students how to tap into this information and familiarizing them with the library go hand in hand.

Library books are organized into three categories: fiction books; nonfiction books; and reference books, such as dictionaries and encyclopedias. In most libraries, fiction books are organized alphabetically by the author's last name, while nonfiction books are organized by subject.

Most libraries have either a card catalog or an electronic card catalog to help people search for books by title, author, or subject. Many libraries also have access to the Internet. Online search engines are a valuable resource, but with their advantages come pitfalls. Inappropriate and unreliable information is often included in search results. Encouraging students to use kid-friendly search engines not only is an effective way to avoid such information, it also promotes Internet safety.

Librarians are also an excellent resource. Librarians can help find the best sources for information and are there to answer any questions that may arise.

Common Errors

Otherwise Known as "Search Smarts"

Some students, when searching for a word in a dictionary or an encyclopedia, forget to consider where the first letter of the word falls in the alphabet, and consequently where the word will fall in the book. These students waste time paging through the entire book instead of narrowing their search to the beginning, the middle, or the end of the dictionary.

To help students avoid this common error, display the visual on page 210a. Remind students to use this visual as a reference before looking up a word in a dictionary or an encyclopedia.

For Kids Who Are Ready

Or "Meet and Greet"

For students who are comfortable using a dictionary and an encyclopedia, introduce the thesaurus. The following is a sample entry from a thesaurus:

exciting Causing strong feelings of happiness, eagerness, or interest
Synonyms **thrilling, inspiring, stirring**

Explain that a thesaurus lists synonyms. Remind students that synonyms are words that have the same or almost the same meaning. Tell students that a thesaurus can help them find the exact word that they need and that many thesauruses are arranged like dictionaries. Keep a thesaurus in the classroom. Invite students to use it to find synonyms for words that they commonly repeat in their writing.

Ask a Mentor

Real Situations, Real Solutions

Dear Library Luminary,

My students are confused about when to use an encyclopedia instead of a dictionary. What should I tell them?

To use or not to use,
Miss Merrin

Dear Miss Merrin,

That is the question! Students should use an encyclopedia instead of a dictionary when they are interested in learning more about a word than just its meaning—but only if the word is a noun. Encyclopedias contain general information about people, places, things, and events, and are usually used for research. Point out that an encyclopedia is a good place to look up proper nouns.

Ponder the purpose,
Library Luminary

Dear Loyal Librarian,

In addition to using kid-friendly search engines, how can I help students be sure that a Web site is legitimate and that the information is reliable?

Filtering facts,
Frank

Dear Frank,

To decide whether a Web site is reliable, tell students to check the letters at the end of the address. Sites developed by organizations, which end in *.org*, or by the government, which end in *.gov*, are usually accurate. A site ending in *.edu* is often a reliable source if the pages were created by professors or a university. Encourage students to also check when a Web site was last updated.

You can rely on me,
Loyal Librarian

"That's the best pop-up I've ever seen."

Research Tools

Teacher's Toolbox

Try the following ideas to help your students get the most out of this chapter:

- Encourage students to use journals and magazines as research tools.

- Have the school librarian make a presentation for students on how to use an electronic card catalog and online search engine.

- Supply students with the following kid-friendly search engines: www.ajkids.com, www.kidsclick.org, www.yahooligans.com.

Reasons to Research

Share with students the following situations in which the research tools learned in this chapter may be applied to writing projects throughout the year:

- using a nonfiction book about kites to write a how-to article about flying a kite

- looking up an adjective in a dictionary to see if it is appropriate to use in a description

- finding in the library a fiction book to use for a book report

- finding in the library a map of Florida to include with a personal narrative about a trip there

- using a kid-friendly search engine to find a Web site about tigers to use for a research report

- using the Internet to look up the correct Zip Code when mailing a friendly letter

Chapter Adaptors

SPEAKING & LISTENING

Form the class into small groups and assign each group a simple encyclopedia article. Have students read the article and take notes on note cards. Then have each group give an oral summary of the article. Be sure that each student in the group shares at least one fact with the class. When each group is finished, invite the rest of the class to tell facts they learned from the presentation.

FACT-FINDING MISSION

Invite students to go on a scavenger hunt for interesting facts. Provide small groups with encyclopedias or set aside time for students to use the library. Photocopy and distribute the following list of questions: *In what year was the first airplane invented? Which planet is farthest from the sun? Where did the Pilgrims land in 1620? Where is Kuala Lumpur? What do pandas eat?* Have students work together to find the answers to the questions. Award a prize to the first group to finish the list of questions correctly.

DICTIONARY SCAVENGER HUNT

Once students are comfortable using a beginning dictionary, explain that dictionaries for grown-ups work in the same way. Provide advanced dictionaries to groups of students and have them go on a scavenger hunt. Photocopy and distribute the following questions: *What is a googol? What is a brooch? What is a sphinx? What is a mosaic? What is a lynx? What is a solarium? What is a caboose? What is a hippodrome? What is a tempest? What is a manatee?* Have students work together to find the definitions of the words. Award a prize to the first group to finish defining the list of words correctly.

RETEACHING

Provide students with fiction and nonfiction books that feature similar topics. *(Examples: bears, trees, the moon)* Have students identify which books are fiction and which books are nonfiction. Ask students how they know. Remind students that fiction books tell about made-up people, places, things, or events and that nonfiction books contain facts about real people, places, things, or events.

RETEACHING

Pick a letter and assign each student a word that begins with that letter. Have students make signs that show their words. Designate two students as guide words and have them stand at the front of the room. Have the remaining students determine whether their words come between the guide words, before the guide words, or after the guide words. Have students stand in their appropriate places at the front of the room.

ENGLISH-LANGUAGE LEARNERS

Invite English-language learners to create their own translation dictionaries. Have students choose five nouns and draw those nouns on separate sheets of paper. *(Examples: bicycle, dog, girl, house, park)* For each drawing, have students write the noun in their primary language under the picture and in English above the picture. Then have students alphabetize their pages in English. You might have students who share a primary language work together to choose different nouns and build a bigger dictionary.

CHAPTER 7

Research Tools

Quotation Station

Writing is the best way to talk without being interrupted.

—*Jules Renard*
author

Computer Area

Fiction Section

A-L

Librarian

Circulation Desk

Book Return

210 • Chapter 7

Nonfiction Section

Reference Area

Reading Area

Research Tools • 211

Name _____

Alphabetical Order

Words in **alphabetical order** are in the order of the letters of the alphabet. These words are in order by the first letter of each word.

*a*stronaut   *m*oon   *p*lanets   *s*pace

These children have to line up in alphabetical order. Write their names in alphabetical order. Use their last names.

1. Audrey Anders
2. Seth Baker
3. Miguel Covas
4. Brandon Deane
5. Sarah Fowler
6. Luis Gonzalez
7. Jenna Roth
8. Nancy Wright

Brandon Deane

Sarah Fowler

Nancy Wright

Miguel Covas

Audrey Anders

Luis Gonzalez

Jenna Roth

Seth Baker

Name

More Alphabetical Order

Words that start with the same letter are put in alphabetical order by the second letter.

b**a**ll   be**e**p   b**i**g   b**o**x

A Are these names in alphabetical order? Write **yes** or **no**.

1. Aiden, Abigail, Andrew   *no*

2. Ella, Emma, Ethan   *yes*

3. Caleb, Chloe, Connor   *yes*

4. Molly, Mitch, Matt   *no*

5. Gerry, Gia, Grace   *yes*

B Look at the words in the word bank. Write them in alphabetical order.

| bear | bison | bat |
| bobcat | bumblebee | bluebird |

1. *bat*
2. *bear*
3. *bison*
4. *bluebird*
5. *bobcat*
6. *bumblebee*

Name

Practice with Alphabetical Order

A Put each group of words in alphabetical order. Write 1, 2, 3, or 4 next to each word to show the correct order.

1. squid 3
   sea 2
   orca 1
   turtle 4

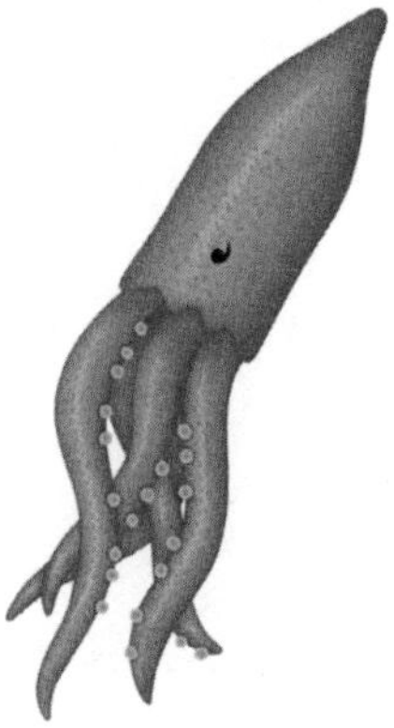

2. bat 1
   tiger 4
   fox 3
   bear 2

B Write each group of words in alphabetical order.

1. almost *add*
   add *almost*
   any *any*
   apple *apple*

2. grass *gave*
   goat *get*
   gave *goat*
   get *grass*

3. more *meet*
   music *miss*
   miss *more*
   meet *music*

4. she *seal*
   snow *she*
   story *snow*
   seal *story*

Name

Dictionary Skills

A **dictionary** is a book of words. A dictionary tells you how to spell a word and what a word means. The words in a dictionary are in alphabetical order.

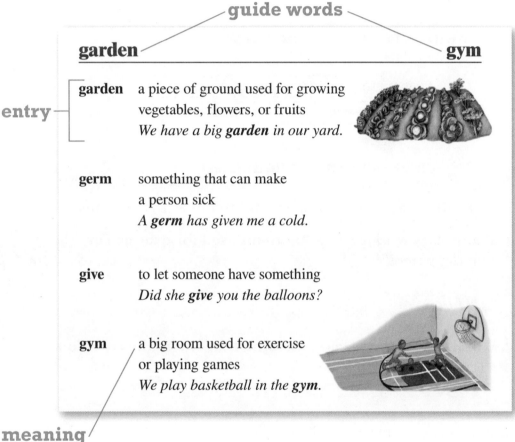

guide words

garden   **gym**

entry — **garden**   a piece of ground used for growing vegetables, flowers, or fruits
*We have a big **garden** in our yard.*

germ   something that can make a person sick
*A **germ** has given me a cold.*

give   to let someone have something
*Did she **give** you the balloons?*

gym   a big room used for exercise or playing games
*We play basketball in the **gym**.*

meaning

1. What letter does each word start with? *g*

2. Which word comes before **give** in the dictionary? *germ*

3. Which word comes after **give** in the dictionary? *gym*

Name _____

Dictionary Skills—Parts of an Entry

A dictionary **entry** has at least two parts: the **entry word** and the **meaning**. A dictionary may use a picture or an example sentence to help you understand what the word means. This is a dictionary entry.

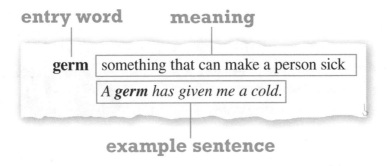

entry word   **meaning**

germ | something that can make a person sick |
| *A germ has given me a cold.* |

example sentence

Use the dictionary page on page 215 to answer these questions.

1. Which entry word means **a big room used for exercise or playing games**?

    gym

2. Which entry word means **something that can make a person sick**?

    germ

3. Write the meaning of the word **give**.

    to let someone have something

4. Write your own example sentence for the word **garden**.

    Answers will vary.

Name _____

Dictionary Skills—Guide Words

Guide words help you find a word in a dictionary. Guide words are at the top corners of each page. They tell the first and last words on a dictionary page.

When you look for a word in a dictionary, do the following:

1. Decide if the word is in the beginning, the middle, or the end of the dictionary.
2. Look at the guide words.
3. Decide if your word comes alphabetically between the two guide words.
4. If it does, look for the word on the page.

A Where would you find each word? Write **beginning**, **middle**, or **end**.

1. ball *beginning*   4. yawn *end*
2. maid *middle*   5. zoo *end*
3. dog *beginning*   6. limp *middle*

B Read each pair of guide words. Underline the word that you might find on a page with those guide words.

1. caterpillar—check   <u>cent</u>   hold   build
2. dragon—dust   salad   <u>dress</u>   nurse
3. fall—finger   horse   <u>fast</u>   barn
4. hair—heart   <u>head</u>   bird   carrot
5. idea—invent   tree   gate   <u>insect</u>
6. pig—pizza   <u>pill</u>   flower   pull

Name

Encyclopedia Skills

An **encyclopedia** is a group of books that has information. The information is about people, places, things, and events. Each book is called a **volume**. The topics in an encyclopedia are in alphabetical order. Each topic is called an **entry**.

entry

Frog, Northern Cricket
Cricket frogs are tree frogs. They do not climb, and they have no pads on their toes. Northern cricket frogs can vary in color from frog to frog. They are small, with warty skin and a dark triangle between their eyes. Often they have dark spots or stripes. They make a sound like two small stones being quickly tapped together.

The northern cricket frog breeds in spring and early summer. Even though these frogs come out during the day, their small size can make them difficult to find.

volume

Encyclopedia of Knowledge — F volume 6

Answer these questions about the encyclopedia entry above.

1. What is the topic of this entry?

northern cricket frogs

2. In which volume can this entry be found? *6*

3. What type of frog is the northern cricket frog? *tree frog*

4. Write one interesting fact you learned about the northern cricket frog.

Answers will vary.

Name _____

Fiction and Nonfiction Books

Fiction books tell about make-believe people, places, things, or events. These books are on library shelves in alphabetical order by the author's last name. Fiction books are in a special part of the library.

Nonfiction books tell about real people, places, things, and events. These books tell facts. They are on library shelves by topic. They are in a different part of the library.

Can you tell which books are nonfiction and which books are fiction? Write nonfiction or fiction after each title.

1. Perry and the Pink Lion — *fiction*

2. Lions in Africa — *nonfiction*

3. Where Lions Live — *nonfiction*

4. A Lion's Wearing My Shoes! — *fiction*

5. How Lions Live — *nonfiction*

6. The Lion's Tea Party — *fiction*

7. The Tale of the Lion and the Ant — *fiction*

8. The Truth About Lions — *nonfiction*

Name

Parts of a Book

A book has many parts. The **cover** tells the title and the author of the book. The **contents page** tells where to find information about a topic.

title

page

topic

Contents

Chapter

1. Earthworms 1

2. Worms That Recycle 15

3. Leeches 27

4. Tapeworms 40

by James Carlson

author

Answer these questions about the parts of a book.

1. What is the title of the book?

All About Worms

2. Who is the author of the book?

James Carlson

3. Which chapter has facts about worms that recycle?

Chapter 2

4. On what page would you start looking for facts about leeches?

page 27

Name

Using the Internet

Some people call the **Internet** the world's biggest library. You can use the Internet to find facts about any topic that you research.

Make sure that the information you find on the Internet is true. Sometimes what you read on the Internet is made up. Use **search engines** made for kids. A kids' search engine helps you find Web sites that have true information.

Internet safety is very important. Don't give out information about yourself, such as your name or your address. Make sure a grown-up is nearby when you are using the Internet. If you see something that makes you uncomfortable, tell a grown-up.

Research Tools • 221

Grammar Review

A **Read these sentences. Tell what kind of sentence each sentence is.**

t = telling   c = commanding   a = asking   e = exclaiming

1. The thunder scared me! __e__   5. We drink lemonade. __t__

2. I caught a fish. __t__   6. Call your grandma. __c__

3. Go to bed. __c__   7. What time is it? __a__

4. Do you have a pet? __a__   8. I love this song! __e__

B **Underline the correct month in each sentence.**

1. It is cold in (October Oktobur).   4. Flowers grow in (May Mae).

2. We swim in (Jewly July).   5. School is out in (January June).

3. (March June) is before April.   6. (December May) is the last month.

C **Circle the abbreviation or the initials in each sentence. Then add periods.**

1. T.M.S. are his initials.   4. Mar. means March.

2. J.J.B. are her initials.   5. Thur. means Thursday.

3. Mr. Martinez has a garden.   6. Dr. Roy will see you now.

D **Read these sentences. Write p if the underlined word is a pronoun. Write a if the underlined word is an adjective.**

1. His name is Mark. __p__   4. Are you going home? __p__

2. Kat ate the crunchy apple. __a__   5. What bright snow! __a__

3. Where did she go? __p__   6. Jay has nine plums. __a__

Name _____

E **Read each sentence. Underline the common noun. Circle the proper noun.**

1. (Molly) reads a lot of books.
2. The snake looked at (Ellie).
3. The nearby (lake) is Lake Michigan.
4. Julian found a (quarter).
5. The (dog) jumped on Sophia.
6. Ellie bought a (camera).

F **Underline the correct contraction for the two words.**

1. could not   can't   couldn't
2. I have   I've   I'll
3. has not   hasn't   hadn't
4. I am   I'll   I'm
5. we had   we're   we'd
6. they are   they'd   they're
7. we have   we've   we'd
8. you are   you'd   you're

G **Underline the correct verb in each sentence.**

1. Eve (open opens) the jar.
2. I (have has) a map.
3. A pumpkin (have has) seeds.
4. I (climbs climbed) the tree yesterday.
5. Grandpa (will was) build a fire.
6. The team is (play playing) well.
7. Who has (saw seen) my mitten?
8. They have (ate eaten) breakfast.
9. Tomas has (gave given) me a gift.
10. He was (went gone) that day.
11. Our chores were (did done) early.
12. The pizza (is am) cold.
13. I (is am) a fast runner.
14. A fish (was were) in the pond.

CHAPTER 1
Sentences and Personal Narratives

Introducing the Chapter
Pages 6–7

Students Should
- have a basic understanding of personal narratives
- have a basic understanding of sentences

Reading the Model

Talk with students about what writing is. Say: *Writing is a way that people share information, ideas, and stories so that anyone can read and enjoy them.* Explain that when we write our thoughts as sentences, we can share our thoughts with others. Point out that a piece of writing is like a photo of a person's thoughts. Tell students that the writer puts thoughts and memories on paper so that they will last.

Read aloud the quotation and ask students what it means to them. Ask students if they have ever seen a photo that was blurry or too dark. Say: *The biggest difference between a photo and a piece of writing is that you have time to make your writing as good as it can be. Even the best writers do not write perfectly the first time they put their ideas into sentences. Good writers often erase and rewrite. Any sentence you read in a book was probably written and erased and improved many times.*

Direct students to look at the opening picture. Invite volunteers to tell how the picture makes them feel. *(scared, nervous)* Invite volunteers to tell about times when they were scared or nervous. Ask students questions that will elicit additional details about their stories. *(Examples: What was the weather like? Who else was there? What did you hear?)* Point out that each story is a true story that happened to the student who told it. Say: *A personal narrative is a true story that the writer tells about himself or herself.*

Read aloud the personal narrative title and model. Ask students what words in the story show that it story is about something that happened to the writer. *(I, my)* Guide students to understand that words such as *I, me,* and *my* are used in a personal narrative. Ask students to tell how the writer felt about the experience. *(He felt scared. He felt silly for being scared.)* Explain that writers write personal narratives to share their true stories with others. Ask what words in the story show that it is scary. *(loud, rainy, night, scary, shadows, monster)* Invite volunteers to name other words and phrases they might find in a scary story. Write on the board students' words and phrases.

Explain that when we write stories, we write by using sentences. Read aloud a sentence from the model. Point out that the sentence tells one complete thought. Explain that sentences go together to tell many complete thoughts, and that those thoughts make up the whole story. Point out that the words and phrases on the board do not tell complete thoughts. Help students use the words on the board to form sentences. Explain that a piece of writing is like a brick house and that sentences are the bricks that the house is made of.

A little black dot that you can see.
Period is my name.
A telling sentence ends with me,
I play a telling game.

The Sentence   Page 8

Students Should

- recognize that a sentence is a complete thought
- know that an end mark comes at the end of a sentence

Teaching the Lesson

Guide students through the first two paragraphs and example. Explain that the example is not a complete sentence because it does not express a complete thought. Tell students that the example only names something—the bear. Go over the next two paragraphs and example. Point out that this example also names the bear, but it says what the bear did. Ask students what this example says about the bear. *(that it ate honey)* Tell students that this is a complete sentence.

Guide students through the rest of the teaching. Explain that an end mark shows where the sentence ends. Write the following in a column on the board: *The cat, The pig, The cow, The bird.* Ask students whether these word groups are complete sentences. Model for students how to make the word group *The cat* into a complete sentence. *(Example: The cat yawned.)* Then ask students to suggest things that each of the remaining animals might do. Write on the board students' responses without end marks. *(Examples: The pig snorted, The cow chewed grass, The bird flew away)* Explain that because these word groups name something and tell what it did, they are complete thoughts, which means they are complete sentences. Invite volunteers to add periods to the sentences on the board.

Go over the activity directions. When students have completed the activity, review their answers.

Extension

Have the class recite the poem on page 8. Then call on a student to say a sentence and to say *period* when he or she reaches the end of the sentence. Repeat with additional volunteers.

More About Sentences *and* Capital Letters and End Marks   Pages 9–10

Students Should

- recognize that a sentence begins with a capital letter and ends with an end mark

Teaching the Lesson

Write on the board *the dog ran* without capital letters or end marks. Guide students to understand that *the dog ran* is a sentence because it tells a complete thought. Read aloud the paragraph on page 9. Explain that capital letters let readers know that a sentence is beginning and that end marks let readers know that a sentence is ending. Have volunteers add a capital letter and an end mark to the sentence on the board.

Go over the activity directions on page 9. When students have finished the activity, ask them to share their answers by reading the sentences aloud, beginning each sentence by telling the capital letter and ending each sentence by telling the end mark. *(Example: "Capital T, the dog eats its dinner, period.")*

Go over the activity directions on page 10. When students have finished the activity, review their answers.

Extension

Have students stand in a line at the front of the classroom. Read aloud word groups, one at a time, taken from classroom texts or other available materials. Some word groups should form complete sentences, and some should not. Starting at one end of the line, have a student tell whether the word group tells a complete sentence. If a student gives an incorrect answer, have him or her sit down. Continue until there is only one student standing. For an added challenge, allow sitting students to make an incomplete sentence into a complete sentence to be able to return to the line.

Words Working Together
and
More Words Working Together
Pages 11–12

Students Should
- recognize complete sentences

Teaching the Lesson
Explain that all writing is made up of sentences and that sentences are made up of words. Go over the teaching on page 11. Review the concept of a complete sentence. Write on the board the word groups *the car, made a yellow cake,* and *the fish swim away* without capitalization or punctuation. Ask students to identify the word group that tells a complete thought. *(the fish swim away)* Have volunteers add correct punctuation and capitalization. Then help students form the other word groups into complete sentences.

Go over the activity directions on pages 11 and 12. When students have finished each activity, review their answers.

Extension
Ask students to choose a word group from the left column of activity A on page 12. Have students make the incomplete sentence into a complete sentence by adding their own second part. Then have students choose a word group from the right column of activity B and make it into a complete sentence, using their own words. Invite volunteers to share their sentences.

Telling Sentences
Page 13

Students Should
- recognize a telling sentence
- understand that a telling sentence begins with a capital letter and ends with a period

Teaching the Lesson
Review what students have learned about a sentence. *(tells a complete thought, has a capital letter, has an end mark)* Then go over the teaching and examples. Guide students to understand that the examples are complete sentences because they both tell something about honey. Ask volunteers to tell one thing that they did last night, using a complete sentence. Write their responses on the board. Explain that these sentences are called telling sentences because students are telling something about themselves. Emphasize that the end mark for a telling sentence is a period.

Go over the activity directions. When students have finished the activity, review their answers.

Read aloud the Writer's Corner. Allow time for students to write their sentences. Invite volunteers to share their work.

Extension
Have students write a telling sentence about something imaginary that might have happened this morning. *(Examples: A dragon got on the school bus. A talking monkey made breakfast.)* Have students draw a picture to accompany the sentence. Invite volunteers to share their sentences and pictures.

Making Telling Sentences
Page 14

Students Should
- recognize telling sentences

Teaching the Lesson
Write on the board *The tiny car.* Have students use this sentence starter to say a variety of telling sentences. Write on the board students' sentences. Review what makes each sentence a telling sentence. *(tells about something, starts with a capital letter, ends with a period)*

Go over the activity directions. When students have finished the activity, review their answers.

Extension
Have students close their books. Then read aloud the first sentence in the activity. Prompt students to suggest words to put in the blank. *(Examples: zoo, beach, library, pool)* Choose one word and have the student who suggested that word write the telling sentence on the board. Repeat with other sentences from the activity.

Commanding Sentences
and
More Commanding Sentences
Pages 15–16

Students Should
- recognize a commanding sentence
- understand that a commanding sentence begins with a capital letter and ends with a period

Teaching the Lesson
Play a game of Simon Says with the class. Explain to students that when you tell them to do something, you are giving a commanding sentence. Go over the teaching and examples on page 15. Remind students that all sentences begin with a capital letter and end with an end mark. Point out that a period is one kind of end mark. Ask students what other kind of sentence ends with a period. *(a telling sentence)* Use the examples to help students understand the definition of a commanding sentence.

Go over the directions for activity **A** on page 15. Help students identify the commanding sentences. Then allow time for students to color the appropriate signs. Explain the directions for activity **B** on page 15. When students have finished the activity, review their answers.

Commanding Sentence is my name.
Giving directions is my aim.
I help you know the things to do
at home, at play, and in school too!

Read aloud the Writer's Corner on page 15. Allow time for students to write their commanding sentences. Have students draw a cartoon of the scene with one person expressing the sentence in a speech bubble. Invite volunteers to share their work.

Go over the activity directions on page 16. When students have finished each activity, review their answers.

Extension

Have the class recite the poem on page 16. Then call on a student to say a commanding sentence and to say *period* when he or she reaches the end of the sentence. Repeat with additional volunteers.

Sentence Review
and
More Sentence Review
Pages 17–18

Students Should

· distinguish between telling sentences and commanding sentences

Teaching the Lesson

Read aloud the teaching on page 17. Invite volunteers to give examples of each kind of sentence. Write students' suggestions on the board. Remind students that both kinds of sentences begin with capital letters and end with periods.

Go over the activity directions on pages 17 and 18. When students have finished each activity, review their answers.

Extension

Have students write one commanding sentence on a sentence strip and one telling sentence on a sentence strip. Collect students' sentences and place them in a container. Draw sentence strips from the container and read them aloud. Have students tell whether each sentence is a commanding sentence or a telling sentence.

Asking Sentences
and
More Asking Sentences
Pages 19–20

Students Should

· recognize an asking sentence

· understand that an asking sentence begins with a capital letter and ends with a question mark

· recognize that some asking sentences begin with question words

Teaching the Lesson

Write on the board six asking sentences, each beginning with a different question word. (*Who, What, When, Where, Why, How*) Ask volunteers to point out what the sentences have in common. (*They ask questions. They end with question marks. They begin with capital letters.*) Remind students that all sentences begin with a capital letter and end with an end mark. Explain that the end mark for these sentences is a question mark. Tell students that these sentences are called asking sentences.

Guide students through the paragraph on page 19. Point to a question mark on the board and have students make the mark in the air, then on paper. Ask students to think of questions that they might like to ask one another. Write their asking sentences on the board. (*Examples: When is your birthday? How old are you? Where is the library?*) Draw boxes around the question words in your sentences and in the students' sentences. Point out that many questions use question words.

Go over the directions for the activity on page 19. When students have finished the activity, review their answers. For items with more than one answer, guide students to understand what other question words fit the sentence.

Go over the activity directions on page 20. When students have finished each activity, review their answers.

Extension

Have the class recite the poem on page 19. Then call on a student to say an asking sentence and to say *question mark* when he or she reaches the end of the sentence. Repeat with additional volunteers.

Exclaiming Sentences
and
More Exclaiming Sentences
Pages 21–22

Students Should

- recognize an exclaiming sentence
- understand that an exclaiming sentence begins with a capital letter and ends with an exclamation point

Teaching the Lesson

Briefly review telling, commanding, and asking sentences. Then ask students to imagine they are watching a TV show about alligators. Ask a volunteer to say a telling sentence that he or she might use if someone asked what was on TV. *(Examples: I am watching a show about alligators. There is an alligator on TV.)* Write the sentence on the board. Then invite a volunteer to say how he or she might say the sentence after discovering an alligator in the kitchen. *(Example: There is an alligator in the kitchen!)* Point out that the sentence about discovering an alligator in the kitchen was said with excitement and surprise.

Guide students through the teaching and examples on page 21. Write an exclamation point on the board. Explain that this end mark can be used to show excitement or surprise. Tell students that adding an exclamation point to a sentence makes it an exclaiming sentence. Write on the board a few of these sentences without end marks. Have volunteers add exclamation points to the sentences.

Go over the activity directions on pages 21 and 22. When students have finished each activity, review their answers.

Read aloud the Writer's Corner on page 22. Have students write their exclaiming sentences. Invite volunteers to share their sentences.

Extension

Have the class recite the poem on page 21. Then call on a student to say a telling sentence and to say *period* when he or she reaches the end of the sentence. Then have the student say the same sentence as an exclaiming sentence, saying *exclamation point* at the end. Repeat with additional volunteers.

Asking and Exclaiming Sentences
and
More Asking and Exclaiming Sentences
Pages 23–24

Students Should

- distinguish between asking and exclaiming sentences

Teaching the Lesson

Write on the board examples of both asking and exclaiming sentences without end marks. Review the definitions of both kinds of sentences. Then have a volunteer draw a large question mark and a large exclamation point to the right of your sentences. Read each sentence aloud and have volunteers draw a line from the sentence you read to the correct end mark. Then have other volunteers draw the correct end marks at the end of each sentence.

Go over the activity directions on pages 23 and 24. When students have finished each activity, review their answers.

Extension

Distribute a note card to each student. Have students write on the note card one word that names a person, place, or thing. Then have half the class write the letter *A* at the tops of their cards and have the other half write the letter *E*. Collect and shuffle the note cards. Distribute the cards. Tell students that *A* stands for asking sentence and *E* stands for exclaiming sentence. Have students write on the back of the card an asking or exclaiming sentence that uses the word on the card. Have students read aloud their sentences. Ask the class to identify what kind of sentence it is.

The Naming Part of a Sentence
Page 25

Students Should
- recognize the naming part of telling sentences

Teaching the Lesson
Write the following on the board: *The brown cow. The jet.* Ask students if the examples are complete sentences. Reinforce the idea that a sentence must tell a complete thought and that these examples only name things. Erase the periods from the examples and ask volunteers to make the word groups into complete sentences. *(Examples: The brown cow ate grass. The jet landed on the ground.)*

Guide students through the teaching. Ask students what the sentences on the board tell about. *(a brown cow, a jet)* Draw circles around the naming parts of the examples. Explain that the naming part of the first sentence is *The brown cow* because that part of the sentence names who or what the sentence is about. Reinforce this idea with the second sentence.

Go over the activity directions. Then complete the activity with students by reading aloud each item and asking *Who or what is the sentence telling about?*

Extension
Have students draw a picture of someone they know and write the person's name below it. Then have students use a different pencil color to write a telling sentence that uses the person's name as the naming part of the sentence.

The Action Part of a Sentence
Page 26

Students Should
- recognize the action part of a telling sentence

Teaching the Lesson
Write telling sentences on the board. *(Examples: Brian wrote a letter. The trees lost their leaves.)* Remind students that a telling sentence tells a complete thought and has a naming part. Point out that they can find the naming part of a telling sentence by asking who or what the sentence is telling about. Invite volunteers to draw circles around the naming parts of the sentences on the board. Then have volunteers read aloud the parts of the sentences that are not circled. Explain that these are the action parts of sentences.

Go over the teaching and examples. Use the sentences on the board to reinforce that the action part tells what a person or thing does. Write on the board a few action parts. *(Examples: eats nuts. sleep during the day. flies over the trees.)* Explain that these are action parts and that they are not complete sentences. Help students to make complete sentences by adding naming parts to the action parts. *(Examples: A squirrel eats nuts. Bats sleep during the day. The eagle flies over the trees.)* Have students underline the action parts of the sentences on the board.

Go over the activity directions. When students have finished, review their answers.

Extension
Have students choose one animal from the following list: cat, frog, monkey, fish. Tell students to write telling sentences that use their chosen animal and that tell something the animal does. *(Examples: A cat purrs. A cat drinks milk. A cat licks its paws.)* When students have finished, ask them to underline the action part of each sentence. Ask a volunteer to read aloud only the action parts of his or her sentences. Ask the class to guess what kind of animal the student wrote about. Repeat with additional volunteers.

Naming Parts and Action Parts
Page 27

Students Should

- recognize how naming parts and action parts work together

Teaching the Lesson

Review the naming parts and action parts of sentences. Then guide students through the teaching. Explain that for a sentence to be complete, it must have a naming part and an action part. List the following on the board: *the dancer, the cook, the singer, the farmer, the actor, the swimmer.* Ask students to complete the sentence starters. Write on the board their responses. *(Examples: the dancer bowed after the show, the singer sang a beautiful song, the actor gave a speech)* Have students identify which is the naming part and which is the action part. Ask students what else these word groups need to be sentences. *(a capital letter at the beginning, an end mark at the end)* Allow volunteers to make the appropriate changes to the word groups on the board.

Go over the directions for the activities. When students have finished each activity, review their answers.

Extension

Photocopy for each student a page from student reading materials. Read aloud the text and ask students to underline the naming parts and circle the action parts of the sentences. Help students understand that a sentence must have both parts to express a complete thought.

Show What You Know
Pages 28–29

Students Should

- recognize the different kinds of sentences
- know the correct end mark for each kind of sentence

Teaching the Lesson

Explain the directions for each activity. Assist students if necessary. When students have finished each activity, review their answers. Show What You Know may be used as a review or as a test.

Get Ready to Write

What Is a Personal Narrative?—The Beginning Page 30

Students Should

- understand the purpose of a personal narrative
- understand the function of a beginning

Teaching the Lesson

Ask a volunteer to read aloud the title. Say: *The word* personal *means "belonging to a person." The word* narrative *means "story." So a personal narrative is a story that belongs to a person. It is a story about that person.* Review the personal narrative students read on page 7. Then guide students through the first two paragraphs of the teaching. Tell students that no matter how long or how short a story is, it always has a beginning, a middle, and an ending.

Go over the first paragraph of the section The Beginning. Tell students that the beginning is where writers say what the story is about. Then read aloud the first sentence of the example. Ask: *What do you think this story is about?* (the wind playing a trick) Go over the rest of the example. Talk to students about how the beginning fits with rest of the story.

Go over the activity directions. Have students complete the activity as a class. Invite volunteers to explain how they know which beginning fits with each personal narrative.

Extension

Have students write their own beginnings for each of the personal narratives in the right column of the activity. *(Example:* I love to ride my bike *for the first narrative)* Encourage students to imagine that what happened in each story happened to them. When students have finished, invite volunteers to share their work.

The Middle Page 31

Students Should

- understand the purpose of a middle

Teaching the Lesson

Remind students that a personal narrative is a true story about the writer. Review the words that writers use in a personal narrative. *(I, me, my)* Then ask: *What does a beginning do?* (tells what the story is about)

Go over the first paragraph. Tell students that the middle is where you tell your story. Ask students to imagine that they are telling a story about their last birthday party or about what they did on a field trip. Explain that the middle would tell what happened at the party or on the field trip. Tell students that the middle is usually the longest part of the story.

Guide students through the example. Then direct students' attention to the sentences labeled *middle.* Use the example to illustrate that the middle describes the important events of the story. Tell students that the beginning and the middle tie together, and that the middle tells more about what is told in the beginning.

Go over the activity directions. Ask students to remember or to imagine a trip to a lake. Have students complete the activity as a class. Emphasize the importance of relating the beginning and ending sentences to the middle of the story.

Extension

To provide students with extra practice writing middles, write on the board the following beginnings and endings:

Today was the best day!/I can't wait for tomorrow.

I was really scared about the first day of school./I was silly to be so worried!

Have students write two or three middle sentences for each beginning and ending. Remind students to write about themselves. As students write, circulate through the class to check their progress and to offer encouragement and support. When they have finished, invite volunteers to share their stories.

The Ending   Page 32

Students Should

- understand the purpose of an ending

Teaching the Lesson

Guide students to explain what a personal narrative is. *(a story about me; a true story; a story that uses the words* I, me, *and* my*)* Then ask students to explain what beginnings and middles do. *(Beginnings tell what the story is about. Middles tell what happens in the story.)*

Read aloud the first paragraph. Tell students that the ending tells how a story turns out. Explain that endings let people know that the story is over and sometimes tell what the story meant or why it is important.

Read aloud the example. Then direct students' attention to the sentence labeled *ending*. Use the example to emphasize that the ending tells how the story turns out.

Go over the activity directions. Have students complete the activity as a class. Ask students to explain their answers.

Extension

Have students write their own endings for each of the personal narratives in the left column of the activity. *(Example:* I'll have to remember not to add so much sugar! *for the first narrative)* Encourage students to imagine that what happened in each story happened to them. When students have finished, invite volunteers to share their work.

Write a Story   Page 33

Students Should

- understand how to combine the beginning, middle, and ending to form a personal narrative

Teaching the Lesson

Go over the first paragraph. Ask students to explain what a personal narrative is. *(a story about me; a true story; a story that uses the words* I, me, *and* my*)* Then go over the activity directions. Allow time for students to write their stories.

As students work, circulate among them to offer assistance and support. Help students as they write, guiding them to write complete sentences. When students have finished, invite them to share their personal narratives with the class.

Extension

Before students complete the activity on this page, encourage them to draw pictures of what they want to write in the beginning, middle, and ending of their stories. *(Example: Students who decide to write about the first day of school might draw a picture of themselves walking into the classroom or trying to decide where to sit. This picture could represent the beginning of their personal narrative.)* When students have drawn pictures to go with each part of their story, encourage them to write sentences about each picture.

Writer's Workshop

Prewriting— Pick a Topic — Page 34

Students Should

- understand how to brainstorm topics
- identify appropriate topics for their personal narratives

Ask students to name things that they have done, things that they were excited about, or things that they were worried about. Have students tell why the events were important to them. Then invite a volunteer to read aloud the title. Say: *Prewriting is when we think about and pick topics for our personal narratives. A topic is what the narrative is about. When we do prewriting, we write down a lot of topics. That way we can pick the best one.*

Go over the first paragraph. Say: *A topic is what a personal narrative is about. A topic might be* I went to the bowling alley, my first baseball game, *or* what I did after school yesterday. *These would all be good personal narrative topics.* Emphasize that before they write, students will first have to pick topics.

Read aloud the second paragraph. Explain that Raj is a second-grade student who is writing a personal narrative. Tell students that they will follow Raj through each step of the writing process as he writes his own personal narrative. Have students read aloud Raj's topics. Explain that Raj wrote down many different topics for his personal narrative so that he could choose the best one. Help students understand that each item on the list is a possible topic for a personal narrative because each topic is something that happened to him. Explain that Raj circled the topic he wanted to write about.

Guide students through the third paragraph and the topic prompts. Ask students to share their own possible topics. For each topic ask the following questions: *What did you do? How did you feel?*

Model for students how to brainstorm a list of topics for your own personal narrative. Use the topic prompts on the page to guide your brainstorming list. As you work, explain to students why you think each topic might make a good personal narrative. Then choose one topic and circle it. Talk to students about how the topic relates to the personal narrative that you will write.

Go over the last paragraph. Then allow time for students to write their topic ideas in their notebooks. Encourage students to pick the topic that seems most interesting.

Circulate among students to provide encouragement and to be sure that they are listing appropriate topics. Help students to understand which topics are appropriate for personal narratives and why those topics are appropriate.

Prewriting— Plan Your Story — Page 35

Students Should

- use drawings to plan and organize their personal narratives

Invite a volunteer to read aloud the title. Say: *First we chose our topics. The next step of prewriting is to organize our ideas.* Explain that *organize* means "to put the parts of our story in order." Tell students that when we do this part of prewriting, we figure out what we want to say.

Go over the first paragraph. Explain that a good way to plan and organize a personal narrative is to draw pictures of the story. Tell students that pictures can help them keep the story in order. Explain that pictures can also help students make sure their stories have all the important parts. Point out each of Raj's pictures and have students describe what is in the picture. Review that the beginning of a personal narrative tells what the story is about, that the middle tells what happens in the story, and that the ending lets readers know the story is over. Remind students that the ending might tell the last thing that happens, might ask a question, or might tell about a special feeling the writer has.

Remind students of the topic that you chose for your personal narrative. Model on the board pictures that represent the beginning, middle, and ending of your personal narrative. Explain how you can use the pictures to help plan your personal narrative. Say: *Drawing pictures can help me remember what happened. Drawing pictures also helps me figure out what parts of the story are important. Once I know what parts of my story I want to include, the pictures can help me put the parts in the right order.* Save these pictures for the drafting stage of the writing process.

Go over the last paragraph. Tell students that they can draw more than three pictures if they wish. Then allow time for students to draw their pictures. Circulate through the class to provide students with help and support. Guide students in choosing which parts of their personal narrative to include in their pictures. Help students understand the difference between details that are important to the story and details that do not belong.

Drafting   Page 36

Students Should
- use their prewriting pictures to write first drafts
- write first drafts using complete sentences

Ask volunteers to share the pictures they drew and to explain what part of their stories each picture represents. As volunteers share, prompt them to say complete sentences about their stories. Explain that these sentences might go in their written personal narratives.

Invite a volunteer to read aloud the title. Say: *During prewriting we drew pictures about our ideas. During drafting we will write sentences about our topics.*

Read aloud the first paragraph. Direct students' attention to Raj's draft. Ask students to identify in the draft words Raj used to talk about himself. *(I, my)* Tell students that Raj turned his ideas into sentences. Point out that later he will have time to make his draft better.

Read aloud the paragraph following Raj's draft. Review the pictures you drew during prewriting. Model for students drawing additional pictures or adding details. Tell students that sometimes we remember other things about a story after we have finished prewriting. Explain that students can add more pictures or details to their story, as long as the pictures and details relate to the topic. Allow students time to add additional pictures or details to their notebooks. As students work, check that they are adding relevant details.

Model writing sentences for each of your pictures. Explain how each sentence goes with each picture. Then have students write a sentence to go with each of their pictures.

Model for students how to use your prewriting pictures to write your own personal narrative. Write on the board sentences that are part of the beginning, middle, and ending of your personal narrative. Explain to students how the sentences connect to the prewriting pictures. Include in your model draft at least one mistake from the Editing Checklist on page 37 and one mistake from the Proofreading Checklist on page 38. Save your draft for use during the Editing stage.

Read aloud the rest of the teaching. Invite volunteers to read aloud the words in the word bank. Then allow time for students to complete their drafts. Circulate through the class to provide students with encouragement and support. Explain that there are steps to complete before finishing a personal narrative. Tell students that later they will have time to look closely at correcting their mistakes.

Editing Page 37

Students Should
- edit their personal narratives

Have a volunteer read aloud the title. Say: *During editing you make sure that your writing makes sense. When you edit, you look for places where someone else might get confused, and you fix the problems.*

Read aloud the first paragraph. Explain that a checklist can help writers remember the important things to check as they edit. Invite volunteers to read aloud the items on the Editing Checklist. After each item is read, pause to clarify students' understanding of the question and to explain how students might check for that item in their drafts.

Read aloud the next paragraph and direct students' attention to the thought bubble. Ask students which item on the checklist helped Raj find the mistake in his draft. *(Do I have a beginning?)* Ask students how Raj fixed his draft. *(He added the sentences It was a loud, rainy night. Scary shadows were everywhere.)* Talk with students about why the sentences make the draft better. *(They tell what the story is about.)*

Direct students' attention to your personal narrative. Guide them to use the Editor's Checklist to edit your personal narrative. Help students answer the checklist questions to find the mistake in your draft. Tell students that everyone makes mistakes when they write and that is why we edit. Say: *Now that we have found this mistake, I can correct it and make my story better.*

Read aloud the last paragraph of this section. Tell students that a friend can often catch mistakes that the writer missed. Emphasize the importance of appropriate behavior and language for peer-editing sessions. Say: *When we edit other people's writing, we use helpful words. We always start by saying what we liked about the story. Tell the writer if you thought it was funny or interesting. If you see a mistake, say "I think you could make your story better if you made this change." Never use hurtful words like* bad, boring, *or* I didn't like it.

Choose a volunteer to model appropriate peer-editing behavior, using your personal narrative as a model. Use appropriate language to reinforce how students should interact during peer-editing conferences.

Allow time for students to edit their drafts. Circulate among students to be sure that they are giving consideration to each item on the checklist. Ask students to give reasons for making or not making changes to their work. Then allow time for partners to read and talk about each other's drafts. Observe students as they meet to be sure that they are using appropriate peer-editing behavior and language. When they have finished, say: *When a friend edits your work, check it over. Your friend might suggest a change that you don't agree with. It is a good idea to check your friend's changes by using the checklist. You can also ask a teacher, a parent, or another friend for help. You want your writing to be correct, but it is your story and you should decide what to change.*

Revising Page 37

Students Should
- use editing changes to revise their drafts

Ask a volunteer to read aloud the title of this section. Say: *When we revise our writing, we change it to make it better. Some changes are our own ideas. Some changes come from suggestions that a friend or a teacher has made.*

Read aloud the first paragraph. Point out the partial student model. Guide students to notice the use of proofreading marks to add a sentence. Point to the thought bubble above Raj's head. Explain that by using the checklist, Raj discovered that he had forgotten to write a beginning, so he added two sentences. Say: *When we edit, we mark changes in the whole draft. When we revise, we rewrite those changes correctly. Marks like this help us show where we want to change things. This mark means to add something to the story.*

Guide students through the Proofreading Marks chart on the inside back cover of the book. Help students understand the function of each proofreading mark, using the examples in the chart and additional examples of your own.

Point out the mistake in your draft that the class found during editing. Demonstrate how to mark the correction. Talk about how making this change helps to make the story clearer. Then rewrite your draft on the board, incorporating into the new copy your marked change. Remember to include your mistake from the Proofreading Checklist on page 38. Tell students that a new copy of the draft can help us see any other mistakes. Explain that this story is not the best it can be yet, but now it will be easier to spot mistakes.

Read aloud the rest of this section. Then allow time for students to revise their drafts. As they work, circulate among students to check that they are making their editing changes correctly.

Proofreading   Page 38

Students Should

- understand the function of proofreading marks
- proofread their revised drafts

Invite a volunteer to read aloud the title. Say: *During proofreading we make sure that all the words are spelled the right way and that the sentences are correct. Proofreading is important because misspelled words and mistakes in sentences can bother the reader. Readers might not pay attention to the story because they are looking at misspelled words or other mistakes.*

Read aloud the first paragraph. Then have volunteers read aloud the Proofreading Checklist. As students read, guide them to explain what each question means.

Read aloud the paragraph following the checklist and direct students' attention to the partial student model. Ask students what mistake Raj found in his story and which item on the checklist helped him

find the mistake. *(an incomplete sentence; Are the sentences complete?)* Help students explain why the sentence is incomplete. *(It does not tell an action.)* Ask students how Raj fixed the mistake. *(He added an action—turned.)* Point out the proofreading mark Raj used to add a word to his draft. Say: *Proofreading marks are marks we use to show what changes we want to make to a draft.* Go over the Proofreading Marks chart and review the function of each proofreading mark.

Guide students to proofread your revised draft, using the Proofreading Checklist. Help students use the questions to find the mistake in your personal narrative. Remind students that everyone makes mistakes when they write, and that by proofreading they make their stories better. Demonstrate how to use proofreading marks to correct your error.

Go over the last paragraph. Then allow time for students to proofread their drafts. Tell students to check for only one kind of mistake at a time. Circulate through the class to offer students assistance and support. Tell students that they can use references, such as a picture dictionary, a word wall, and this book, to check and correct mistakes.

If time allows, have partners trade drafts and proofread each other's work. Remind students that a friend might catch mistakes that they have missed. If you choose this option, circulate among students to be sure that they are using appropriate peer-conferencing language. When students have finished, remind them to double-check their partner's suggestions.

Page 6e provides a full-sized, reproducible copy of the student's Personal Narrative scoring rubric. Students can use the rubric when assessing their own personal narratives.

Page 6f provides a full-sized, reproducible copy of the Teacher's Scoring Rubric for personal narratives. The rubric can be used when assessing students' understanding of the genre.

Students Should
- understand what publishing means
- produce final copies of their personal narratives

Have a volunteer read aloud the title. Tell students that publishing happens when a writer decides to share his or her work with an audience. Explain that an audience is the people who read their writing. Tell students that their audience might be you. It might be their parents, their brothers or sisters, or their friends. Explain that their audience is anyone with whom students share the final copy of their writing. Then tell students that publishing might mean handing in the personal narrative to a teacher, giving it to their parents, or sharing it with the class. Say: *Publishing is an exciting time for writers. After all that hard work, it is nice to share your work with an audience.*

Go over the first two paragraphs. Allow students to answer the question. (*Raj will publish his story by reading it to his mom.*) Talk with students about ways they could publish their work. Then model for students how to produce a final copy. You might write your final copy on the board, or you might use one of the publishing ideas listed in the student book. As you work, say: *First I wrote this personal narrative. Then I edited it, revised it, and proofread it. Now I am ready to share my personal narrative with an audience.*

Go over the rest of the page. Talk with students about how they will publish their own personal narratives. Then allow time for students to make their final copies. Remind students to write slowly and carefully, and to check each sentence to make sure they do not make any new mistakes. Allow time for students to create artwork or other items to accompany their published pieces.

When students have finished, distribute copies of the student's Personal Narrative scoring rubric. Read aloud each item on the rubric. Guide students to understand what each item means and how to apply it to their own writing. Then allow time for students to self-evaluate their personal narratives.

Have students begin keeping a portfolio of their finished drafts. Distribute folders or have students use their own. Ask students to decorate their folders in any way they choose. Tell students that a portfolio will help them see what they are learning and how far they have come since the beginning of the year.

I want to read my story to my mom!

Stormy Night
It was a loud, rainy night.
Scary shadows were everywhere.
My chair looked like it had a
monster on it! So I turned on
the light. Then I laughed.
It was just my fuzzy bear.
Funny to be scared
of a fuzzy bear.

CHAPTER 2

Nouns and Friendly Letters

Introducing the Chapter   Pages 40–41

Students Should

- have a basic understanding of friendly letters
- have a basic understanding of nouns

Reading the Model

Talk with students about the personal narratives they wrote. Have students summarize some of their stories. Then read aloud the quotation. Say: *When we write our ideas, we can share them with almost anyone anywhere.* Ask students about ways we can share written ideas with people who are far away. *(e-mail, the Internet, letters)*

Tell students that when they write messages to people they know, they are writing friendly letters. Talk about ways that students may have communicated with people by using written messages. *(holiday cards, e-mails, letters, notes at home)* Invite volunteers to tell about messages they have written and received. Guide students to understand that many messages we write share a story, thank someone, or ask for something.

Direct students' attention to the pictures on pages 40 and 41. Say: *Ava was so excited when she got her new puppy that she wanted to share the news. She decided to write a friendly letter to her grandma.* Read aloud the friendly letter model. Say: *Friendly letters can be about many different things. But all friendly letters have the same parts.* Point out the date, greeting, body, closing, and signature. Explain that friendly letters all have these parts. Help students identify the sender and receiver of the letter. *(Ava, Ava's grandmother)* Then ask students to tell what the message is. *(that Ava has a new*

puppy) Ask volunteers to tell about things they have received recently that they are excited about. Help volunteers suggest people they would like to write to. Guide students to say in complete sentences some things they might like to write.

Write on the board *puppy* and other common nouns. Say: *Friendly letters can be about many things. Maybe you want to ask to borrow something. Maybe you want to thank someone for a gift. Maybe you want to tell someone about a new toy or book you have.* Point out that the words on the board are words that name people, places, and things. Explain that words that name people, places, and things are called nouns. Tell students that nouns are important words. Then read aloud the friendly letter model, pausing and not reading aloud the nouns in the letter. Say: *Without nouns we couldn't talk or write about the things around us.*

Nouns and More Nouns   Pages 42–43

Students Should

- recognize nouns

Teaching the Lesson

Point to people, places, and things in the classroom and ask students to name them. Explain that all words that name people, places, and things are nouns.

Go over the teaching on page 42. Write on the board *person*. Have students identify which picture at the top of the page is of a person. Then have students offer nouns that name people. *(Examples:*

teacher, student, clown) Write students' suggestions on the board. Repeat with examples for places and things.

Go over the activity directions on pages 42 and 43. When students have finished each activity, review their answers.

Read aloud the Writer's Corner on page 43. Then allow time for students to write their sentences. Invite volunteers to read aloud their sentences, and have the rest of the class identify the nouns.

Extension

Have the class recite the poem on page 42. Then ask students to fold a sheet of paper into three parts. Tell students to label the sections *person, place,* and *thing.* Have students draw pictures appropriate to each section. Then invite a volunteer to bring his or her work to the front of the room. As the rest of the class recites the poem, have the student point to the appropriate picture whenever the poem says *person, place,* or *thing.* Have the volunteer say what is in each picture. Repeat with other volunteers.

Proper Nouns   Page 44

Students Should

- recognize proper nouns
- understand that a proper noun begins with a capital letter

Teaching the Lesson

Review that nouns name people, places, and things. Then list on the board various nouns that name you. *(Examples: teacher, man/woman, runner)* End the list by writing your name. Tell students that all of these nouns name people. Explain that most of these nouns can name lots of people. Tell students that nouns such as *teacher* and *runner* could be used to name other teachers or people. Guide students to understand that only one noun—your name—names just you. Explain that a person's name is a special noun called a proper noun. Tell students that

because a proper noun names one special person, place, or thing, it begins with a capital letter.

Guide students through the teaching and example. Create a list similar to the one on the board, using a student as the subject without capitalizing the student's name. *(Example: student, boy, robert)* Ask students to tell which noun is a proper noun and what needs to be done to make it correct. Have that student capitalize the first letter of his or her name.

Write on the board the name of your school without capital letters. Tell students that this noun names a special place. Guide students to understand that it is a proper noun. Explain that when a name has more than one word, each important word begins with a capital letter. Add capital letters to the name of your school. Then ask students to name things. Write on the board students' suggestions. Guide students to name a proper noun for a thing.

Go over the activity directions. When students have finished each activity, review their answers.

Extension

Write the following sentences, including the errors, on the board: *My sister is going to chicago. his sailboat is named Whistlefoot. Give this note to diana. Have you been to africa? your coat looks warm.* Read aloud the sentences, stopping after each to help students determine which letter needs to be capitalized and why. Then have a volunteer add the capital letter while the rest of the class says *sentence* or *proper noun* as appropriate.

The Days of the Week
and
Practice the Days of the Week
Pages 45–46

Students Should

- recognize the names of the days of the week
- understand that the names of the days of the week are proper nouns

Teaching the Lesson

Review that proper nouns name particular people, places, and things. Go over the teaching on page 45. Write on the board *day*. Guide students to understand that this is not a proper noun because it does not name a special day. Then ask a volunteer to name today's day of the week. Write on the board the name of the day. Point out that this noun names a special day, so it is a proper noun and begins with a capital letter. Help students name the other days of the week. Then display a calendar. Have students recite the names of the days as you point to them on the calendar. Ask students to use the calendar to help you list on the board the seven days in order. Emphasize the use of capital letters.

Go over the activity directions on page 45. When students have finished the activity, review their answers.

Have students look at the weather forecast on page 46. Explain that many TV shows and newspapers use pictures like these to tell people what the weather might be like for the next several days. Guide students to understand how to read the weather forecast. Go over the activity directions and help students use the chart to answer the questions. When students have finished, review their answers.

Extension

Have students make a blank one-week calendar by drawing seven boxes side by side. Ask students to label the boxes with the names of the days. Then have students write in each box one thing that they do that day. Allow students to color and decorate their weekly schedules.

The Months of the Year
and
Practice the Months of the Year
Page 47–48

Students Should

- recognize the names of the months of the year
- understand that the names of the months of the year are proper nouns

Teaching the Lesson

Write on the board *month*. Ask volunteers to tell what months their birthdays are in. Write their answers on the board. Guide students to understand that *month* is not a proper noun because it names a large group of things. Then go over the teaching on page 47.

Show students the names of the months on a calendar. Then distribute 12 note cards with the name of one month on each card. Tell students that they are going to be in a parade of the months. Have a leader with a calendar begin to march around the room. Ask the student who has the *January* card to stand up and say *I am January, the first month.* Then allow that student to follow the leader. Ask students who have subsequent month cards to repeat this procedure until the 12 students are marching in the parade. When the parade is complete, have the 12 students stop in front of the room. Have the student with the *January* card say *I am January, capital* J and be seated. Repeat with the subsequent months.

Go over the activity directions on pages 47 and 48. When students have finished each activity, review their answers.

Read aloud the Writer's Corner on page 47 and have students write their sentences. When they have finished, invite volunteers to share their sentences. Have volunteers write on the board their birthdays in month-date format. *(Example: February 9)*

Extension

Have the class recite the poem on page 47. Then distribute note cards with the names of the months on them. Call out a month. Have the student with that month's card stand and say the month's name, the capital letter, and one special thing about that month. *(Example: This month is July. The capital letter is J. July is a special month because we can go swimming.)* Then ask the class how many days are in that month. Allow students to use a calendar or the poem if they need help. Repeat with the other months.

Abbreviations   Page 49

Students Should

- recognize the abbreviations for days, months, and common titles
- understand that most abbreviations begin with capital letters

Teaching the Lesson

Ask students to name the days of the week and the months of the year. Write on the board students' responses. Invite volunteers to tell why these words begin with a capital letter. *(They are proper nouns. They name a special day or month.)* Point out that many of the words are long. Explain that months and days can be written in a shorter form.

Go over the teaching. Then write the abbreviations for the months and days listed on the board. Explain that abbreviations begin with a capital letter because they stand for proper nouns. Tell students that the period shows that the rest of the word was shortened.

Go over the directions for activities **A** and **B**. When students have finished each activity, invite volunteers to share their answers by spelling the abbreviations, including the capital letter and period. *(Example: "capital S, a, t, period")*

Go over the directions for activity **C**. Write on the board the abbreviations *Mr., Mrs.,* and *Ms.* Explain what each one stands for and when each one is used. Then add *Dr.* to the list. Have students complete the activity.

Go over the directions for activity **D**. When students have finished the activity, review their answers.

Extension

Make flash cards for the days of the week and the months of the year. On one side of each card, print the complete word and on the other side, the abbreviation. Show the cards, sometimes the full word, sometimes the abbreviation. Have students give the abbreviation for full words by spelling them, including the period. Have students say the full word when the abbreviation is shown.

Initials   Page 50

Students Should

- recognize that initials stand for names
- understand that an initial is always a capital letter and is followed by a period

Teaching the Lesson

Briefly review that abbreviations begin with a capital letter and end with a period. Write on the board the initials of three students. Explain that people's names can also be shortened through the use of initials. Guide students through the teaching. Use the examples to show how each letter corresponds to the first letter in each part of a person's name. Emphasize that each letter is capitalized and that there is a period after each letter.

Point to the first set of initials on the board. Have students whose first name begins with the first letter raise their hands. Invite those students to say their last names. Help the class match the initials to the correct student. Repeat with the other sets of initials.

Go over the directions for activity **A**. When students have finished the activity, review their answers and help students distinguish between initials and abbreviations.

Go over the directions for activities **B** and **C**. When students have finished each activity, review their answers.

Extension

Give students short newspaper articles that include names. Ask students to underline each name that appears in the article. Then have students write those names as initials on a separate sheet of paper.

Common Nouns

Page 51

Students Should

- recognize common nouns

Teaching the Lesson

Write on the board a short list of proper nouns that name people, places, and things. *(Examples: Mike, Woodlawn School, Ohio River)* Review that proper nouns name special people, places, and things. Guide students to give more general names for each proper noun. *(Examples: boy, building, river)* Point out that these nouns are not capitalized because they name one of a large group of things, not special things. Explain that nouns that name any one of a group of things are called common nouns.

Guide students through the teaching. Have volunteers label the common nouns on the board as person, place, or thing.

Go over the activity directions. When students have finished each activity, review their answers.

Extension

Play a noun riddle game. Call on students to use an object in the classroom as the subject of a riddle. *(Example: I am white. I am used to write on the board. What am I? You are chalk. Chalk is a common noun.)*

Common Nouns and Proper Nouns

Page 52

Students Should

- distinguish between common nouns and proper nouns

Teaching the Lesson

List on the board several common nouns. Challenge students to suggest a proper noun for each one. *(Examples: girl, Beth; boy, Scott; city, Toledo)* Go over the teaching and examples. Then have volunteers label the nouns on the board as proper or common. Ask students how proper nouns are written differently from common nouns. *(Proper nouns begin with capital letters.)*

Guide students through the activity directions. When students have finished the activity, review their answers.

Extension

Have students search classroom reading materials for proper nouns. Invite volunteers to share the proper nouns they find. Write on the board students' responses. Then have students name common nouns for each proper noun. *(Example: Harry Potter; boy, student, wizard, friend, nephew)* Keep track of how many common nouns students come up with for each proper noun.

A noun names a person, a place, or a thing—
a friend, the park, or a bell that rings,
a boy, a building, a bat, or a ball.
Nouns are words that name them all.

Singular and Plural Nouns
and
More Singular and Plural Nouns   Pages 53–54

Students Should

- recognize singular nouns and plural nouns
- understand that the plural of most nouns is formed by adding -*s* to the singular form

Teaching the Lesson

Make two sets of flash cards, one set with some pictures showing one object and some showing more than one object and the other set naming the object or objects in the pictures. Distribute the cards to students and have those with picture cards take turns showing their cards and asking the class *Who has my noun?* Have the student with the corresponding word card answer *I have your noun. You are _____.* Have students with singular objects and singular nouns place their cards on one side of the ledge of the board and students with plural objects and plural nouns place their cards on the other side.

Go over the teaching on page 53. Ask a volunteer to tell which group of cards names one thing. Write *singular* over that group of cards. Ask a volunteer to tell which group of cards names more than one thing. Write *plural* above that group of cards. Select

pairs of cards that have the singular and plural forms of the same word and read aloud each pair. Guide students to understand that the plural form of each pair adds -*s* to the singular form.

Go over the activity directions on pages 53 and 54. When students have finished each activity, review their answers.

Read aloud the Writer's Corner on page 54 and allow time for students to write their sentences. When students have finished, invite volunteers to share their sentences. Have volunteers tell the singular form of the animal they wrote about.

Extension

Prepare a bulletin board or wall space by dividing it into two sections labeled *Singular* and *Plural.* Have students draw a picture of their favorite kind of transportation. *(Examples: car, train, boat, airplane)* Collect students' drawings, shuffle them, and redistribute to the class. Have students identify the kind of transportation in the drawing and write the common noun for it on the bottom of the drawing. Ask students to label the picture *singular* at the top. Then have students draw a new picture of multiple examples of the kind of transportation. When students have finished, have them label their new drawings with the correct plural form of the common noun at the bottom and with the word *plural* at the top. Invite students to attach their drawings to the correct sections of the bulletin board.

To show belonging and ownership,
a possessive is what to use.
An apostrophe and the letter s
will tell you whose is whose.

Possessives *and* Singular Possessives
Pages 55–56

Students Should

- recognize possessives
- understand how to use *'s* to show possession by one person or animal

Teaching the Lesson

Have volunteers tell something they have in their desks or backpacks. Write on the board the name of the student and the common noun for the item the student named. Explain that there is a way to show in writing that something belongs to a person or an animal. Guide students through the teaching and examples on page 55. Emphasize the use of *'s* in each example. Use the names and nouns on the board to form sentences like the examples in the student book. *(Example: Barry has a lunchbox. It is Barry's lunchbox.)* Circle the *'s* on the board for each example.

Explain that animals can also possess something. Display a picture of an animal. Point to various parts of the animal or things in the picture and help students form the possessive, using the animal's name. *(Example: This is the elephant's trunk. These are the elephant's tusks.)*

Go over the activity directions on page 55. When students have finished each activity, review their answers.

Review the difference between singular and plural nouns. Then go over the teaching and examples on page 56. Guide students through the directions for the activity. When students have finished the activity, review their answers.

Extension

Have students give an object they own to a nearby student. Have each student say a telling sentence that tells who the object belongs to. *(Example: This is Jamie's eraser.)*

Plural Possessives *and* Possessive Practice
Pages 57–58

Students Should

- understand how to form the possessive of a plural noun

Teaching the Lesson

Go over the first paragraph and examples on page 57. Review how to form the plural of people and animals. Write on the board a list of singular nouns. Then write *+s* after each singular noun. Have volunteers write the plural form of the noun next the singular form.

Explain that more than one person or animal can own something. Guide students through the second paragraph of the teaching and the examples on page 57. Model for students how to form the plural possessive of the plural nouns on the board. Then have students suggest more plural nouns. Add nouns that could be an object of possession for that noun. *(Examples: players' gloves, students' books)* Have volunteers write the possessive form.

Go over the activity directions on pages 57 and 58. When students have finished each activity, review their answers.

Read aloud the Writer's Corner on page 57. Allow time for students to write their sentences. When students have finished, invite volunteers to read aloud their sentences. Have the rest of the class identify the plural possessives.

Extension

Have students choose one of the possessive plural nouns from the activity on page 57. Ask students to write their own sentence using the word and to draw a picture representing the sentence. Check that students are using the plural forms correctly. Then have the class recite the poem on page 57. Point out the last two lines of the poem. Explain that usually an apostrophe is used before *s* with singular nouns and after *s* with plural nouns.

Compound Words
and
More Compound Words
and
Practice
Compound Words   Pages 59–61

Students Should

- recognize compound words

Teaching the Lesson

List on the board *blue, rain,* and *hair* in one column and *bird, coat,* and *brush* in another column. Ask volunteers to tell what each word means. Explain that sometimes two words can be put together into one word to make something new. Go over the first paragraph of the teaching on page 59. Then have students read aloud the examples. Invite volunteers to tell what each compound word means. Help students distinguish between the meaning of each compound word and the two words combined to make it. Guide students through the second paragraph. Write on the board additional examples of compound words and have volunteers draw a line between the two words that make up the compound word. Say complete sentences that show how the meanings of the two words that make up a compound word relate to the meaning of that compound word. *(Example: An earthworm is a worm that crawls in the earth.)* Encourage students to use a dictionary to find out whether two words can form a compound word.

Go over the activity directions on pages 59–61. When students have finished each activity, review their answers.

Extension

Have the class recite the poem on page 60. Then say several words, some that are compound words and some that are not. For each word, invite a volunteer to tell whether it is a compound word. If it is a compound word, have the student identify the two words that make it up. Then have the student tell what the compound word means. Guide the student to use the meanings of the two words that make up the compound word to determine the compound word's meaning. Use the compound words on pages 59–61 and some compound words not studied in the book.

Show What
You Know   Pages 62–63

Students Should

- identify proper nouns and common nouns
- write correctly the names of the days of the week and months of the year
- write abbreviations and initials correctly
- recognize plural nouns
- write singular and plural possessives
- recognize compound words

Teaching the Lesson

Explain the directions for each activity. Assist students if necessary. When students have finished each activity, review their answers. Show What You Know may be used as a review or a test.

When you join two words together, you make a compound word. *Butterfly, snowball,* and *bluebird* are compound words that you have heard.

Get Ready to Write

What Is a Friendly Letter?   Page 64

Students Should

- understand what friendly letters are
- understand the purpose of a friendly letter

Teaching the Lesson

Have a volunteer read aloud the title. Ask students to share times that they have sent or received cards, e-mails, or letters. Talk about why each of these were sent and how students felt when they received these things. Then tell students that these are all forms of friendly letters. Say: *Friendly letters are letters that we send to people we know. Friendly letters can share a story or a message, say thank you, ask a favor.* Have students look back at the friendly letter on page 41. Review what Ava told her grandma. Ask a volunteer why Ava wrote her letter. *(to tell her grandma about her new puppy)*

Go over the first paragraph and the examples. Explain that when students write their own friendly letters, they might share a story, say thank you, or ask a favor. Talk about how each example fits with each purpose listed. Direct students' attention to the words in each example that signal what the purpose of the friendly letter is. *(a telling sentence for sharing a story,* thanks *or* thank you *for saying thank you, and an asking sentence for asking a favor)* Guide students to understand that the purpose should fit the person to whom they are writing.

Go over the activity directions. Guide students to complete the activity as a class. Talk about how each example fits the purpose listed.

Extension

Encourage students to think of someone to whom they might write a friendly letter. Then have students choose a purpose for that friendly letter and write a sentence that would fit the purpose. *(Example: for saying thank you:* Thank you for taking me to the football game.*)* When students have finished, invite volunteers to share their work.

The Parts of a Friendly Letter   Page 65

Students Should

- recognize the parts of a friendly letter

Teaching the Lesson

Remind students that friendly letters are letters that we send to people we know. Review the reasons friendly letters are written. *(to share a story, to say thank you, to ask a favor)* Ask students to look back at the letter on page 41. Direct students' attention to the date, the greeting, the body, the closing, and the signature of the letter. Explain that students will include all of these parts in the friendly letters they will write.

Ask a volunteer to read aloud the title. Go over the teaching and the example letter. Help students understand how each part functions and what should be included. Then explain that no matter how long or short a friendly letter is, it should always have these parts.

Help students complete the activity as a class. Then guide students to answer the following questions: *Why is the date written on the letter?* (to show when the letter was written) *Why does the greeting begin with* Dear Ms. Lee? (because all letters should be polite and respectful and because it shows the name of the person receiving the letter) *Why does the letter end with* Your friend, Mr. Cooper? (to tell the reader who wrote the letter)

Extension

Ask students to imagine they are writing to a second grader in another country to tell him or her about what the class is doing today. Guide students to fill in each part of the letter, using the model on page 65 as a guide. Assist students as they compose the body of the letter. Repeat the activity with different recipients and topics to provide extra practice.

The Five Parts — Page 66

Students Should

- identify the parts of a friendly letter

Teaching the Lesson

Remind students that every friendly letter has five parts: the date, the greeting, the body, the closing, and the signature. Review the function of each part. Go over the model friendly letter on page 65 and indicate where each part is placed.

Ask a volunteer to read aloud the title. Go over the teaching. Guide students to understand that the audience of the letter helps to determine why the letter is being written. Say: *If you wanted to thank your uncle for a new bike, you would write to your uncle. You would not write to your grandmother.* Tell students that using *Dear* is polite and respectful and that friendly letters usually begin with *Dear*.

Help students understand that the body of a letter is where they write the message. Explain that the body tells the reader what the writer wants to say and is the most important part of the letter. Ask students to suggest some things they might write about in the body of a letter. Talk about who would receive these letters and have students suggest sentences that might be part of the body of their letters.

Explain that the closing of a letter is a polite way to let the reader know that the letter has ended. Tell students that the signature is the place where the writer signs his or her name. Explain that the signature is important because it shows who wrote the letter.

Go over the directions for activity A. Guide students to complete this activity as a class. Point out the importance of knowing the order that the parts of a letter should follow.

Go over the directions for activity B. When students have finished the activity, invite volunteers to share their answers.

Extension

Write on the board a friendly letter with blank lines next to each part. Invite volunteers to write the name of each part in the appropriate blank.

Putting the Letter Together — Page 67

Students Should

- understand how to put a friendly letter together

Teaching the Lesson

Review the parts of a friendly letter. Emphasize that the parts of a letter must be in a certain order so that the person who receives the letter knows when it was sent, to whom it was written, why it was written, and who sent it.

Invite a volunteer to read aloud the title. Explain that now that they know the parts of a friendly letter, students will learn how to put the parts together to form a complete letter. Then go over the activity directions. Help students complete this activity as a class.

Extension

Write on separate note cards the parts of a letter. Make enough sets of cards to distribute to small groups of students. Have groups work together to place the cards in the correct order. Monitor students as they work to be sure that each part is in the correct place.

date   January 21, 2007

greeting   Dear Gina,

body   I am sorry you are not feeling well. Will you be back soon? We are doing some fun projects in school. We all miss you.

closing   Your friend,

signature   Rebecca

Writer's Workshop

Prewriting— Pick a Topic
Page 68

Students Should

- brainstorm friendly letter topics
- identify appropriate topics for their friendly letters

Ask students to name people to whom they might write a friendly letter. Have volunteers tell why they might write that person a friendly letter. Then invite a volunteer to read aloud the title. Say: *During prewriting we think about the person we will write to and what we want to say. The topic is what the letter is about.*

Go over the first two paragraphs and direct students' attention to Ava's list of friendly letter ideas. Explain that each idea is information that Ava wants to share with someone she knows. Have students identify which idea shares a message, which thanks someone, and which asks a favor. Point out that Ava decided to write to her grandmother because she is so excited about her new puppy.

Go over the third paragraph and the topic prompts. On the board, model for students how to brainstorm a list of receivers and topics for your own friendly letter. Use the topic prompts on the page to guide your brainstorming list. As you work, explain why you think each topic might make a good friendly letter. Talk about how the topic relates to the letter that you will write.

Read aloud the rest of the page. Then allow time for students to brainstorm ideas in their notebooks. As students work, circulate among them to provide encouragement and to be sure that they are listing appropriate topics. Help students to understand which topics are appropriate for friendly letters. Encourage students to pick the topic that seems most interesting to them.

Prewriting— Plan Your Letter
Page 69

Students Should

- use a chart to plan their friendly letters

Invite a volunteer to read aloud the title. Say: *First we chose our topics. The next step of prewriting is to plan our letters and organize our ideas.* Tell students that when we do this part of prewriting, we figure out what we want to say and we put the parts of our letter in order.

Go over the first paragraph. Use Ava's chart to review what information belongs in each part of a friendly letter. Explain that by using a chart Ava will be sure to include all the parts of her friendly letter.

Model planning your friendly letter by drawing on the board a chart and writing the information that relates to the friendly letter topic you chose on page 68. Explain how using a chart helps you plan your friendly letter. Say: *Filling in this chart helps me remember important parts of my letter. It also helps me remember the correct order of the parts of the letter. Writing ideas for the body helps me remember what I want to say to the person I am sending this letter to.* Save your chart for the Drafting stage of the writing process.

Go over the last paragraph. Then allow time for students to copy and fill in their charts. Circulate through the class to provide students with help and support. Explain that later they will have time to draft their friendly letters.

Drafting

Students Should
- use their prewriting charts to write their first drafts

Invite a volunteer to read aloud the title. Say: *Drafting is the time we first put our ideas into sentences. First we planned our ideas. Now we will write our letters.*

Go over the first paragraph and Ava's draft. Ask students the following: *What part tells to whom the letter is written? What part tells what the letter says? What part says goodbye?* Tell students that Ava used her chart to help write her friendly letter. Remind students that Ava may have made mistakes in her first draft but that she will look for mistakes later.

Invite volunteers to share their prewriting charts with the class. Invite students to explain what they want to say in their letters and to whom they will write. As volunteers share, prompt them to say complete sentences. Explain that these sentences might go in their friendly letters.

Go over the paragraph following Ava's draft. Tell students that they might have more ideas for their letters after they have finished prewriting. Allow time for students to add to their charts any other ideas that they have. Monitor students as they work to be sure that the additional details stay on the topic and do not add unnecessary information.

On the board, model for students how to use your prewriting chart to write a draft of your own friendly letter. As you write, have students identify which part of the letter you are writing and its purpose. Include in your draft at least one mistake from the Editing Checklist on page 71 and one mistake from the Proofreading Checklist on page 72. Save your draft to use during the Editing stage.

Go over the rest of the teaching. Allow time for students to complete their drafts. Circulate through the class to provide students with encouragement and support. Tell students that they might make mistakes but that they can look for them later.

Editing

Students Should
- edit their friendly letters

Invite a volunteer to read aloud the title. Say: *Editing is the time you make sure that your writing makes sense. When you edit, you look for places where someone else might get confused and then you fix the problems.*

Go over the first paragraph. Ask volunteers to read aloud each item on the Editing Checklist. After each item, talk about what it means and how students might check their drafts to answer the question.

Go over the next paragraph and the thought bubble. Ask students which item on the checklist helped Ava find the mistake in her draft. *(Do I have a date?)* Talk with students about why a date is important in a friendly letter. *(It tells when the letter was written.)*

Direct students' attention to the draft of your friendly letter. Guide students to use the Editing Checklist to help you find the mistake. Invite volunteers to suggest ways to fix the mistake and improve your draft. Remind students that everyone makes mistakes when drafting and that is why we edit. Say: *Now that we have found this mistake, I can correct it. My letter will be better, and the person who receives it will understand what I want to say.*

Go over the third paragraph. Tell students that reading their drafts aloud is a good way to catch mistakes that were made while drafting. Tell students to make sure that their letter has all the parts of a friendly letter. Then allow time for students to edit their drafts. Circulate among students to be sure that they are giving consideration to each item on the checklist. Ask students to give reasons for making or not making changes to their work.

If time allows, have students read one another's drafts. Remind students that a friend can often catch mistakes that the writer missed. If necessary, model again appropriate language and behavior for peer-editing sessions.

When students have finished, say: *When a friend edits your work, check it over. Your friend might suggest a change that you don't agree with. It is a good idea to check your friend's changes, using the checklist. You can also ask a teacher, a parent, or another friend for help. You want your writing to be correct, but it is your letter and you should always decide what to change.*

Revising   Page 71

Students Should

- use editing changes to revise their drafts

Ask a volunteer to read aloud the title of this section. Say: *When we revise our writing, we change it to make it better. Some changes are our own ideas. Some changes may come from suggestions that a friend or a teacher has made.*

Go over the first paragraph and direct students' attention to the partial student model. Remind students that Ava forgot to include a date in her letter. Invite a volunteer to explain how she fixed her draft. *(She used the insert mark to add a date at the beginning of the letter.)* Say: *When we edit, we mark changes in the whole draft. When we revise, we rewrite those changes correctly. Marks like this help us show where we want to change things. This mark means to add something to the draft. What is Ava adding to her draft?* (June 1, 2007)

Point out the mistake in your draft found during editing. Demonstrate how to mark your correction. Talk about how making this change improves your draft. Then rewrite your draft on the board, incorporating into the new copy your marked change. Remember to include your mistake from the Proofreading Checklist on page 72. Tell students that a new copy of the draft can help them see any other mistakes that might be in the letter. Explain that this draft is not the best it can be yet, but now it will be easier to spot mistakes.

Read aloud the last paragraph. Then allow time for students to revise their drafts. As they work,

circulate among them to be sure that they are correctly writing their editing changes.

Proofreading   Page 72

Students Should

- proofread their revised drafts

Have a volunteer read aloud the title. Say: *Proofreading is the time we make sure that the words are spelled correctly and that the sentences are correct. Proofreading is important because spelling mistakes and sentences that are wrong can draw the reader's attention away from what the message says.*

Go over the first paragraph. Then have volunteers read aloud the Proofreading Checklist. After each item, help students understand what the question means and how check the question in their drafts.

Read aloud the next paragraph. Invite a volunteer to identify Ava's mistake. (Buttercups *should have an apostrophe to show possession.)* Ask a volunteer to tell which question from the Proofreading Checklist helped Ava find her mistake. *(Are all the words spelled correctly?)* Point out the proofreading mark Ava used to correct the mistake. If time allows, write on the board additional examples of proofreading errors, and invite volunteers to correct the sentences with the appropriate proofreading marks.

Guide students to use the Proofreading Checklist to find the proofreading mistake in your draft. Remind students that people make mistakes when they write, and that by proofreading you have made your draft better. Demonstrate how to use a proofreading mark to correct the mistake.

Read aloud the last paragraph. Then allow time for students to proofread their drafts. Tell students to check for only one kind of mistake at a time. Circulate through the class to offer students assistance and support. Guide students to understand how to use references, such as a picture dictionary, a word wall, and their book, to check and correct mistakes.

If time allows, have partners trade drafts and proofread each other's work. Remind students that a friend might catch mistakes that they have missed. If you choose this option, circulate among students to be sure that they are using appropriate peer-conferencing language. When students have finished, remind them to double-check their partner's suggestions.

Publishing   Page 73

Page 40e provides a full-sized, reproducible copy of the student's Friendly Letter scoring rubric. Students can use the rubric when assessing their own friendly letters.

Page 40f provides a full-sized, reproducible copy of the Teacher's Scoring Rubric for friendly letters. The rubric can be used when assessing students' understanding of the genre.

Students Should

- produce final copies of their friendly letters

Have a volunteer read aloud the title. Tell students that publishing happens when a writer decides to share his or her work with an audience. Remind students that an audience is the people who read their writing. Tell students that the audience for a friendly letter is the person who receives the letter. Explain that publishing a friendly letter usually means mailing it to the person it is addressed to. Say: *Publishing is an exciting time for writers. After all that hard work, it's nice to share your letter with the person you wrote it to.*

Go over the first two paragraphs and allow students to answer the question. *(Ava will mail the letter to her grandma.)* Model for students how to produce a clean copy of your friendly letter. You might write your final copy on the board, or you might use one of the publishing ideas listed in the student book. As you work, say: *First I wrote my friendly letter. Then I edited it, revised it, and proofread it. Now I am ready to share this letter with the person I wrote it to.*

Read aloud the third paragraph. Then allow time for students to make final copies of their letters. Remind students to write slowly and carefully, and to check each sentence to make sure they do not make any new mistakes.

When students have finished, go over the rest of the page. Talk about how they would like to publish their letters. If you intend to have students mail their letters, model on the board how to address an envelope. Emphasize that students should not send their letters to people they do not know. Tell students that it is important to let a parent or teacher read over any letters they write before they mail them. Then talk about other ways to publish a friendly letter, such as bringing it home, putting it on the class bulletin board, or personally delivering it to the person it is addressed to. If necessary, allow time for students to make drawings to go with their letters or to address envelopes.

When students have finished, distribute copies of the student's Friendly Letter scoring rubric. Guide students to understand what each item means and how to apply it to their own writing. Then allow time for students to self-evaluate their letters.

Remind students to add their finished letters to their portfolios. Explain that their portfolios will help them see what they are learning and how their writing has improved throughout the year.

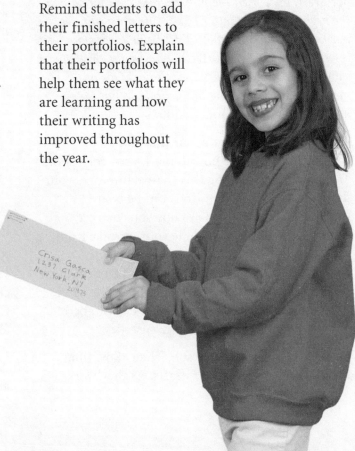

CHAPTER 3
Verbs and How-to Articles

Introducing the Chapter
Pages 74–75

Students Should
- have a basic understanding of how-to articles
- have a basic understanding of verbs

Reading the Model

Read aloud the quotation. Say: *When you take the time to write carefully, you have many chances to make sure your work is the best it can be. When you write, you are trying to tell someone something. It is always important to tell about things clearly.* Talk about why it is important to write or speak clearly when teaching someone how to make or to do something new. *(The person being taught may get confused.)* Illustrate the point by giving students mixed-up directions for something simple. *(Example: frosting a cake)*

Direct students' attention to the picture. Invite volunteers to tell what the children are making. *(ice-cream sundaes)* Say: *The boy in the picture is named Ben. He likes to make ice-cream sundaes.* Invite volunteers to name snacks that they enjoy and know how to make. Ask volunteers to tell how to make those snacks. Say: *When you know how to make or to do something, you can teach others. One way to teach others is to write a how-to article. How-to articles tell how to make or to do something.* Talk about different kinds of how-to articles students may have seen. *(Examples: recipes, game directions, instructions for assembling a toy)*

Read aloud the title of the how-to article model. Explain that Ben has made many ice-cream sundaes and that he decided to write a how-to article to teach others. Read aloud the how-to article model. Point out the list and ask a volunteer

to tell what the list is. *(a list of things you need to make an ice-cream sundae)* Explain that how-to articles often list the things someone would need to do the activity. Then point out the numbered steps. Explain that in a how-to article it is important that the steps be written in the correct order. Tell students that numbering the steps makes it easier for readers to follow the order of the steps. Then point out the words *first, next, then,* and *last.* Explain that these are called order words. Tell students that order words also help readers follow the order of the steps.

Ask volunteers to tell other things they could teach people to make or to do. As students suggest ideas, write on the board verbs taken from their answers. *(Examples: make, build, play)* Read aloud the list of verbs. Tell students that these words tell what something or someone does. Explain that these words are called verbs. Point out the verbs in the steps of the how-to article model. Say: *Without verbs, it would be hard to learn anything from this how-to article. Verbs tell what someone or something does. Verbs are important in how-to articles.*

Action Verbs   Page 76

Students Should

- recognize verbs that express action
- understand that every sentence needs a verb

Teaching the Lesson

Write on the board examples of telling sentences. (*Examples: Sharon eats soup for lunch. Jasper writes poetry for fun. Kelly jumped over a puddle.*) Use the examples to review naming parts and action parts of sentences. Have volunteers underline the naming part of each sentence and circle the action part. Remind students that the action part of a telling sentence tells what someone or something does.

Write on the board examples of naming parts of sentences. (*Examples: The birds, Many dishes, Some children*) Point out that these naming parts are not complete sentences. Help students think of words they could use to make the examples into complete sentences. (*Examples: The birds sing. Many dishes cracked. Some children dance.*) Underline the verbs added to the examples. Explain that these words are verbs and that they show action.

Guide students through the teaching. Write on the board the verbs *walk, talk, play,* and *read.* Help students use the verbs in telling sentences. Then erase the verbs from the sentences. Read aloud what is left and emphasize that every sentence must have a verb to be complete.

Go over the activity directions. When students have finished the activity, review their answers.

Read aloud the Writer's Corner. Invite volunteers to tell actions they like to do. Help students determine appropriate verbs. Write their suggestions on the board. Then allow time for students to write their sentences. Invite volunteers to share their work.

Extension

Have students choose one sentence from the activity. Ask students to rewrite the sentence, using a verb of their own. Have the class recite the poem on page 76. Then invite volunteers to share their sentences. Ask each one to recite the poem again,

substituting the verb in his or her sentence for the word *run* in the first line of the poem.

More Action Verbs   Page 77

Students Should

- recognize action verbs

Teaching the Lesson

Go over the teaching. Invite a volunteer to tell what an action verb does. *(shows action)* Then have students read aloud the verbs on the fish. Invite volunteers to use each verb in a sentence.

Go over the activity directions. When students have finished each activity, review their answers.

Extension

Have students draw and name their own superheroes. Encourage students to think about what super powers their heroes have. Then invite volunteers to share their drawings. Ask each volunteer to explain in complete sentences what his or her superhero can do. Help students identify the action verbs in the sentences.

Run and *jump* and *play* and *sing*— these are action words. When you want to show what happens, use an action verb.

Verbs in the Present Tense

Students Should

- understand that verbs tell when an action happens
- recognize verbs that tell what happens often
- understand that the letter *s* is added to verbs that show what one person or thing often does

Teaching the Lesson

Ask volunteers to name things they do every day or every week. Write students' suggestions on the board as complete sentences in the present tense. (*Examples: Steven eats cereal. Claire writes poems.*) Underline the verbs. Explain that verbs tell *when* something happens. Tell students that verbs can show that something happens often. Point out that verbs that are written to tell what happens often are used in the present tense.

Guide students through the teaching and examples. Have students identify who the first example sentence is about. *(Devin)* Have students identify who the second example sentence is about. *(Rene and Ana)* Point out the sentences on the board and ask if any other students do those activities often. Rewrite the sentences to include more than one student. (*Examples: Steven and Karla eat cereal. Claire and Jake write poems.*) Point out that these sentences tell about more than one and that the verbs do not add the letter *s*.

Go over the activity directions. When students have finished each activity, review their answers.

Extension

Write on the board the verbs *ring, read,* and *chirp* and the nouns *phones, people,* and *birds.* Read aloud each of the three nouns and have the class answer with the corresponding verb. Then mix up the order of the nouns and say them aloud, some singular and some plural. Be sure that students are responding with the correct form of the verb.

Has and *Have*

Students Should

- recognize when to use *have* and *has*

Teaching the Lesson

Review action verbs in the present tense. Then write on the board sentence starters that use the verb *has*. (*Examples: The horse has, The clown has*) Invite volunteers to complete the sentence starters. Write on the board their responses. Explain that *has* is used with nouns that name one. Next to the sentences rewrite the sentence starters with plural subjects and the verb *have*. (*Examples: The horses have, The clowns have*) Help students complete the sentence starters. Explain that *have* is used when a sentence tells about more than one.

Guide students through the first three paragraphs of the teaching and examples. Then invite volunteers to say sentences that use *has* and *have*.

Go over the last paragraph of the teaching. Tell students that *I* and *you* follow a different rule. Invite volunteers to say sentences that begin with *I have* and *You have*.

Go over the activity directions. When students have finished each activity, review their answers.

Extension

Have small groups work together to make posters featuring Olympic events. Encourage students to draw and color people doing a variety of events. When students have finished, display the posters around the room. Invite volunteers to describe their posters, using sentences with *has* and *have*. (*Examples: The soccer player has white shoes. The swimmers have yellow swimsuits.*)

Verbs in the Past Tense
Page 80

Students Should

- understand that verbs can tell an action that happened in the past
- recognize that the letters *ed* are added to many verbs to tell about an action in the past
- recognize how to add the letters *ed* to verbs that end with a silent *e*

Teaching the Lesson

Review present tense action verbs. Write on the board a sentence in the present tense. *(Example: I walk to school.)* Explain that verbs can also tell about something that happened in the past. Erase the verb from the sentence and replace it with the past tense form of the verb. *(Example: I walked to school.)* Read aloud the sentence. Explain that this sentence tells about something that happened in the past. Invite a volunteer to tell what you did to the verb to make it tell about the past. *(added the letters* ed*)*

Guide students through the first paragraph of the teaching and examples. Say more sentences that use regular present tense action verbs and ask students to say the sentences in the past tense.

Write on the board *smile*. Have students say a sentence that uses *smile* in the past tense. *(Example: Joe smiled when he got to school this morning.)* Go over the next paragraph of the teaching and examples. Point out that *smile* and *dance* both end with a silent *e*. Erase the letter *e* from the word *smile* and write *ed*. Explain that verbs ending in a silent *e* drop the silent *e* before the *-ed* is added. Write on the board other verbs that end in a silent *e*. *(Examples: change, glue, move, pile)* Allow volunteers to practice erasing the silent *e* and adding *-ed* to each word. Invite other volunteers to say sentences that use the words.

Go over the activity directions. When students have finished the activity, review their answers.

Extension

Ask students to search classroom reading materials for sentences that tell about the past. Invite volunteers to read aloud the sentences they find, identify the verb, and spell it aloud. Point out any verbs that end in silent *e*.

More Verbs in the Past Tense
Page 81

Students Should

- recognize that some verbs double the consonant before adding the letters *ed*

Teaching the Lesson

Review past tense action verbs students have studied. Write on the board the present tense forms of the verbs from the word bank on page 80. Invite volunteers to say sentences in the past tense that use the verbs on the board. Write on the board their sentences, leaving a blank for the verb. Invite volunteers to write the verb in the blank.

Write on the board the verbs *trim, flip, tip,* and *mop.* Invite volunteers to say sentences in the past tense that use these verbs. Explain that when *-ed* is added to these verbs they change spelling. Point out that each verb ends in a consonant and that a vowel comes before the final consonant. Explain that when *-ed* is added to words like these, the final consonant is doubled.

Go over the teaching and example. Invite a volunteer to tell what the final consonant in the word *skip* is and what vowel comes before it. Point out that the letter *p* is doubled when the letters *ed* are added. Invite volunteers to write the past tense form of each of the verbs on the board.

Go over the activity directions. When students have finished each activity, review their answers.

Read aloud the Writer's Corner. Allow time for students to write their sentences. Invite volunteers to read aloud their sentences. Help the class determine how the past tense verb in each sentence should be spelled.

Extension

Assign partners a verb that ends in silent *e* or that ends in a consonant that follows a vowel. *(Examples: like, stop)* Have partners write on the board their assigned verb in the present tense and demonstrate for the class how to write that verb in the past tense.

Working with Verbs *and* More Work with Verbs
Pages 82–83

Students Should

- understand how to write verbs in the past tense
- distinguish between *has* and *have*

Teaching the Lesson

Invite volunteers to name things they did yesterday. Help students form each suggestion into a complete sentence in the past tense. Write on the board students' sentences. Then invite volunteers to name things they do every day. Help students form each suggestion into a complete sentence in the present tense. Write on the board students' sentences and emphasize the difference between sentences that show action that happens often and sentences that show action in the past.

Go over the activity directions on pages 82 and 83. When students have finished each activity, review their answers.

Extension

Write each of the following phrases on a separate note card: *played tennis, plays tennis, dances with his friends, danced with his friends, skips stones, skipped stones.* Then write on the board the following: *Every Saturday Otto Von Breek _____. Yesterday Otto Von Breek _____.* Pass out the note cards to volunteers. Have students come to the board to match their note cards to the appropriate sentence. Have the student read the sentence aloud and tell whether the sentence tells about something that happened in the past or about something that happens often. Repeat with other students.

Hurrah for Helping Verbs
Page 84

Students Should

- recognize helping verbs

Teaching the Lesson

Write on the board in a column the following sentences: *I helped Talisha. Tony wrote the poem. Chris plays the flute.* In a second column, write the following sentences: *I will help Talisha. The poem was written by Tony. Chris is playing the flute.* Invite volunteers to underline the verbs in the sentences in the first column.

Point out that the sentences in the first column have one verb. Explain that some actions need only one verb. Tell students that some sentences need more than one verb to tell about an action. Underline both verbs in each sentence in the second column. Point out that these sentences have two verbs. Guide students to identify which verb describes the action in the sentence. *(help, written, playing)* Circle the helping verbs. Explain that these verbs are called helping verbs because they help other verbs.

Guide students through the teaching and example. Write on the board other examples of sentences with helping verbs. Have students identify which verb is the helping verb.

Go over the activity directions. When students have finished each activity, review their answers.

Extension

Draw on the board a simple house consisting of a square and a triangular roof. Next to it list in a column the helping verbs *is, am, are, was, were, may, can, have,* and *will.* Tell students that Carpenter Carl is building a house and he needs helpers. Invite volunteers to use in a sentence one of the helping verbs on the board with the verb *build* that tells what they will add to the house. *(Examples: I am building a door. We are building a porch. He was building a chimney.)* When students use a helping verb correctly, allow them to draw part of the house. Then erase that helping verb and repeat with the helping verbs that remain. Then have students recite the poem.

Verbs That Tell What Is Happening Now

Students Should

- recognize verbs that show an action that is happening now

Teaching the Lesson

Write on the board the column headings *Verb* and *In the Past*. Write in the first column *cook*. Review that a verb can tell about the past if *-ed* is added. Invite a volunteer to write in the second column *cook* in the past tense. Then have volunteers say a sentence that uses *cooked*. Repeat with the words *work* and *play*. Review that helping verbs help other verbs. Explain that the helping verbs *am, is,* and *are* can be used to make a verb tell about an action that is happening now. Write a third column heading *Happening Now*. Write *is cooking* in the third column. Explain that the letters *ing* are added to verbs to show that the action is happening now. Have a volunteer say a sentence that uses *is cooking*.

Guide students through the teaching and examples. Help students form the verbs *work* and *play* into verbs that show an action that is happening now. Invite volunteers to say sentences that use the verbs correctly.

Go over the activity directions. When students have finished the activity, review their answers.

Read aloud the Writer's Corner. Invite volunteers to say sentences that describe things that are happening now. *(Examples: The clock is ticking. The heater is blowing. The students are listening.)* Allow time for students to write their sentences. Invite volunteers to share their work. Emphasize the difference between sentences that tell about the past and sentences that tell about something that is happening now.

Extension

Draw on the board a tick-tack-toe grid. Write in each square of the grid a verb from page 85. Assign half the class as Team Past and half the class as Team Now. Have one team member rewrite one of the verbs on the board either to show something happened in the past or to show something happening now. The first team to create a vertical, horizontal, or diagonal line wins. Then switch students' teams and repeat the game with other verbs.

More Things That Are Happening Now
Page 86

Students Should

- recognize how to add the letters *ing* to verbs that end in silent *e*
- recognize how to add the letters *ing* to verbs that end with a consonant that follows a vowel

Teaching the Lesson

Write on the board the column headings *Often, In the Past,* and *Happening Now*. Write *join* in the first column. Review how to change the verb to show the past and to show something happening now. Then go over the first paragraph of the teaching and examples. Write in the first column *move* and *love*. Review how to add the letters *ed* to a verb that ends in a silent *e*. Explain that these verbs follow the same rules when adding the letters *ing*. Show students how to write the *-ing* form of *move*. Have students predict how *love* should be spelled in each column.

Go over the second paragraph of the teaching and examples. Write in the first column *dip* and *nod*. Review how to add the letters *ed* to verbs that end with a consonant following a vowel. Explain that these verbs follow the same rules when adding the letters *ing*. Show students how to write the *-ing* form of *dip*. Have students predict how *nod* should be spelled in each column.

Go over the activity directions. When students have finished each activity, review their answers.

Extension

Have students search classroom reading materials for verbs that end in the letters *ing*. Invite volunteers to read aloud sentences they find. For each sentence, have one volunteer write on the board the helping verb they heard in the sentence and have another volunteer write the *-ing* verb. Then invite another volunteer to use the verb and helping verb in a new sentence.

Verb Review *and* More Verb Review — Pages 87–88

Students Should

- practice adding the letters *ing* to verbs

Teaching the Lesson

Use the teaching on pages 87 and 88 to review how to add the letters *ing* to verbs. Then go over the activity directions on pages 87 and 88. When students have finished each activity, review their answers.

Extension

Assign students some verbs that end in silent *e*, some that double the final consonant, and some that add *-ed* and *-ing* without spelling changes. Have students write their verbs with *-ed* and *-ing* endings. Then have students draw pictures of the verbs they were assigned. Help students create three displays for their drawings—one for verbs that end in silent *e*, one for verbs that double the final consonant, and one for verbs that add *-ed* and *-ing* without any spelling change.

Saw and Seen — Page 89

Students Should

- understand when to use *saw* and *seen*
- recognize that *seen* needs a helping verb

Teaching the Lesson

Review that many verbs can show an action in the past by adding the letters *ed*. Invite volunteers to say sentences that show verbs in the past. Explain that some verbs change spelling when they tell about the past. Write on the board *I see a spooky lighthouse.* Explain that the verb *see* changes spelling to tell about the past. Erase *see* from the sentence and write *saw.* Have a volunteer read aloud the sentence. Invite other students to say sentences that use *saw.*

Tell students that another way to use *see* to tell about the past is *seen.* Explain that *seen* is different from *saw* because it needs a helping verb to do its job. Review that helping verbs can help other verbs show the action in a sentence. Explain that some verbs are strong and do not need to use helping verbs. Tell students that other verbs need helping verbs.

Go over the teaching and example. Then write on the board the following sentences: *The sailors see a big whale. The sailors saw a big whale. The sailors have seen a big whale.* Have volunteers underline the verbs in the first two sentences. Then have another volunteer circle the helping verb in the third sentence and underline the verb it is helping. Invite volunteers to say sentences that use *saw.* Then have students say sentences that use *seen* with helping verbs.

Go over the activity directions. When students have finished each activity, review their answers.

Extension

Fill a container with note cards on which you have written either *saw* or *seen.* Then fill another container with note cards that name the helping verbs *has, have, is, are, was,* and *were.* Have a student draw from the first container. If the student draws *saw,* he or she should give a sentence using the word. If the student draws *seen,* he or she should call on another student to be a helper. Have the helper draw a card from the second container. Ask the pair to say a sentence that uses their verb and helping verb.

Ate and *Eaten*, Gave and *Given*   Page 90

Students Should

- understand when to use *ate* and *eaten*
- understand when to use *gave* and *given*
- recognize that *eaten* and *given* need helping verbs

Teaching the Lesson

Review that many verbs can show an action in the past by adding the letters *ed*. Remind students that some verbs change their spellings to tell about the past. Go over the first paragraph of the teaching. Review that *saw* is a strong verb that tells about the past and that *seen* needs a helping verb. Invite volunteers to say sentences that use *saw* and *seen*. Write on the board the column headings *Strong Verbs* and *Verbs That Are Not Strong*. Have a volunteer write *saw* and *seen* in the appropriate columns.

Go over the next paragraph of the teaching and example. Explain that *eat* is another verb that changes spelling to tell about the past. Write on the board *We eat cereal*. Invite a volunteer to change the sentence to tell about the past. *(We ate cereal.)* Tell students that *eaten* is another way to tell about the past, but *eaten* needs a helping verb. Explain that *ate* and *eaten* are like *see* and *saw*—one is strong and one is not. Write *ate* and *eaten* in the appropriate columns on the board. Use each word in a sentence. Then invite volunteers to say sentences using *ate* and *eaten*.

Go over the next paragraph of the teaching and example. Explain that *give* tells about the past by changing to *gave* or *given*. Write *gave* and *given* in the appropriate columns on the board. Use each word in a sentence. Then invite volunteers to say sentences of their own.

Go over the activity directions. When students have finished each activity, review their answers.

Extension

Make paper fish with the verbs *ate, has eaten, have eaten, gave, has given,* and *have given* written on them. Put a paper clip on each one and put it in a fish bowl. Have students go fishing with a magnet on a string. When a student draws a fish, help him or her form a sentence using the verb.

Went and *Gone*, Did and *Done*   Page 91

Students Should

- understand when to use *went* and *gone*
- understand when to use *did* and *done*
- recognize that *gone* and *done* need helping verbs

Teaching the Lesson

Go over the first paragraph of the teaching. Review that *saw, ate,* and *gave* are strong verbs and that *seen, eaten,* and *given* need helpers. Write on the board the column headings *Strong Verbs* and *Verbs That Are Not Strong*. Write on the board in the appropriate columns the six verbs. Invite volunteers to say a sentence for each verb.

Explain that the verb *go* is a verb that changes spelling to show the past. Guide students through the second paragraph of the teaching and example. Add *went* and *gone* to the appropriate columns on the board. Invite volunteers to say sentences for *went* and *gone*.

Go over the next paragraph of the teaching and example. Write *did* and *done* in the appropriate columns on the board. Use each word in a sentence. Then invite volunteers to say sentences of their own. Encourage students to say sentences for *done* that use a variety of helping verbs.

Go over the activity directions. When students have finished each activity, review their answers.

Extension

Post signs in different parts of the room that read *Mountains, Beach, Amusement Park,* and *Antarctica.* Call on a student to go to one of the posted locations. Then ask the student where he or she went. Have the student answer *I went to the mountains.* Then ask the class where the student went and have them answer *Sue has gone to the mountains.* Write on a slip of paper either *did* or *done.* Explain that this is the student's ticket home and that to get home, the student must use the word in a sentence. Help the student correctly use the word. Repeat with other students.

Am and *Is*   Page 92

Students Should

- understand that some verbs express being
- recognize *am* and *is* as being verbs

Teaching the Lesson

Write on the board sentences that use action verbs but have a blank in place of the action verb. *(Examples: Bill _____ a house. The alligator _____ up the river.)* Invite volunteers to complete these sentences with action verbs. Point out that these verbs show action and can be pantomimed. Explain that there is another kind of verb that does not show action. Tell students that a being verb does not show action.

Go over the first paragraph of the teaching. Tell students that being verbs cannot be pantomimed. Write on the board the verbs *am* and *is* and explain that these verbs cannot be acted out. Then write sentences that use each of the being verbs. *(Examples: Saul is our best singer. I am a good swimmer.)* Ask the class to identify the being verb in each sentence.

Guide students through the rest of the teaching and examples. Use the sentences on the board to emphasize the use of *am* with *I* and the use of *is* with a sentence about one person, place, or thing.

Go over the activity directions. When students have finished each activity, review their answers.

Extension

Invite volunteers to say sentences about themselves, using *I am.* (Example: *I am hungry.*) For each sentence, have another volunteer repeat the sentence substituting the first student's name and the verb *is* for *I am.* (Example: *Daniel is hungry.*)

Are   Page 93

Students Should

- recognize *are* as a being verb
- distinguish among *am, is,* and *are*

Teaching the Lesson

Go over the first paragraph of the teaching. Write on the board the verbs *am* and *is* and invite volunteers to use the words in sentences. Remind students that *am* is used with the word *I,* and *is* is used to tell about one person, place, or thing. Then explain that the verb *are* is another being verb. Invite volunteers to use *are* in sentences.

Go over the rest of the teaching and examples. Write on the board a list of singular and plural nouns, along with the pronouns *I* and *you.* *(Example: cow, building, farmers, I, streets, you)* In a second list, write the being verbs *am, is,* and *are.* Invite volunteers to draw a line from each word in the first list to the appropriate being verb in the second list. Invite volunteers to use each pair in a sentence.

Go over the activity directions. When students have finished each activity, review their answers.

Extension

Distribute to students pictures from nature magazines. Have students use *is* or *are* to write a complete sentence about their picture. *(Examples: The sharks are underwater. The tree is enormous.)* Invite volunteers to share their pictures and sentences. As students present their pictures, ask them to give a sentence that uses *am* and tells how they feel about the picture. *(Examples: I am afraid of sharks. I am excited to climb this tree.)* Have the rest of the class repeat the sentence, using *you are.* *(Examples: You are afraid of sharks. You are excited to climb this tree.)*

Was and Were   Page 94

Students Should

- recognize *was* and *were* as being verbs that tell about the past
- understand when to use *was* and *were*

Teaching the Lesson

Review that being verbs are verbs that do not show action. Write on the board *am, is,* and *are* and have students use each in a sentence. Explain that being verbs can also tell about the past. Write on the board *was* and *were.* Explain that these are two being verbs that tell about the past.

Invite a volunteer to tell what day today is and write the student's response on the board as a complete sentence. *(Example: Today is Tuesday.)* Ask students to identify the being verb in the sentence. Then ask what day yesterday was and write the answer as a complete sentence. *(Example: Yesterday was Monday.)* Underline *was* and explain that it is a being verb that tells about the past. Ask volunteers to tell about other things from the past, using *was.* *(Examples: Last Tuesday was a holiday. Our guest last week was nice.)*

Go over the teaching and examples. Explain that *were* is used with *you* and in sentences about more than one thing. Say sentences that use *were* to tell about the past. Then invite volunteers to say sentences of their own.

Go over the activity directions. When students have finished each activity, review their answers.

Extension

Move around the room and collect an object or a set of objects one at a time. *(Examples: a pencil or pencils, a book or books, a flowerpot or flowerpots)* Pick up the object and say from where you are picking it up. *(Example: I'm taking these books from the bookshelf. I'm taking this flowerpot from the corner.)* Ask students to remember the place from which you took the object. Then move the object or objects to a central location, such as your desk, and write on the board the name of the object or objects. When you have collected a few objects or sets of objects, have students use the prompts on the board to write sentences using *was* or *were* to tell where the objects or sets of objects were. *(Examples: The books were on the bookshelf. The flowerpot was in the corner.)* When students have finished, invite volunteers to share their sentences. Then have students recite the poem on page 94.

Watching for Helping Verbs   Page 95

Students Should

- recognize helping verbs
- identify the correct form of a verb that is used with a helping verb

Teaching the Lesson

List on the board in a column the verbs *saw, ate, gave, went,* and *did.* In a second column, list the verbs *seen, eaten, given, gone,* and *done.* Invite volunteers to identify which column lists strong verbs and which column lists verbs that need helping verbs.

Go over the teaching. Then have volunteers say sentences that use the verbs from the second column. For each sentence, invite another volunteer to identify the helping verb used in the sentence.

Go over the activity directions. When students have finished each activity, review their answers.

Extension

Write on separate note cards the verbs *seen, eaten, given, gone,* and *done.* Make enough note cards for each student to receive one. Distribute the note cards and have students write a sentence using the verb they receive along with one of the helping verbs listed on page 95.

Post signs assigning different parts of the room to each of the helping verbs listed. Then call on students to read aloud their sentences. Have the rest of the class identify the helping verb and tell the student who read the sentence which part of the room to go to. When all students have read a sentence and gathered in groups, offer volunteers a chance to change groups by having them say a sentence that uses their verb along with the helping verb of the group they wish to move to.

Is and was and will and can—these verbs help other verbs. When the action in a sentence needs a hand, you use a helping verb.

Students Should

- recognize being verbs

Teaching the Lesson

Go over the teaching. Then review that being verbs do not show action. Remind students of a familiar story. *(Examples: Little Red Riding Hood, Cinderella)* Then call on students to say something about the story, using a being verb that you assign. Help students use *am* in sentences about the story. *(I am glad that the prince found Cinderella.)* Have students use present and past tense forms in sentences about the story. *(Examples: The wolf is a mean creature. The wolf was hungry.)*

Go over the activity directions. When students have finished each activity, review their answers.

Extension

Have students form an even number of small groups. Ask half the groups to work together to write several sentences that use the verbs *am, is,* and *are.* Have the other groups work together to write several sentences that use the verbs *was* and *were.* When students have finished their sentences, have groups using *am, is,* and *are* exchange sentences with groups using *was* and *were.* Have students rewrite the sentences they receive, using their set of verbs. *(Example: The clouds are puffy. The clouds were puffy. The train is red. The train was red.)*

Students Should

- recognize adverbs

Teaching the Lesson

Write on the board the words *gently, loudly, quickly, slowly,* and *proudly.* For each word, ask students to tell what actions they can do in that manner. *(Example: What can you do gently?)* Write on the board students' responses. *(Examples: pet gently, play loudly, eat quickly)* Underline the adverbs. Tell students that these words are called adverbs.

Go over the first paragraph of the teaching. Point out the verb in each phrase on the board. Then write on the board *walk.* Have a volunteer pantomime the action. Then write on the board *walk quickly* and have the student pantomime the action. Write on the board *walk slowly.* Have the student pantomime the action. Continue adding new adverbs to emphasize how adverbs can tell more about verbs. *(Examples: happily, lightly, quietly, carefully)*

Guide students through the rest of the teaching and examples. Emphasize that adverbs tell *how.* Whisper to a student a way of walking that is listed on the board. Have the student pantomime the action. Then ask *How is this student walking?* Allow the class to guess the adverb.

Go over the activity directions. When students have finished the activity, review their answers.

Read aloud the Writer's Corner. Allow time for students to write their sentences. Invite volunteers to share their sentences. Write on the board the verbs students used in their sentences. Point out that adverbs can be used with many different verbs.

Extension

Choose four adverbs from those in the word bank on page 97. Write each adverb at the top of a sheet of poster board. Then have students search in magazines for pictures of people or things that are doing the actions as the adverbs suggest. Have students make a collage for each adverb.

Students Should

- distinguish between past tense and present tense
- recognize how to write verbs to show that something is happening now
- identify helping verbs
- understand how to use being verbs and action verbs in the past tense
- recognize adverbs

Teaching the Lesson

Explain the directions for each activity. Assist students if necessary. When students have finished each activity, review their answers. Show What You Know may be used as a review or a test.

Get Ready to Write

What Is a How-to Article?   Page 100

Students Should

- identify the parts of a how-to article
- understand the purpose of a how-to article

Teaching the Lesson

Talk with students about times they have followed recipes, read the directions for a game, or completed a science experiment they read about in a book. Ask students to describe what they made or did and to explain why the instructions or directions were important to completing the activity. Talk about what might have happened if students had not followed the directions. *(The project would have been harder. They might not have finished the project.)* Then have a student read aloud the title. Say: *Each of the examples we have talked about is a how-to article. How-to articles teach others how to make something or how to do something.*

Have students turn back to the how-to article on page 75. Ask students to explain what the how-to article teaches. *(how to make an ice-cream sundae)* Tell students that this writer knew how to make an ice-cream sundae and wanted to teach others how to make it.

Go over the first paragraph. Guide students to understand that when they write their own how-to articles, they should teach something that they know how to make or to do. Ask volunteers to name things they know how to make or to do about which they might write a how-to article.

Direct students' attention to the how-to article and the callouts. Go over the first three parts of the article. Explain that the title of a how-to article tells what the article will teach or show how to do. Guide students to understand that the beginning of a how-to article tells what the topic of the article is.

Tell students that the What You Need list tells readers what supplies, ingredients, or things they will need to complete the project.

Go over the Steps. Guide students to understand that the steps tell readers exactly what they must do to complete the project. Tell students that the steps must all be written down because missing steps may keep readers from being able to finish the project. Explain that the steps must be in the correct order, because if they are not, readers may get confused and give up the project.

Guide students to complete the activity as a class. Have students explain their answers.

Extension

Have students think of things they know how to make or to do. *(Examples: turning somersaults, making lemonade, tying a bow)* Invite students to tell the class what steps are needed to make or to do each thing. As each student speaks, guide him or her to say complete sentences and to be sure that the steps are accurate and in the correct order.

Order in a How-to Article   Page 101

Students Should

- understand order in a how-to article
- recognize order words

Teaching the Lesson

Invite students to explain what a how-to article is. Then review the parts of a how-to article. *(Title, Beginning, What You Need list, Steps)* Use the model how-to article on page 100 to reinforce students' understanding of the parts. Guide students to explain the role of each part of a how-to article.

Invite a volunteer to read aloud the title. Go over the teaching. Explain that order in a how-to article is the order that the steps should be in. Have students look at the how-to article on page 100.

Guide students to understand how the words *first, next, then,* and *last* help tell the order in which the steps happen. Explain that before writers write how-to articles, they think about the order the steps should be in. Say: *After writers have thought about the order of the steps, they write the steps using order words. The order words help tell the reader the order of the steps.*

Go over the activity directions. Complete the first set of steps as a class. Have students complete the second set of steps independently. When students have finished, invite volunteers to explain their answers to the class.

Extension

Write on the board in a column the following steps, which are out of order: *Move the toothbrush over your teeth. Put toothpaste on the brush. Rinse your mouth. Put the toothbrush in your mouth.* Invite a volunteer to pantomime the steps in the order in which they are written. Emphasize the importance of putting steps in the correct order. Then invite volunteers to write *First, Next, Then,* and *Last* in front of the steps on the board to put them in the correct order. Repeat the activity with other simple sets of steps, such as sharpening a pencil, combing hair, or pouring a bowl of cereal.

Steps in a How-to Article   Page 102

Students Should
- understand the steps of a how-to article

Teaching the Lesson
Review the order words *first, next, then,* and *last,* and how these words show readers the order of the steps in a how-to article. Ask students why knowing the order of steps is important. *(If readers don't know the order of the steps, they cannot complete the activity or project.)* Invite volunteers to say directions for getting from one part of the school to another, using order words to show the order of the steps. Talk about what might happen if the steps were out of order.

Have a volunteer read aloud the title. Go over the directions and the phrases in the first word bank. Guide students to complete the activity as a class. Encourage students to explain why the steps belong in the order they have chosen.

Go through the phrases in the second word bank. Allow time for students to complete the activity independently. Circulate among students to be sure that they are writing the steps in the correct order. When they have finished, invite volunteers to share their work and to explain their answers.

Extension

Play a storytelling game with students by making stories one sentence at a time, using order words. Begin a simple story with a sentence that uses *first*. *(Examples: First Annie lost her necklace. First the giant woke up.)* Ask a volunteer to tell the next sentence of the story by saying a sentence with *next*. Then have a third volunteer tell another sentence of the story by saying a sentence with *then*. Have a volunteer use *last* and finish the story.

Plan a How-to Article   Page 103

Students Should
- understand how to plan a how-to article

Teaching the Lesson
Remind students of the importance of writing the steps of a how-to article in the correct order. Invite volunteers to explain why the order of the steps in a how-to article is important.

Ask a volunteer to read aloud the title. Talk about ways that students have learned to plan personal narratives and friendly letters. *(brainstorming, using a chart to organize ideas)* Help students describe how planning their personal narratives and friendly letters helped them to write their drafts. Tell students that planning a how-to article means thinking about what to write and the order that the information will be in.

Go over the activity directions. Invite volunteers to name things about which they might write. Have students complete the title by filling in the blank after *How to.* Then direct students' attention to the beginning *Making _____ is easy and fun.* Encourage students to fill in the blank with their topic.

Allow time for students to complete the rest of the activity independently. Circulate among students to be sure that they are including all of the materials needed and that their pictures are in the right order. When students have finished, invite volunteers to share their work with the class.

Extension

Have the class choose a simple activity, such as building a snowman. Model on the board planning a how-to article by copying the graphic organizer on page 103. Encourage students to think of items they would need for the What You Need list. Write on the board students' responses. Then invite them to tell the steps needed. Write on the board the steps that students provide.

When the organizer is complete, ask a volunteer to demonstrate what the article is teaching, following the list and steps as he or she pantomimes the activity. If any materials or steps are missing, have students write on the board what should be included so that the volunteer can successfully complete the activity.

Writer's Workshop

Prewriting— Pick a Topic   Page 104

Students Should

- brainstorm topics for their how-to articles
- identify appropriate how-to article topics

Ask students to name things they know how to do or to make. *(Examples: making a sandwich, drawing a picture, braiding hair, taking care of a pet)* Talk about times students have taught someone else to do or to make something. Ask students to describe how they taught another person their special skill.

Invite a volunteer to read aloud the title. Ask students to explain what they did during prewriting when they wrote their personal narratives and friendly letters. *(wrote lists of possible topics, chose the best topic, used a chart or graphic to organize ideas)* Say: *When we do prewriting for how-to articles, we think about special things we can do or make. Then we decide if we can teach someone else how to do or to make that thing.*

Go over the first two paragraphs and direct students' attention to the notebook graphic. Explain that to think of a topic for his how-to article, Ben brainstormed a list of things he knew how to do or to make. Go over each item on Ben's list. Point out that each item is something that Ben knows how to do and that it would be a good topic for a how-to article. Tell students that Ben brainstormed a lot of topics so that he could choose the best one. Ask a volunteer which topic Ben chose. *(how to make an ice-cream sundae)*

Model on the board brainstorming a list of topics for your own how-to article. For each topic, explain why it might be a good topic for a how-to article.

Include on your list a topic that would be inappropriate for a how-to article, such as *My vacation in Maine*. Guide students to understand why that topic would not be appropriate for a how-to article. Then choose one topic by circling it. Talk with students about why you chose that topic.

Go over the rest of the page. Write on the board the three questions from the paragraph. Encourage students to ask themselves these questions as they are brainstorming topics. Explain that if students can answer yes to these questions, then they probably have a good topic idea for their how-to articles.

Allow time for students to write their topic ideas in their notebooks. As they work, circulate among students to provide encouragement and to be sure that they are listing appropriate topics. Help them to understand which topics are appropriate for how-to articles and why those topics are appropriate. Encourage students to pick the topic that seems most interesting to them.

Prewriting—Plan Your How-to Article   Page 105

Students Should

· use sentence strips to plan their how-to articles

Have a volunteer read aloud the title. Say: *Now that we have picked topics for our how-to articles, we must plan what we want to write. This is the second step in prewriting.* Review ways in which students planned or organized their personal narratives and friendly letters. Tell students that planning a how-to article means thinking about the parts to include, such as the What You Need list and the steps it will take to complete the activity.

Go over the first paragraph. Have a volunteer explain what a What You Need list is. *(a list of all the things a person needs to do or to make something)* Review the importance of writing clear, ordered steps. Then go over Ben's steps. Tell students that

Ben has chosen to write his steps on sentence strips because they are easy to reorder.

Model on the board writing a What You Need list for the topic that you chose for your how-to article. As you write your list, explain why you are including each item. Invite students to help you identify any other things a person might need to make or to do what is in your how-to article.

Write on large sentence strips the steps of your how-to article. Demonstrate how you can move the strips around to be sure that the steps are in the correct order. Invite students to help you place the steps in the correct order. Say: *Writing a What You Need list and making sure that my steps are in order help me to write a better first draft. I can make sure that the most important things are included. Later I can look at ways to make my article better.* Tape the strips to the board next to your What You Need list. Save both for the Drafting stage.

Go over the last paragraph. Allow time for students to write their What You Need lists in their notebooks. Circulate through the room to provide assistance and support. Help students make sure that they have included all the necessary items on their lists.

Allow time for students to write their steps. Have students write their steps on sheets of paper and cut the sentences into sentence strips. Guide students to arrange their steps in the correct order and to tape or glue the arranged steps in their notebooks.

Drafting   Page 106

Students Should
* use their prewriting notes to write their first drafts

Invite a volunteer to read aloud the title. Talk about students' experiences drafting their personal narratives and friendly letters. Emphasize how students used their prewriting notes when writing their first drafts. Say: *Drafting is our first opportunity to put together our ideas. When we write a draft of a how-to article, we make sure that we have included all the parts.* Ask students to name the parts of a how-to article. *(Title, Beginning, What You Need, Steps)*

Read aloud the first paragraph. Direct students' attention to Ben's draft. Explain how each part of the draft is connected to the notes that Ben made during prewriting. *(Examples: The items in the What You Need list came from the list Ben made during prewriting. The steps came from the steps that Ben wrote and rearranged during prewriting.)*

Point out the parts of the draft that were added after prewriting. *(title, beginning)* Tell students that these parts give readers a hint of what they will learn. Invite volunteers to suggest other titles that Ben might have used for his how-to article. *(Example: Make Sundaes for Your Friends!)*

Model how to use your What You Need list and sentence strips to write your how-to article. Write on the board the title of your how-to article and a beginning that tells about your topic. As you work, explain why you chose your title and what you want your beginning to say. Then write your What You Need list and steps. As you write your steps, remember to include order words. Explain that students can end their articles with a sentence that encourages readers to do what the article teaches. Emphasize how the parts of your how-to article are connected to your prewriting notes. Be sure to include in your draft at least one mistake from the Editing Checklist on page 107 and one mistake from the Proofreading Checklist on page 108. Save your draft to use during the Editing stage.

Guide students through the rest of the page. Then allow time for them to complete their drafts. Circulate through the class to provide students with help and advice. Emphasize the importance of using order words as students write their steps. Remind students that during drafting they should write all of their ideas. Tell students that they will have time to look closely at spelling and complete sentences when they edit and proofread.

Editing   Page 107

Students Should
* edit their how-to articles

Ask a volunteer to read aloud the title. Talk about how editing students' personal narratives and friendly letters made their writing better. Then say: *When you edit a how-to article, you look for places where readers might get confused and you fix the problems.* Explain that when students edit their how-to articles, they should pay special attention to missing items in the What You Need list. Tell students to look carefully at the steps to be sure none are missing or out of order.

Guide students through the first paragraph and each item on the checklist. After you read each item, help students understand what each question means and how they should check for it in their drafts.

Go over the next paragraph and the thought bubble. Ask students which item on the checklist helped Ben find the mistake in his draft. *(Do I use order words?)* Ask students how Ben fixed his draft. *(He added the order word* Then.*)*

Direct students' attention to your how-to article. Guide students to use the Editing Checklist to edit your draft. When students find your mistake, invite volunteers to suggest ways that you might fix the draft. Remind students that they edit their drafts because everyone makes mistakes. Tell students that even the best writers have to edit.

Go over the next paragraph. Remind students that reading their drafts aloud is a good way to catch mistakes. Encourage students to first make sure that their drafts are complete. Then allow time for students to edit their drafts. As they work, circulate through the class to be sure that students are giving consideration to each item on the checklist. Check students' justifications for making changes to their work.

If students read each other's drafts, remind them of the proper language and behavior for peer-editing sessions. Emphasize that when a friend edits their work, they should check over what the friend marks in the draft. Remind students that it is a good idea to check any changes by using the checklist or by asking a teacher or a parent for help.

Revising   Page 107

Students Should
- use editing changes to revise their drafts

Invite a volunteer to read aloud the title. Talk about students' experiences revising their personal narratives and friendly letters. Remind students that when we revise, we change our writing to make it better.

Go over the first paragraph. Point out the mistake in your draft that the class found during Editing. Demonstrate how to mark the correction. Talk about how making this change improves the draft. Then rewrite your draft on the board, incorporating into the new copy your marked change. Remember to include your mistake from the Proofreading Checklist on page 108. Remind students that a new copy of the draft can help them see any other mistakes that might be in their how-to articles.

Read aloud the last paragraph. Allow time for students to revise their drafts. As they work, circulate among students to be sure that they are correctly writing their editing changes.

Proofreading   Page 108

Students Should
- proofread their revised drafts

Ask a volunteer to read aloud the title. Say: *Remember that we proofread to check for spelling, punctuation, capitalization, and grammar. We look at whether verbs are used correctly. We make sure each sentence begins with a capital letter and ends with the right end mark.* Talk about why proofreading is important. *(Mistakes in spelling, punctuation, capitalization, and grammar might distract or confuse the readers.)*

Guide students through the first paragraph and the Proofreading Checklist. As you go over the checklist, talk about what each question means and help students understand how to check for each item in their drafts.

Read aloud the next paragraph and direct students' attention to the partial student model. Point out Ben's correction and invite a volunteer to tell what was wrong with the original sentence. *(Ben used the wrong verb.)* Talk with students about why *covered* should be *cover. (The verb* covered *tells about the past.)* Point out that Ben deleted the incorrect verb and inserted the correct one.

Guide students to find the mistake in your draft, using the Proofreading Checklist. Invite volunteers to suggest how you might fix the mistake. Ask students to explain how you could use proofreading marks to correct the mistake. Demonstrate how to make the correction, using proofreading marks.

Go over the last paragraph and allow time for students to proofread their drafts. Remind students to check for only one kind of mistake at a time. Circulate through the class to offer students assistance and support. Remind students that they may use references such as a picture dictionary, a word wall, and this book to check and correct mistakes.

If time allows, have partners exchange drafts and proofread each other's work. Remind students that a friend might catch mistakes that they have missed. Be sure that students are using appropriate peer-conferencing language. When students have finished, remind them to double-check their partner's suggestions.

Publishing   Page 109

Page 74e provides a full-sized, reproducible copy of the student's How-to Article scoring rubric. Students can use the rubric when assessing their own how-to articles.

Page 74f provides a full-sized, reproducible copy of the Teacher's Scoring Rubric for how-to articles. The rubric can be used when assessing students' understanding of the genre.

Students Should
• produce final copies of their how-to articles

Invite a volunteer to read aloud the title. Remind students that publishing happens when a writer shares his or her work with an audience. Invite students to share ways that they published their personal narratives and friendly letters. Ask students how their audience reacted to their published work. Tell students that the audience for a how-to article is someone who wants to make or to do what the article teaches.

Make a poster.

Do a demonstration.

Put in a class How-to Book.

Read it to the class.

Give it to a friend who wants to learn something new.

Go over the first paragraph. Point out Ben and his published draft. Talk about why an audience might enjoy reading Ben's published how-to article.

Model how to produce a final copy of your how-to article. You might write your final copy on the board, or you might use one of the publishing ideas listed in the book. As you work, say: *First I picked a topic and organized my ideas about the topic. Then I wrote a draft. I edited, revised, and proofread my draft. Now I am ready to share my how-to article with my audience. My audience is anyone who wants to learn to do or to make what my article teaches.* Discuss ways you might publish your article and people who might enjoy learning about your topic.

Go over the second paragraph. Allow time for students to make a final copy of their how-to articles. Tell students to write slowly and carefully and to check each sentence to make sure they do not make any new mistakes.

CHAPTER 4
Pronouns, Adjectives, and Descriptions

Introducing the Chapter
Pages 110–111

Students Should

- have a basic understanding of descriptions
- have a basic understanding of pronouns
- have a basic understanding of adjectives

Reading the Model

Read aloud the quotation. Talk with students about the kinds of writing they have done so far. (*personal narratives, friendly letters, how-to articles*) Invite volunteers to tell things they learned from writing those pieces. Say: *When you write, you have to think about what you want to say. When you do that, sometimes you learn new things about your topic or about yourself. That is what* exploration *means: discovering new things.* Explain that when they write personal narratives, they might discover things that they forgot. Tell students that friendly letters can help them discover important messages they want to share with others. Point out that how-to articles can help them discover talents and skills they may not even know they have. Say: *You also discover how to write by writing often. When you edit and proofread, you learn from your mistakes. Every time you write something new, you become a better writer.*

Direct students' attention to the picture. Invite volunteers to tell about the scene. Explain that this pond is next to someone's house. Then point out the model description. Say: *This is a description. The writer likes the pretty pond outside her house. She wrote a description to tell others what the pond is like.* Point out that as students talked about the picture, they were describing the scene.

Invite volunteers to tell about their favorite toys, people, and places. If necessary, ask questions to prompt students to provide more details. (*Examples: What color is your model train? What does it sound like at the bowling alley?*) Point out that students are describing some of their favorite things. Say: *Descriptions help us tell others about people, places, things, and events. A good description allows a reader to imagine what something or someone looks like, sounds like, smells like, feels like, and tastes like.*

Ask students to close their eyes. Tell them to listen as you read and to try to imagine what you are describing. Then read aloud the model description, placing emphasis on sensory words and images. Have students open their eyes. Ask a volunteer to tell where in the description it says that the writer is describing a pond. (*in the first sentence*) List on the board the five senses. (*sight, sound, smell, taste, touch*) Explain that these are the five senses. Read aloud the description again, pausing after each sentence to help students identify which of the five senses that sentence is about. Say: *A good description tells about our senses.*

Point out the word *We* in the second to last sentence of the model. Ask students to tell who *we* is. (*the writer and Liam*) Read aloud the sentence, substituting *Liam and I* for *We.* Explain that *We* takes the place of *Liam and I.* Point out *Pronouns* in the chapter title and explain that words that take the place of nouns and groups of nouns are called pronouns.

Read aloud adjectives from the model. (*Examples: big, cool, sweet, tangy*) For each adjective invite a volunteer to name the word that the adjective is telling about. Point out *Adjectives* in the chapter title and explain that adjectives are words that tell about, or describe, nouns. Say: *Pronouns make our writing more interesting. They help us avoid repeating the same nouns over and over. Adjectives help our readers imagine what we are describing. Adjectives make our descriptions clearer and more interesting.*

Pronouns *and* More Pronouns Pages 112–113

Students Should

- identify pronouns

Teaching the Lesson

Review that a noun names a person, place, or thing. Have students suggest nouns that name people, places, and things. Explain that pronouns are words that can take the place of nouns.

Go over the teaching on page 112. Read aloud the pronouns. Write on the board the sentence *Peter likes it.* Have a volunteer underline the pronoun. Then have students suggest words that *it* might replace. *(Examples: school, TV, Friday)* List students' responses on the board. Then explain that nouns can only be replaced by certain pronouns. Emphasize this point by asking students whether the sentence on the board could apply to people. *(Example:* Peter likes his teacher *cannot be represented by* Peter likes it.*)* Write on the board *He is going home.* Help students suggest possible nouns that *He* might replace. *(Examples: George, a soldier, a clown)* Emphasize the difference between *he* and *she* by using *She is going home.* Then use this sentence structure to guide students to understand the difference between *we* and *they.* *(We are going home. They are going home.)*

Go over the activity directions on pages 112 and 113. Help students distinguish between subject pronouns and object pronouns by having them

listen for what sounds correct. If students ask or are prepared to learn how to use subject pronouns and object pronouns besides *I* and *me,* refer to For Kids Who Are Ready on page 110b. When students have finished each activity, review their answers.

Read aloud the Writer's Corner on page 113. Talk with students about things they like to do with their best friends. Then allow time for students to write their sentences. Have students draw pictures to go with their sentences. Encourage students to label the people in their pictures.

Extension

Help students come up with gestures for each of the pronouns in the poem on page 112. *(Examples: pointing to themselves for* I *and* me, *pointing to a girl for* she, *pointing to a book for* it, *pointing to everyone for* we*)* Then have students recite the poem, using the appropriate gestures when they read the pronouns.

Practice with Pronouns *and* Pronouns Review Pages 114–115

Students Should

- recognize pronouns
- understand which pronouns to use

Teaching the Lesson

Have signs prepared, each showing one of the following pronouns: *he, she, it, him, her, they, them, we* and *you.* Display the pronouns and read aloud the teaching on page 114. Write on the board sentences with nouns that could be replaced by one of the pronouns displayed. *(Examples: Chad and I*

rode an elephant. *The elephants circled around the pen.*) Read aloud each sentence and help students choose a noun or noun phrase that could be replaced by a pronoun. Underline the noun or noun phrase and invite a volunteer to tell what pronoun can be used. When students suggest the correct pronoun, erase the underlined word or words and replace with the pronoun. Have a volunteer read aloud the sentence. Repeat with the remaining sentences. Help students distinguish between *he/him, she/her,* and *they/them* by reading the sentence once with each pronoun and helping students choose the correct pronoun.

Go over the activity directions on pages 114 and 115. Help students distinguish between subject pronouns and object pronouns by having them listen for what sounds correct. If students ask or are prepared to learn how to use subject pronouns and object pronouns besides *I* and *me,* refer to For Kids Who Are Ready on page 110b. When students have finished each activity, review their answers.

Extension

Review a story that students have recently read or with which they are familiar. Write on the board the sentence starters *First, Then,* and *Finally.* Choose a character from the story. Help students complete the sentences by telling in complete sentences that use pronouns what that character did in the story. *(Example: First he built a house of straw. Then he hid from the wolf in his house. Finally he lost his house and ran away.)* Repeat with other characters and stories.

Pronouns *I* and *Me* and More Work with *I* and *Me*   Pages 116–117

Students Should

- understand when to use the pronoun *I* and when to use the pronoun *me*

Teaching the Lesson

Review that pronouns are words that take the place of nouns. Write on the board *Ava likes the color yellow. She loves bananas.* Invite a volunteer to identify the pronoun. Help students determine which noun *She* takes the place of. Then ask volunteers to tell about their favorite colors with sentences that use *I* similar to the one on the board. *(I like the color purple. I love grapes.)* Have students say additional sentences about themselves that use *me.* Tell students that when we talk about ourselves, we use the pronouns *I* and *me.*

Go over the first paragraph of the teaching on page 116. Then review the naming part and action part of sentences. Underline the naming part of the sentence on the board and circle the action part. Then go over the example sentences in the student book. Help students identify the naming part and action part of each sentence. Emphasize where *I* and *me* are placed in each sentence.

Read aloud the activity directions on page 116. Emphasize that *I* is always capitalized. Complete the activity by having students first identify the naming part and action part of each sentence and then having them read aloud the sentence to identify where *I* and *me* are placed.

Go over the activity directions on page 117. When students have finished each activity, review their answers.

Extension

Prepare several sentences, some that use *I* and some that use *me*. Assign half of the class as Team Naming Part and the other half as Team Action Part. Review with each team that *I* is used in the naming part of sentences about yourself and that *me* is used in the action part of sentences about yourself. Then have students listen as you read aloud sentences. Ask that Team Naming Part raise their hands when they hear *I* and that Team Action Part raise their hands when they hear *me*.

Using *I* in Sentences
and
Practice Using *I* in Sentences   Pages 118–119

Students Should

- understand how to vary the position of the pronoun *I* in a sentence

Teaching the Lesson

Write on the board the following sentence starters: *At the park, In my backyard, On the way to school.* Invite volunteers to complete the sentence starters by using *I* to tell what they do at these places. *(Example: At the park I play on the swings.)* Write on the board several responses. Explain that when people talk about themselves, they often use *I* at the beginning of the sentence. Tell students that their writing can be more interesting if they sometimes put *I* in the middle of the sentence. Use the sentences on the board to help students understand how *I* can sometimes be used in the middle of a sentence. Emphasize that *I* is still used before the verb even though it is not at the beginning of the sentence.

Guide students through the teaching and example on page 118. Then help volunteers form sentences by using the procedure described in the numbered list.

Go over the activity directions on pages 118 and 119. When students have finished each activity, review their answers.

Read aloud the Writer's Corner on page 119. Have students draw a picture of the place they want to write about. Then have students write their sentences. Invite volunteers to share their pictures and sentences with the class.

Extension

Write on the board several sentences that begin with *I*. *(Examples: I found five eggs. I read a sports magazine.)* For each sentence, help the class decide on a place where the action described might have occurred. Invite volunteers to form new sentences that use the places and sentences on the board. *(Examples: In the henhouse I found five eggs. At the library I read a sports magazine.)*

Pronoun Review
and
More Pronoun Review   Pages 120–121

Students Should

- understand how to use pronouns

Teaching the Lesson

Use the teaching on page 120 to review what pronouns are. Write on the board the pronouns students have studied. For each pronoun invite a volunteer to use the word in a sentence. Talk with students about nouns that each pronoun can replace in a sentence.

Go over the activity directions on pages 120 and 121. Help students distinguish between subject and object pronouns by listening for what sounds correct. If the class or individual students seem prepared to understand how to use subject and object pronouns besides *I* and *me*, refer to For Kids Who Are Ready on page 110b. When students have finished each activity, review their answers.

Extension

Review pronouns that students have studied by playing a guessing game. Say sentences that begin with *I am thinking of a pronoun* to prompt students to answer with the pronouns they have studied. *(Examples: I am thinking of a pronoun that can be used in place of boy. I am thinking of a pronoun that can be used in place of children.)*

Adjectives   Page 122

Students Should
- identify adjectives

Teaching the Lesson

Ask students to close their eyes and imagine an elephant standing in the room. Have students suggest words to describe the elephant. *(Examples: big, gray, smelly, loud)* Write on the board students' responses. Point out that each word on the board describes the elephant. Explain that words that describe nouns are called adjectives. For each adjective on the board, invite a volunteer to tell another noun that the adjective might describe. *(Examples: a big mountain, a gray mouse, a smelly swamp)* Explain that adjectives help people to imagine things. Emphasize the point by having students close their eyes and imagine a car. Then tell students to imagine a red car. Point out that they can now see the car more clearly. Suggest other adjectives for the car to help students form a clearer picture. *(Examples: shiny, fast, small, striped)*

Guide students through the teaching and examples. Play a game with students in which one volunteer suggests a noun and another volunteer suggests an adjective that might describe it. Point out that adjectives can make nouns more interesting.

Go over the activity directions. When students have finished the activity, review their answers.

Extension

Have each student cut out an interesting picture from a magazine and glue the picture to a sheet of paper. Ask students to write in the space around the picture several adjectives that describe it and to draw lines from their adjectives to what they describe in their pictures. Invite volunteers to present their work to the class. Then have the class recite the poem on page 122.

More Adjectives *and* Practice with Adjectives   Pages 123–124

Students Should
- recognize adjectives

Teaching the Lesson

Review that adjectives describe nouns. Have students suggest examples of nouns and adjectives that describe them. *(Examples: red rose, shiny watch, happy child)* Then write on the board a sentence with blanks where adjectives might go. *(Example: The _____ whale swam in the _____ ocean.)* Invite volunteers to suggest adjectives that could go in the blanks. Write in the blanks students' suggestions. Then erase the adjectives and have another volunteer suggest other adjectives. For each set of adjectives, invite students to identify which noun each adjective is describing. Repeat with other sentences. Use the sentences on the board to help students understand that adjectives make sentences clearer and more interesting.

Go over the activity directions on pages 123 and 124. When students have finished each activity, review their answers.

Read aloud the Writer's Corner on page 123. Have students write their sentences. Then invite volunteers to read aloud their sentences. List on a poster the adjectives that students use. Write at the top of the poster *Our school is*. Then help students think of more adjectives to describe their school.

Extension

Ask students to close their eyes and imagine a castle at the beginning of a ghost story. Call on students to name one thing they imagine in their scene. *(clouds, spiders, alligators in the moat, guards)* For each suggestion, have a volunteer give an adjective that describes what other students named. *(dark clouds, black spiders, scaly alligators, mean guards)* Continue until several students have had a turn. Then ask students to imagine a different castle that belongs to the princess in a fairy tale. Repeat the procedure with the new castle.

Sensory Words
and
More
Sensory Words   Pages 125–126

Students Should

- recognize adjectives that tell about sight, sound, smell, taste, and touch

Teaching the Lesson

Review that adjectives tell about nouns. Write on the board the word *popcorn*. Invite volunteers to say adjectives that describe popcorn. Guide students to give adjectives that describe the five senses by asking questions. *(Examples: What does popcorn taste like? How does it sound when you make it? How does it sound when you eat it? How does it feel in your hands?)* Write on the board the adjectives that students suggest. Explain that there are many different kinds of adjectives. Then tell students that some adjectives tell about our senses. Ask students to name the five senses. Write their responses on the board.

Go over the teaching and examples on page 125. Explain that sensory words tell about the five senses. Point out how each of the example sentences on page 125 tells about one of the five senses. Ask volunteers to name things they like to look at. Then ask volunteers to name things they like to smell. Continue with the other senses.

Go through the adjectives describing popcorn that are listed on the board. Help students determine which sense each word tells about. Choose other topics and have students suggest words that tell about each of the five senses. *(Examples: an airplane, cotton candy)* Use your topics to point out that not every topic can be described by using all five senses. *(Example: taste for an airplane, sound for cotton candy)*

Go over the activity directions on pages 125 and 126. When students have finished each activity, review their answers.

Extension

Have students recite the poem on page 126. Then write on the board as column headings *see, smell, taste, touch,* and *hear.* Play a guessing game in which you write sensory words in the appropriate columns that describe a common object. As you write each sensory word, invite students to guess the object. Continue adding sensory words to each column until students guess the object. To help students guess objects for which not all five senses would be appropriate, mark an *X* in that sense's column. *(Example: mark X under taste for an airplane)*

Five senses help us describe the world
we see, we smell, we taste, we touch, we hear.
Use sensory words when you write,
and your description will be loud and clear.

Adjectives That Compare

Page 127

Students Should

- understand that adjectives can compare by adding *-er* or *-est*

Teaching the Lesson

Draw on the board three trees, each tree smaller than the previous one. Then write to the side of the trees the words *small, smaller,* and *smallest.* Invite volunteers to read aloud the words and to draw a line from each word to the appropriate tree. When students have finished, write the appropriate word under each tree. Underline *small* in each word and circle *er* and *est.* Remind students that adjectives tell about nouns. Explain that the circled letters help adjectives compare nouns.

Go over the teaching and examples. Write on the board *The refrigerator is cold.* Point out that *cold* is an adjective that tells about the refrigerator. Then write on the board *The freezer is _____ than the refrigerator.* Invite volunteers to predict what word should go in the blank. Point out that this sentence only compares two things—a refrigerator and a freezer. Then write *The South Pole is the _____ place on Earth.* Invite volunteers to predict what word should go in the blank. Point out that there are many cold places on Earth. Invite volunteers to suggest other cold places they have heard of. Then explain that this sentence is saying that the South Pole is the coldest place of all these cold places.

Go over the directions for activity **A.** When students have finished the activity, review their answers and help them determine how many things are being compared in each sentence. Go over the directions for activity **B.** When students have finished the activity, review their answers.

Extension

Assign half the class *-er* endings and half the class *-est* endings. Write on the board an adjective to which the letters *er* or *est* can be added without spelling changes. Say either *compares two things* or *compares three or more things.* Invite the appropriate

group to send a volunteer to write the correct ending at the end of the word on the board. Then invite another member of that group to use the word in a sentence. Repeat with other adjectives.

More Adjectives That Compare

Page 128

Students Should

- understand how to add *-er* and *-est* to adjectives that end in a consonant that follows a short vowel
- understand how to add *-er* and *-est* to adjectives that end in silent *e*

Teaching the Lesson

Review that adjectives can compare things. Write on the board *er* and *est.* Ask volunteers which ending is used to compare two things and which ending is used to compare three or more things. Point out that *er* has only two letters and that *est* has three letters. Encourage students to use this tip to help them remember when to use *er* and when to use *est.* Review adjectives that compare that students studied on page 127.

Explain that some adjectives change spelling when adding the letters *er* and *est.* Go over the first paragraph of the teaching and examples. Write on the board *flat, short, steep, fat,* and *red.* Go through each word and help students determine which adjectives double the final consonant when adding the letters *er* and *est.* Have students spell aloud each adjective with each ending.

Go over the second paragraph of the teaching and examples. Remind students of verbs that drop the silent *e* when adding *-ed* and *-ing. (Examples: like, prove)* Write on the board adjectives that end in silent *e. (Examples: brave, cute, nice)* Invite volunteers to erase the *e* and add the letters *er.* Then have each volunteer write the adjective with the *est* ending.

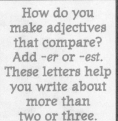

How do you make adjectives that compare? Add *-er* or *-est.* These letters help you write about more than two or three.

describe their pictures to the class. Guide students to use sensory words as they say their descriptions.

Topic Sentences   Page 135

Students Should
- understand the purpose of a topic sentence

Teaching the Lesson
Review that a description tells about a person, a place, a thing, or an event. Have volunteers talk about times they have described their day, a pet that they have, a game that they played, or a person that they know. As students give descriptions, ask questions to prompt them to use words that appeal to the five senses.

Have a volunteer read aloud the title. Review what a topic is. *(what the writing is about)* Invite volunteers to share topics they wrote about for their personal narratives, letters, and how-to articles.

Go over the first paragraph. Tell students that the topic sentence of a description is the sentence that says what the description will be about. Say: *We grab a reader's attention by making a topic sentence interesting. If a topic sentence is not interesting, a reader might decide not to read the whole description. A topic sentence that grabs a reader's attention makes the reader want to read the whole description.*

Read aloud the example topic sentence. Ask students what the description will be about. *(breakfast)* Then read aloud the rest of the description. When you have finished, write on the board the word *breakfast*. Help students point out nouns in the description that go with *breakfast*. *(bacon, toaster, butter, eggs)* Write the words on the board. Tell students that the topic sentence tells readers what to expect in a description. Write on the board *My favorite meal is dinner*. Ask students whether the topic sentence fits the words listed under *breakfast*. Guide students to understand that the topic sentence should give readers a clue to what the description will be about and that it should be related to the adjectives in the description.

Go over the activity directions. Guide students to complete the activity as a class. Help students to justify their answers.

Extension
Have students write a list of *My Favorites*. Invite students to list their favorite foods, toys, books, movies, games, or activities. When they have finished, explain that any of these things could be a topic for a description. Ask students to choose one of their listed items and write an interesting topic sentence for a description about that item.

Sensory Words   Page 136

Students Should
- identify sensory words
- understand how sensory words improve a description

Teaching the Lesson
Review with students what a topic sentence is. *(a sentence that tells what a description will be about)* Guide students to explain why these sentences are important in descriptions. *(They tell readers what the description will be about. They make the reader want to read the description.)*

Ask a volunteer to read aloud the title. Then go over the first paragraph and the examples. Remind students that sensory words tell about how things look, sound, smell, taste, or feel. Invite volunteers to describe their favorite foods. Prompt students to use sensory words by asking questions that appeal to the five senses. *(Examples: What does it look like? How does it smell? How does it taste?)* Tell students that using sensory words in descriptions helps readers to imagine the topic.

Go over the directions for activity A. Guide students to complete the activity as a class. Help students to explain how they knew which sensory word matched each sense.

Go over the directions for activity B. When students have finished the activity, invite volunteers to share their answers with the class.

Extension

Write on the board a list of common nouns. *(Examples: table, cookie, pizza, car, puppy)* Have students write two sensory words that describe each noun. When students have finished, invite volunteers to share their answers with the class. Write their responses on the board. Guide students to understand that different people can think of different words to describe the same things. Talk with students about how sensory words help to create a more complete description of each item.

Sensory Words in a Description   Page 137

Students Should

- understand how sensory words function in a description

Teaching the Lesson

Review what sensory words are and talk about how sensory words improve descriptions. Discuss how sensory words help readers imagine what things look, smell, taste, feel, and sound like. Then invite a volunteer to read aloud the title. Explain that sensory words make descriptions clearer and more interesting.

Go over the directions for activity **A.** Have students complete the activity as a class. Challenge students to say topic sentences about each topic, using the sensory words they have listed.

Go over the directions for activity **B.** When students have finished the activity, invite them to share their answers with the class.

Extension

Choose three objects in the classroom. Select items that have distinct features that can be easily described. Place the objects where they can be seen by the entire class. Have students write four sensory words that describe each object. When students have finished, invite them to write their words on the board. Have students say topic sentences, using the words listed on the board.

Writer's Workshop

Prewriting— Pick a Topic   Page 138

Students Should

- brainstorm description topics
- identify appropriate topics for their descriptions

Review the elements and characteristics of a description. *(tells about a person, place, thing, or event; a topic sentence that tells what the description will be about; sensory words that help the reader imagine what is being described)* Guide students to talk about why topic sentences and sensory words are important in descriptions.

Ask a volunteer to read aloud the title. Invite volunteers to describe their prewriting experiences when they wrote personal narratives, friendly letters, and how-to articles. Say: *Descriptions can be about anything. There are a lot of topics we can choose from. Prewriting can help us think of topics and choose the best topic to write about.*

Go over the first two paragraphs. Then have volunteers read each item on the list. Explain that each item is something that Maya knows how to describe. Talk with students about why each item might be a good topic for a description. Invite students to offer sensory words that Maya might use for each topic. Explain that the topic Maya chose is one that she can describe well and one that she wants most to write about. Help students understand that the best descriptions are the ones that use the most senses.

Model on the board brainstorming your own list of description topics. For each idea explain why it might be a good topic for a description. Help students understand why some topics might make stronger descriptions than others. Then choose one topic by circling it. Talk to students about why the topic you chose is a good one for a description.

Go over the next paragraph. Emphasize that the topics students list should appeal to as many senses as possible. Then allow time for students to brainstorm their lists of topics. As students work, circulate among them to provide encouragement and support. Talk with students about why each topic they list might make a good description.

Go over the last paragraph. Explain that if students can answer yes to these questions, then they probably have a good topic idea for their description. Allow time for students to choose and circle the topic that they like best.

Prewriting—Plan Your Description
Page 139

Students Should
- use a chart to plan their descriptions

Invite a volunteer read aloud the title. Say: *Remember that when we do prewriting, we first pick a topic. Then we plan our drafts. Planning our drafts helps us make sure that we don't forget anything when we begin to write. If we have a well-planned draft, we don't have to add or change as much later.*

Review how students planned the drafts of their personal narratives, friendly letters, and how-to articles. *(drawing pictures, using a chart, writing steps on sentence strips)* Explain that planning a description includes thinking about what sensory words to use in the description.

Go through the first paragraph. Then direct students' attention to Maya's five-senses chart. Ask them to imagine what you are about to read. Then read aloud the five-senses chart. Talk about how the sensory words in Maya's chart helped them to picture what the pond near her house is like. Explain that Maya tried to appeal to each of the five senses to help readers imagine the pond.

Model on the board how to create a five-senses chart for your own description. Use the topic you chose. As you fill in each section, explain why you chose particular words and how those words relate to each sense. Say: *A five-senses chart helps me think about which words I will use in my draft. Thinking*

about the sensory words I will use helps me to write a better, more complete description.

Go over the last paragraph. Then allow time for students to complete their five-senses charts. As students work, circulate among them to provide assistance and support. Guide students who are having trouble by asking questions such as *Does it look like something else? What colors does it have? Does it smell like anything else? Is it made up of different smells?*

Drafting
Page 140

Students Should
- use prewriting notes to write their first drafts

Invite a volunteer to read aloud the title. Talk with students about their experiences writing drafts for their personal narratives, friendly letters, and how-to articles. Review how students' prewriting notes helped them to write their first drafts. Remind students that drafting is their first opportunity to put their thoughts and ideas into sentences.

Go over the first paragraph. Then guide students through Maya's draft. Help students to identify words and phrases in the draft that are from Maya's five-senses chart on page 139. *(Examples: big rocks, tangy huckleberries)* Point out how prewriting helped Maya write her draft.

Go over the next paragraph. Allow time for students to add to their charts additional sensory words. Remind students that using sensory words in their descriptions will help the reader better imagine the topic.

Model for students how to use a five-senses chart to write your draft. Try to include in your draft at least one sentence for each of the five senses. Remember to include sensory words. Emphasize how your topic sentence tells what the description is about. As you work, explain to students how your description relates to the notes you wrote during prewriting. Be sure to include in your model draft at least one mistake from the Editing

Checklist on page 141 and one mistake from the Proofreading Checklist on page 142. Save your draft for use during the Editing stage.

Go over the last paragraph. Allow time for students to complete their drafts. As students work, circulate through the class to provide students with encouragement and support. Emphasize that this is a time to capture ideas and to turn thoughts into sentences. Remind students that they will be able to find and fix mistakes in their drafts during editing and proofreading.

Editing   Page 141

Students Should
* edit their descriptions

Invite a volunteer to read aloud the title. Talk with students about their experiences editing their personal narratives, friendly letters, and how-to articles. Remind students that editing is a time to make sure that the ideas in their descriptions make sense. Say: *When we write descriptions, we want our readers to imagine what we are describing. When we edit, we look for places that might confuse readers or make it hard for readers to imagine what is being described. Then we fix those places so that the description is clearer and more interesting.*

Go through the first paragraph. Say: *Maya uses the Editing Checklist to make sure she checks for all the important parts of a description. She also uses the checklist to help keep track of what she checked as she edits her draft. Using the Editing Checklist helps us make our drafts better.* Then go over the Editing Checklist. Pause after each item to talk with students about what the question means and how they might check for it.

Read aloud the next paragraph and thought bubble. Ask students which item on the checklist helped Maya find the mistake in her draft. (*Do I use sensory words?*) Ask how Maya fixed the mistake. (*She added the sensory word* sweet *to describe the smell of lilacs.*)

Direct students' attention to the description you wrote on the board. Help students use the checklist questions to find the editing mistake that you included in your draft. Say: *When we write, it is important to have good editors. You are good editors because you helped me find this mistake. Now I can correct the mistake and make my draft better.*

Go over the last paragraph of the section. Remind students that reading their drafts aloud is a good way to catch mistakes in their drafts. Say: *Sometimes when we read aloud, we hear things that we don't see when we read to ourselves. Try reading your draft aloud to see if you can hear any mistakes.*

Allow time for students to edit their drafts. As they work, circulate among students to be sure that they are giving consideration to each item on the checklist. Check students' justifications for making or not making changes to their work.

I forgot a sensory word!

If students edit each other's drafts, remind them of the proper language and behavior for peer-editing sessions. Emphasize that when a friend edits their work, they should check over the mistakes their friend marks. Tell students to ask a teacher or a parent for help if they disagree with a mistake marked by their friend.

Revising   Page 141

Students Should

- use editing changes to revise their drafts

Invite a volunteer to read aloud the title of this section. Talk with students about what they did when they revised their personal narratives, friendly letters, and how-to articles. *(wrote new copies of the draft, including changes from editing)* Ask students where writers get editing changes. *(Some ideas are the writer's. Others come from a friend or a teacher.)*

Go over the first paragraph. Point out the mistake in your draft that the class found during editing. Demonstrate how to mark the correction. Talk about how making this change helps to make the draft clearer. Then rewrite your draft on the board, incorporating into the new copy your marked change. Remember to include your mistake from the Proofreading Checklist on page 142. Emphasize that a new copy of the draft can help students see any other mistakes that might be in the description.

Allow time for students to revise their drafts. As they work, circulate among students to be sure that they are correctly writing their editing changes. When students have finished, suggest that they check their draft again, using the Editing Checklist to make sure they did not introduce new mistakes into their drafts.

Proofreading   Page 142

Students Should

- proofread their revised drafts

Ask a volunteer to read aloud the title. Remind students that proofreading happens when they make sure that words are spelled correctly, that capital letters and end marks are correct, and that the sentences are correct. Emphasize that we proofread because these kinds of mistakes can distract readers. Explain that readers might have trouble imagining what is being described because they are noticing spelling or capitalization mistakes.

Go over the first paragraph and the Proofreading Checklist. Pause after each checklist item to talk about what the question means and how students might check for it in their drafts. Encourage students to use what they learned in this chapter about pronouns and adjectives as they check that item in their drafts. Remind students that they can also use references such as a picture dictionary or a word wall to check and correct mistakes.

Read aloud the next paragraph and direct students' attention to the partial student model. Ask what Maya noticed about her draft. *(She used the wrong pronoun. She should have used* I *instead of* me *in the sentence.)* Invite a volunteer to tell why *I* is the correct pronoun in the sentence. *(The pronoun* I *is used in the naming part of a sentence, and the pronoun* me *is used in the action part of a sentence.)* Point out the proofreading marks Maya used to correct her draft.

Guide students to proofread your revised draft, using the Proofreading Checklist. Use the questions as a guide to help students find the mistake in your description. Demonstrate how to use proofreading marks to correct the mistake.

Go over the last two paragraphs. Then allow time for students to proofread their drafts. Remind students to check for only one kind of mistake at a time. As they work, circulate through the class to offer students assistance and support. If students are unsure of what a checklist question means or whether something they find is correct, guide them to use age-appropriate reference materials to check the mistake.

If time allows, have partners trade drafts and proofread each other's work. Remind students that a friend might catch mistakes that they have missed. If you choose this option, circulate among students to be sure that they are using appropriate peer-conferencing language. Remind them to double-check their friend's suggestions.

Publishing   Page 143

Page 110e provides a full-sized, reproducible copy of the student's Description scoring rubric. Students can use the rubric when assessing their own descriptions.

Page 110f provides a full-sized, reproducible copy of the Teacher's Scoring Rubric for descriptions. The rubric can be used when assessing students' understanding of the genre.

Students Should
- produce final copies of their descriptions

Invite a volunteer to read aloud the title. Remind students that publishing happens when a writer shares his or her work with an audience. Ask students what an audience is. (*the people who read your writing*) Say: *There are a lot of people who can be the audience for your description. Anyone who is interested in your topic can be your audience.*

Go over the first paragraph. Explain that Maya's published description does not have any mistakes. Tell students that she carefully copied her description and made sure that no new mistakes were added before she posted it on the bulletin board.

Model how to produce a clean copy. You might write your final copy on the board, or you might use one of the publishing ideas listed in the student book. Talk about who the audience for your description is. Tell students that how you publish your work is another way of getting the attention of

your audience. Explain why you have chosen a particular publishing method, and invite students to name people who might read your description.

Go over the second paragraph. Then allow time for students to make a final copy of their descriptions. Remind students to write slowly and carefully and to check each sentence to make sure they do not make any new mistakes. You may wish to allow students who are familiar with computers to type and print out their descriptions. Remind students to use the computer's spell checker and have them use the Proofreading Checklist once more to make sure that they have not typed any new mistakes.

When students have finished, read aloud the last paragraph and invite students to read the publishing suggestions. Talk about how students might publish their descriptions. Allow time for students to create any additional items they need to publish their work, such as drawings or frames.

When students have finished, distribute copies of the student's Description scoring rubric. Guide students to understand what each item means and how to apply it to their own writing. Then allow time for students to self-evaluate their descriptions.

Have students add their finished descriptions to their portfolios. Remind students that their portfolios will help them see what they have learned and how their writing has improved throughout the year.

CHAPTER 5
Contractions and Book Reports

Introducing the Chapter
Pages 144–145

Students Should
- have a basic understanding of book reports
- have a basic understanding of contractions

Reading the Model

Read aloud the quotation. Write on the board *exercise for the body* =. Ask students to tell what exercise does for the body. *(keeps you healthy, makes you strong and quick)* Write their responses to the right of the equal sign. Then write on the board *reading for the mind* =. Invite volunteers to explain what reading does for the mind. *(keeps the mind healthy and strong)* Explain that reading is exercise for the mind.

Invite volunteers to name books they have recently read. For each response, ask the following questions: *Did you like the book? What was it about? Who were the characters? Where did the story take place?* Then invite volunteers who liked their books to raise their hands. Ask those students if they told others about the book. Say: *We tell others about books because we like the books and want others to enjoy them too. Sometimes we tell others about books because we didn't like them and we think others won't like them either. When you tell someone about a book, you are giving a book report.*

Point out the model book report on page 145. Invite volunteers to read the title and the name of the person who wrote the book report. Read aloud the model book report while students follow along. Explain that book reports tell the most important information about the book, including the title of the book, the name of the person who wrote it, and the names of the people or things in the book. Explain that the people or things in a book are called characters. Ask students the following questions: *What book is this report about?* (The Happy Lion) *Who wrote the book?* (Louise Fatio) *Who are some of the characters in the book?* (The Happy Lion, Francois, Monsieur Dupont, and Madam Pinson) Explain that book reports also tell what the book is about. To emphasize this point, reread the portion of the model that summarizes the plot of *The Happy Lion*.

Explain that book reports tell what the report writer thought about the book. Tell students that the way someone feels about a book is called the person's opinion. Ask students to tell how Julio feels about *The Happy Lion*. *(He likes the book.)* Point out that Julio also gives a reason for his opinion. Ask students to tell why Julio likes the book. *(because of the lion)*

Read aloud in the model the sentence *The Happy Lion can't figure out why.* Write on the board the contraction *can't*. Ask students to tell what this word means. *(cannot)* Explain that this word is called a contraction. Write on the board *cannot*. Say: *A contraction is a short way to write a word or two words. The contraction* can't *is a short way to write* cannot.

Have a volunteer read aloud the last sentence of the model. Challenge the class to find the contraction in the sentence. *(he's)* Explain that *he's* is also a contraction. Invite a volunteer to predict from the context of the sentence what two words make the contraction *he's*. *(he is)* Say: *Contractions help us write sentences that sound more like the way people talk. Contractions can make it seem as if you are talking to the reader.*

Contractions *and* Contractions Practice   Pages 146–147

Students Should
- understand how to form contractions with *not*

Teaching the Lesson
Write on the board the sentence starter *I do not like*. Invite volunteers to complete the sentence. Write on the board three sentences that students offer. Underline *do not* in each sentence. Explain that there is a shorter way to write these sentences. Then write as column headings *contraction, word or words*, and *letter left out*. Under *contraction* write *don't*. Explain that *don't* is a short way of writing *do not*. Tell students that the short way of writing two words is called a contraction. Invite volunteers to read aloud the sentences on the board, using *don't* in place of *do not*. Under *word or words*, write *do not*. Point to *don't* and *do not* and ask students to explain what is different about them. (*The space between words is taken out. The letter* o *is left out and replaced with an apostrophe.*) Under *letter left out*, write *o*.

Go over the first paragraph of the teaching on page 146. Then write *have not* under the heading *word or words*. Explain that *have not* can be written as a contraction. Invite a volunteer to predict how *have not* would be written as a contraction. Under *letter left out*, write *o*.

Go over the rest of the teaching. Point out that both contractions on the board were made with the word *not* and that the missing letter in both contractions is *o*. Write under *word or words*, the words *has not* and *did not*. Have students predict what letter will be left out when forming these words into contractions. Then invite volunteers to predict how the contractions for *has not* and *did not* will be formed.

Go over the activity directions on pages 146 and 147. When students have finished each activity, review their answers.

Read aloud the Writer's Corner on page 147. Allow time for students to write their sentences.

Extension
Write on the board the contractions *don't, didn't, hasn't,* and *haven't*. Invite small groups to work together to write a story. Have groups use each contraction in their stories.

More Contractions with *Not and* Writing Contractions with *Not*   Pages 148–149

Students Should
- recognize contractions formed with *not*

Teaching the Lesson
Review that a contraction is a short way of writing two words. Remind students that some contractions are made with the word *not*. Write on the board a chart like the one used in the previous lesson. Help students to fill in the chart to review the contractions *don't, haven't, hasn't,* and *didn't*. Point out that contractions made with *not* leave out the *o* and add an apostrophe. Then explain that there are other words that make contractions with *not*.

Go over the teaching on page 148 and have students trace the contractions in activity **A**. Guide students to add these contractions to the chart on the board.

Go over the activity directions on pages 148 and 149. When students have finished each activity, review their answers.

Extension
Create a contraction spinner. Between the spokes of the wheel, write the two words that form contractions students have studied. Invite a student to spin the spinner. Have that student spell the contraction. Then invite a volunteer to use the contraction in a sentence. If the volunteer uses the contraction correctly, have him or her take a turn at the spinner. Repeat the game with other volunteers.

Working with Contractions *and* More Working with Contractions

Pages 150–151

Students Should

* recognize contractions formed with *not*

Teaching the Lesson

Create flash cards for the contractions *don't, hasn't, haven't, didn't, couldn't, aren't, doesn't,* and *isn't.* Use the flash cards to review these contractions. Invite volunteers to say sentences that use each contraction. Ask what is the same about all these contractions. *(The letter* o *is left out and replaced by an apostrophe.)* Remind students that these contractions are formed with *not.*

Write on the board the following sentences, including the underlines: *I was not home. I cannot go outside today. We were not playing soccer. I will not be at school tomorrow.* Point out that these sentences use *not* and that the underlined words can be made into contractions. Invite volunteers to read aloud the sentences, saying contractions for the underlined words. Tell students that there are some special contractions. Point out the contraction *can't.* Explain that *can't* is a special contraction because it is made from one word. Then point out the contraction *won't.* Explain that *won't* is a special contraction because it has a spelling change. Tell students that they should always pay close attention to the use and the spelling of special contractions.

Go over the teaching on page 150 and have students trace over the contractions in activity A. Invite volunteers to use the contractions in sentences.

Go over the activity directions on pages 150 and 151. When students have finished each activity, review their answers.

Read aloud the Writer's Corner on page 151. Talk with students about places they will not go. Then have students write their sentences.

Extension

Have students recite the poem on page 151. Then invite students to create contraction mobiles. Assign small groups different contractions. Have students write their contraction on paper glued to a piece of cardboard. Then have students write the two words that make up the contraction each on a separate strip of paper. Help students attach string to hang the words from the contraction. Display the contraction mobiles around the room.

Contractions with *Not* Review *and* More Contractions with *Not* Review

Pages 152–153

Students Should

* recognize contractions formed with *not*

Teaching the Lesson

Go over the teaching on page 152. Use flash cards or help students complete a contraction chart to review the contractions that they have studied. Invite volunteers to say sentences that use the contractions.

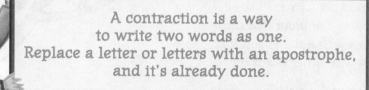

A contraction is a way to write two words as one. Replace a letter or letters with an apostrophe, and it's already done.

Go over the activity directions on pages 152 and 153. When students have finished each activity, review their answers.

Extension

Make a 12-square grid on the floor with tape or string. In each square place a flash card on which you have written a contraction on one side and the two words that form the contraction on the other side. Use the following contractions: *don't, haven't, hasn't, didn't, couldn't, aren't, doesn't, isn't, wasn't, can't, weren't,* and *won't.* Have a student toss a coin into a square, say the contraction, give the two words that make up the contraction, and use it in a sentence. When a student correctly answers, turn the flash card over so that the two words show. Continue the game with other students. If a student lands on a square in which the flash card shows two words, have the student give the contraction, spell it, and use it in a sentence.

Contractions with Am and Is
Page 154

Students Should

- understand how to form contractions with *am* and *is*

Teaching the Lesson

Review that contractions are a short way of writing two words. Remind students that contractions use apostrophes to replace one or more letters from the two words. Write on the board examples of the 12 contractions students have studied. Invite volunteers to tell from what words each contraction is made. Have other students use the contractions in sentences. Point out that these contractions are all formed with *not.* Explain that contractions can be made with other words too.

Go over the first paragraph of the teaching. Point out that *I* is the only word that uses *am.* Then in activity **A** have students trace over the contraction. Ask a volunteer to tell which letter is left out and

replaced with an apostrophe. Invite students to use *I am* and *I'm* in sentences.

Go over the next paragraph of the teaching. Write on the board the following sentences: *Shawn is running. Tyra is walking. The sidewalk is slippery.* Review that pronouns are words that take the place of nouns. Have students suggest pronouns to replace the underlined words in the sentences and write these on the board. Then explain that these pronouns can make contractions with the word *is.* Then invite volunteers to come to the board to replace the pronouns and *is* with the appropriate contraction. Point out that each of these contractions leaves out the letter *i* and replaces it with an apostrophe. Then have students trace over the contractions in activity **B**.

Go over the directions for activity **C**. When students have finished the activity, review their answers.

Extension

Write on the board the following riddles: *He fights fires. What is he? She flies airplanes. What is she? It has no legs and crawls on the ground. What is it? I am soft and purr quietly. What am I?* Have students use the contractions *I'm, he's, she's,* and *it's* in complete sentences to answer the riddles. (*He's a firefighter. She's a pilot. It's a snake. I'm a cat.*) Consider writing more riddles for students to answer.

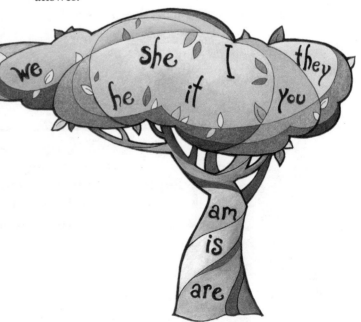

Contractions with *Are* and
Contractions with *Am, Is,* and *Are*   Pages 155–156

Students Should

- understand how to form contractions with *are*
- recognize contractions formed with *am, is,* and *are*

Teaching the Lesson

Write on the board *I* in one column and in another column the pronouns *he, she,* and *it.* Beside the pronoun *I,* write *am* and have volunteers say sentences using *I am.* Write beside the remaining pronouns the verb *is.* Have students use the pronouns in sentences with *is.* Then have students spell each contraction for these words and write their responses on the board.

Go over the teaching on page 155. In a third column write the pronouns *you, we,* and *they.* Explain that these pronouns use the being verb *are.* Write *are* beside each of the new pronouns. Then invite volunteers to use these pronouns and the verb *are* in sentences.

Have students trace over the contractions in activity A. Then have volunteers spell the contraction for each of the new pronouns added to the board. Write students' responses on the board. Invite volunteers to use the new contractions in sentences.

Go over the activity directions on pages 155 and 156. When students have finished each activity, review their answers.

Extension

Cut note cards into shapes such as hearts, squares, circles, and diamonds. Cut those shapes in half and write contractions on one half and the words that form the contraction on the matching half. Include the following contractions: *I'm, you're, he's, she's, it's, we're,* and *they're.* Put four different contractions and the matching words into an envelope. Have a number of different envelopes available with puzzles for students to unscramble.

Contractions with *Have*   Page 157

Students Should

- understand how to form contractions with *have*

Teaching the Lesson

Remind students that when forming a contraction, one or more letters are left out and replaced with an apostrophe. Review some of the contractions students have studied. Explain that the verb *have* can also be used to make contractions with pronouns.

Go over the teaching. Write on the board *I have, you have, we have,* and *they have.* Invite volunteers to use the words on the board to say sentences. Invite volunteers to predict how to form contractions for each of the word pairs on the board. Then have students trace over the contractions in activity A.

Go over the directions for activity B. When students have finished the activity, review their answers.

Extension

Assign each of four groups one of the following word pairs: *I have, you have, we have, they have.* Have each student write his or her word pair on sentence strips. Have students in each group trade strips and cut out the letters that need to be left out from their words to make a contraction. Help students to tape their strips together and to write an apostrophe in the appropriate place. Invite volunteers to hold up their contraction cutouts and use their contractions in sentences.

Contractions with *Has* and Contractions with *Have* and *Has*   Pages 158–159

Students Should

- understand how to form contractions with *has*
- recognize contractions formed with *have* and *has*

Teaching the Lesson

Review contractions formed with *have* by writing on the board a chart with the column headings *contraction, two words,* and *letters left out.* Have students complete the chart for the contractions *I've, you've, we've,* and *they've.* Point out that these contractions are made by leaving out the letters *ha* and replacing those letters with an apostrophe.

Go over the teaching on page 158. Tell students that making contractions with *has* is similar to making contractions with *have.* Write on the chart *he has, she has,* and *it has.* Guide students to complete the rest of the chart for these contractions.

Have students trace over the contractions in activity A. Invite volunteers to use the contractions in sentences.

Go over the activity directions on pages 158 and 159. When students have finished each activity, review their answers.

Extension

Write on separate sentence strips the contractions and the word pairs that form the contractions from activity A on page 159. Put the strips in a box. Have each student choose from the box one strip and write on a sheet of paper a sentence using their words or contraction. When students have finished, invite them to locate their partners by reading their sentences aloud one at a time and finding the student with the matching contraction or words that form the contraction.

Reviewing Contractions and More Reviewing Contractions   Pages 160–161

Students Should

- recognize contractions formed with *am, is, are, have,* and *has*

Teaching the Lesson

Use flash cards or help students complete a contraction chart to review the contractions with *am, is, are, have,* and *has* that they have studied. Invite volunteers to say sentences that use each contraction.

Go over the activity directions on pages 160 and 161. When students have finished each activity, review their answers.

Extension

Have students help you draw a contraction garden. Say a sentence that uses one of the contractions formed with *am, is, are, have,* or *has.* (*Example: We've gone to the store.*) Have a volunteer identify the contraction in the sentence and say the sentence back, replacing the contraction with the words that form it. (*Example: we've; We have gone to the store.*) If the student does so correctly, have him or her write the contraction on the board and draw a stem below the contraction and flower petals around it. Repeat with other students and the contractions they have studied.

Contractions with *Had*
and
More Contractions
with *Had*   Pages 162–163

Students Should

- understand how to form contractions with *had*

Teaching the Lesson

Review with students how to form contractions with *has* and *have* and the pronouns *I, you, he, she, we,* and *they*. Remind students that when making contractions with *have* and *has,* the letters *ha* are replaced with an apostrophe.

Go over the teaching on page 162. Explain that *had* is a verb that tells about the past. Point out that making contractions with *had* is similar to making contractions with the verbs *has* and *have*. Write on the board *I had, he had,* and *she had.* Invite volunteers to use the words on the board to begin sentences. Then invite volunteers to demonstrate on the board how the words form contractions. Have students repeat their sentences using the contractions.

Go over the directions for the activities on page 162. When students have finished each activity, review their answers.

Read aloud the Writer's Corner on page 162. Allow time for students to write their sentences. Invite volunteers to share their work. Ask each student to tell what noun in the sentence is replaced with *he* or *she.*

Go over the teaching on page 163. Write on the board *you had, we had,* and *they had.* Invite volunteers to predict how the contractions for these words should be spelled. Then invite students to use the contractions in sentences.

Go over the directions for the activities on page 163. When students have finished, review their answers.

Extension

Draw a tick-tack-toe grid on the board. Write the pronouns *you, we, they, I, he,* and *she* in the squares. (*Some pronouns will need to be repeated.*) Have the class form two teams, Xs and Os, and invite them to play tick-tack-toe. Have one team choose a square and use the word in that square in a sentence that uses *had*. If the team says a correct sentence a student from the team goes to the board to write in that square the contraction formed with *had*. Another member of the team must use the contraction in a sentence. When a team successfully completes all three steps, it can claim the square. Continue until one team has claimed three squares that form a line horizontally, vertically, or diagonally.

Show What
You Know   Pages 164–165

Students Should

- identify and use contractions correctly

Teaching the Lesson

Explain the directions for each activity. Assist students if necessary. When students have finished each activity, review their answers. Show What You Know may be used as a review or a test.

Get Ready to Write

What Is a Book Report? Page 166

Students Should

- identify the elements and characteristics of a book report
- understand the purpose of writing a book report

Teaching the Lesson

Talk with students about books they have read. Ask students to describe the setting in the book, the characters, what the characters did, and how they acted. Invite volunteers to talk about times they have described a book to a friend or a family member. Tell students that any time they have described a book to someone else, they were giving a book report. Then invite a volunteer to read aloud the title. Say: *A book report is a way to tell people about books. In a book report, you can share what you know about a book. When you write a book report, you tell about the characters and what happens in the book. You also tell if you liked the book or not.*

Review with students the book report on page 145. Ask students to tell what the title of the book is. (*The Happy Lion*) Then ask students to name the lion's friends. (*Francois, Monsieur Dupont, and Madam Pinson*) Talk with students about what happens in the book. (*A lion tries to visit his friends.*) Invite students to tell whether the book-report writer liked the book and to explain why. (*He thought the book was great. He liked the lion.*) Explain that in a book report, a writer tells about a book but does not give away the ending. Tell students that giving away the ending might make people not want to read the book. Talk about whether this book report makes students want to read the book.

Go over the paragraph and the first three listed items. Explain that the title of a book is always underlined. Then invite students to tell who an author is. (*the person who wrote the book*) Tell students that characters are the people or things that a book is about. Guide students to name characters in books they have read. Emphasize that characters aren't always people. Encourage students to talk about characters that are animals or objects, as well as characters that are people.

Read aloud the fourth item. Explain to students that an opinion in a book report is what someone thinks about the book. Tell students that their opinion might be that the book was really great, or their opinion might be that a book was boring. Explain that when they give an opinion, they should tell why they felt the way they did. Point out that in the model book report on page 145, the writer liked the book because he liked the lion.

Go over the model book report and the callouts on page 166. Explain how each part of a book report functions in the model. Then guide students to complete the activity as a class.

Extension

Select a book that you have read with the class. Display the book where the class can see it. Have students identify the title and the author. Then ask students to name and describe characters in the book. Invite volunteers to tell what they thought of the book. Encourage students to give reasons for their opinions.

Parts of a Book Report   Page 167

Students Should

- identify the parts of a book report

Teaching the Lesson

Invite volunteers to explain what a book report is. *(a way to tell an audience about a book; writing that shares what a person knows about a book)* Ask volunteers to name four things that a book report should tell. *(the book's title, the author, the characters, and the writer's opinion)*

Have a volunteer read aloud the title. Then go over the first paragraph and the sentences about the beginning. Direct students' attention to the model book report and the callout labeled *beginning.* Invite students to identify the title, the author, and the main character in the book. *(Second-Grade Sleuth, Jack Ross, Amy)*

Go over the sentence about the middle and direct students' attention to the callout. Ask volunteers to explain what happens in the book. *(Someone plays pranks in Amy's town. Amy makes a plan to trap the prankster.)* Go over the sentence about the ending and direct students' attention to the callout. Ask students whether the book-report writer likes the book and why. *(He or she likes the book because Amy is funny and smart.)* Point out that the book-report writer does not give away the ending of the book.

Go over the activity directions. Have students complete the activity independently. When students have finished, invite volunteers to share their answers.

Extension

Invite volunteers to name books that you have read with the class. Write their responses on the board. Then write the author of each book. Have students choose a book and draw pictures for the beginning, the middle, and the ending of a book report. Encourage students to include in their ending a picture of themselves with a speech balloon that tells their opinion of the book. When students have finished, invite them to share their work with the class.

Opinions in Book Reports
Page 168

Students Should
- identify opinions in a book report

Teaching the Lesson

Review the parts of a book report. Ask students to explain what each part of a book report should contain. *(The beginning tells the title, author, and characters. The middle tells what happens in the book. The ending tells how the writer feels about the book.)*

Invite a volunteer to read aloud the title. Then go over the first paragraph. Explain that an opinion is how someone feels or what someone thinks about something. Ask students whether they like pizza. Explain that their answers are their opinions. Say: *An opinion is not right or wrong. Some people like pizza. Some people do not like pizza. There is no right answer. The right answer is what is right for you. It is OK if people disagree, because people have their own opinions.*

Emphasize the last sentence of the first paragraph. Tell students that when they write a book report, they should tell why they think or feel the way they do. Say: *When you give a reason for your opinion, your readers will know that you have thought about why you feel the way you do. Your readers will be more likely to trust your opinion if they know that you thought about it.*

Go over the next paragraph. Tell students that opinions can be positive or negative. Explain that a positive opinion tells when someone likes something and that a negative opinion tells when someone does not like something. Read aloud each opinion and invite students to identify the opinion as positive or negative. Explain that there is more than one way to give an opinion. Point out that the two positive opinions and the two negative opinions say similar things but in different ways.

Go over the next paragraph and the list of reasons. Emphasize that whether their opinion of a book is positive or negative, they must tell why they think or feel the way they do. Explain that they might like or dislike a book for many different reasons. Invite students to name books that they thought were funny, books that they liked because of the pictures, and books that they liked because of an interesting character. Then ask students to name books they didn't like because they knew what would happen or because the story didn't make sense. Say: *By giving good reasons why you don't like a book, you might convince others not to read it. If you give good reasons for liking it, you might get someone else to read it. Readers often know that if a writer of a book report doesn't like a book, they might not like it either.*

Go over the model book report. Then have students complete the activity independently. When students have finished, invite them to share their answers.

Extension

Have students make a list of books they have read. Tell them to draw a smiling face by the title if they liked the book and a frowning face by the title if they did not like the book. When students have finished, invite volunteers to share their lists. Ask students to choose from their list one book and say one reason why they liked or disliked it.

Organize a Book Report   Page 169

Students Should

- understand how to organize a book report

Teaching the Lesson

Review what an opinion is and how it functions in a book report. (*An opinion is how the writer feels or thinks. The writer's opinion can help readers decide whether they want to read a book.*) Then review the reasons listed on page 168. Remind students that when they write an opinion of a book, they should give a reason for their opinion.

Invite a volunteer to read aloud the title. Explain that organizing a book report means thinking about what to write and making a writing plan. Talk with students about ways they have planned and organized previous writing assignments. (*drawing pictures, making charts, writing on sentence strips*) Tell students that organizing means writing ideas down in a way that makes sense.

Go over the paragraph. Tell students that using a chart can help them organize their book reports. Emphasize that a chart can also help them think about their ideas before they write their first drafts. Then go over the directions and the model chart. Have students complete this activity independently. When students have finished, invite them to share their answers with the class.

Extension

Invite volunteers to list movies that they have seen. Group students who have seen the same movie and have them create a chart similar to the one on page 169. Allow time for students to fill in the chart with information about the movie, leaving the section labeled *Author* blank. Explain that because many people usually help to make a movie, there isn't really one author. When students have finished, invite groups to share their work with the class.

Writer's Workshop

Prewriting— Pick a Topic   Page 170

Students Should

- brainstorm books for a book report
- identify appropriate topics for their book reports

Talk with students about books they have read independently, as well as those you have read together in class. Invite volunteers to describe what happens in the books and to name the main characters. Ask students to explain whether they liked the books and why. Then say: *When we write book reports, the books we choose are our topics. All the books that we have talked about would make good topics for a book report.*

Invite a volunteer to read aloud the title. Say: *When we do prewriting for book reports, we think about books we have read and what we thought or felt about them. Then we decide which book to write about.*

Go over the first paragraph. Direct students' attention to Julio's list. Tell students that to think of a topic for his book report, Julio brainstormed several books. Go over the books on Julio's list. Explain that each book is one that Julio has read and that each book might be a good topic for a book report. Point out that Julio brainstormed many books. Ask a volunteer which book Julio chose and why Julio chose it.

Model on the board how to brainstorm a list of books. Write book titles on the board. Remember to underline each book title. Explain why you think each book might be a good topic for your book report. Then choose one topic by circling it. Choose a book with which students are familiar. It will be helpful later in the Writer's Workshop when you decide which parts of the story you choose to include in your book report. Talk about why you have chosen the book and emphasize why it will make a good topic for a book report.

Go over the last paragraph. Then allow time for students to brainstorm in their notebooks a list of book titles. As students work, circulate among them to provide encouragement and to be sure that they are listing appropriate book titles. Help them to understand which books are appropriate for book reports and why those books are appropriate. Then guide students to choose a book by asking them the questions in the last paragraph.

Prewriting—Plan Your Book Report   Page 171

Students Should

- plan their book reports

Review the importance of planning a book report. Talk about ways students have planned their previous writing assignments. *(drawing pictures, making charts, writing on sentence strips)* Remind students that planning their report means writing and organizing ideas in a way that makes sense.

Invite a volunteer to read aloud the title. Point out that the beginning should name the title of the book, the author, and the characters; the middle should tell what happens; and the ending should tell the book report writer's opinion. Then go over the first paragraph and direct students' attention to the model chart. Invite students to tell the title of the book, the author, and the characters. (*The Happy Lion; Louise Fatio; Lion, Francois, Monsieur Dupont, Madam Pinson*) Then go over the rest of the chart. Tell students that Julio uses the chart to help him think about and organize what he wants to write in each part of his book report.

Model on the board writing a chart for your own book report. Emphasize that the title of the book is underlined. As you complete the Middle section, point out which parts of the story you want to include in your book report. Remind students that they should not give away the ending of the book, so it is better not to write the ending in their charts. In the Ending section, point out the reason for your opinion of the book.

Go over the rest of the page. Allow time for students to write their book-report charts in their notebooks. Circulate around the room to provide students with support and encouragement. Help students make sure that they have written their titles correctly, that they have not given away the ending, and that their opinion has a reason to support it.

Drafting   Page 172

Students Should
- use prewriting notes to write their first drafts

Invite a volunteer to read aloud the title. Talk with students about their experiences drafting previous writing assignments. Remind students that writing a draft is their first opportunity to put their ideas into sentences. Say: *When we write our first drafts, we put the ideas from prewriting on paper. Once we see all the ideas together, we can look for places to make the draft better.*

Go over the first paragraph and direct students' attention to Julio's draft. Guide students to identify in the draft information and ideas from Julio's prewriting chart on page 171. *(Examples: The title of the book comes from the Beginning, the sentences that tell what happens come from the Middle, and the opinion comes from the Ending.)* Point out that Julio has written a title for his book report.

Model for students how you will use your prewriting notes to write the first draft of your book report. As you write, explain how each part of your book report relates to your chart. Be sure to include in your model draft at least one mistake from the Editing Checklist on page 173 and one mistake from the Proofreading Checklist on page 174. Save your draft for use during editing.

Go over the last paragraph. Remind students to include in their drafts all the parts of a book report. Emphasize that using their prewriting charts will help them remember to include all of the important information they have thought about. Then allow time for students to complete

their drafts. As students work, circulate among them to provide guidance and support. Encourage students to include on their drafts a title for their book report.

Editing   Page 173

Students Should
- edit their book reports

Have a volunteer read aloud the title. Talk with students about their experiences editing previous writing assignments. Ask students to give examples of ways that their writing improved after editing. Say: *When we edit book reports, we make sure that all the parts are included. We make sure that the book title is underlined. We make sure that we have written a reason for our opinions. We also look for places where readers might get confused, and we fix those problems.*

Go over the first paragraph and the Editing Checklist. As you read each item on the checklist, pause to clarify students' understanding of the question and to explain how students might check for that item in their drafts.

Read aloud the next paragraph and the thought bubble. Ask students which item on the checklist helped Julio find the mistake in his draft. *(Does the ending tell why I have the opinion I do?)* Ask students how Julio fixed his draft. *(He added the sentence* No matter what happens, he's a happy lion!*)* Talk about why the reason Julio added makes his opinion stronger. *(It tells why Julio liked the book. It shows that Julio thought about his opinion.)*

Direct students' attention to your book report. Help students use the Editing Checklist to edit your book report. Guide them to find the mistake in your draft and to suggest ways of correcting it. Remind students that even the best writers make mistakes when they write, and that all writers edit their work to make it better.

Go over the rest of the section. Then allow time for students to edit their drafts. As they work, circulate through the class to be sure that students are giving appropriate consideration to each item on the checklist. For those students who have grasped the concept and value of editing, check to be sure that they are not making arbitrary changes. Guide these students to understand which editing changes are appropriate.

If students edit each other's drafts, remind them to double-check the mistakes their friend finds. Guide students to use reference materials or to ask questions when they are unsure of a marked change.

Revising   Page 173

Students Should

- use editing changes to revise their drafts

Ask a student to read aloud the title of this section. Talk with students about times they have revised their writing. Ask students to describe good ideas they have received from a family member or friend that helped them to write a better draft. Remind students that some changes are their ideas, while others might come from a friend or a teacher.

Go over the first paragraph. Point out the mistake in your draft that the class found during editing. Demonstrate how to mark the correction. Talk about how making this change helps to make the draft clearer. Then rewrite the draft on the board, incorporating into the new copy your marked change. Remember to include your mistake from the Proofreading Checklist on page 174. Remind students that a new copy of the draft can help them see any other mistakes that might be in the book report.

Go over the last paragraph. Then allow time for students to revise their drafts. As they work, circulate among students to be sure that they are correctly writing their editing changes on their drafts.

Proofreading   Page 174

Students Should

- proofread their revised drafts

Read aloud the title. Remind students that proofreading is when we make sure that the words are spelled correctly and that the sentences are correct. Say: *Proofreading is important because spelling mistakes and sentences that are wrong can confuse readers.* Invite volunteers to describe ways that their previous writing assignments were improved by proofreading.

Go over the first two paragraphs and the Proofreading Checklist. Talk about what each checklist item means and how students can check for it in their drafts.

Go over the partial student model and the paragraph that follows. Ask a volunteer what proofreading mistake Julio found. *(Ca'nt should be can't.)* Go over the way Julio corrected the mistake, reviewing how the proofreading marks function within the draft.

Model on the board proofreading your revised draft. Guide students to find the mistake in your draft, using the Proofreading Checklist. Invite a volunteer to explain how the mistake might be corrected and to mark the correction in your draft.

Go over the rest of the page. Then allow time for students to proofread their drafts. Remind students to check for only one kind of mistake at a time. As they work, circulate through the class to offer students assistance and support. Help them to use reference materials such as a picture dictionary, a word wall, and the student book, to check and correct mistakes.

If time allows, have partners trade drafts and proofread each other's work. Remind students that a friend might catch mistakes that they have missed. If you choose this option, circulate among students to be sure that they are using appropriate peer-conferencing language. When students have finished, remind them to double-check their friend's suggestions.

Page 144e provides a full-sized, reproducible copy of the student's Book Report scoring rubric. Students can use the rubric when assessing their own book reports.

Page 144f provides a full-sized, reproducible copy of the Teacher's Scoring Rubric for book reports. The rubric can be used when assessing students' understanding of the genre.

Students Should

· produce final copies of their book reports

Invite a student to read aloud the title. Ask volunteers to explain what it means to publish. *(to share writing with an audience)* Say: *The audience for a book report is the people who are interested in reading the book you wrote about. Your audience wants to know a little about the book. They are also interested in your opinion of the book. Your opinion may help your audience decide whether to read the book.*

Go over the first paragraph. Tell students that because Julio wants people to read the book he wrote about, he takes special care when publishing his book report. Then direct students' attention to Julio and his published book report. Emphasize that Julio's published book report was recopied carefully to make sure that no new mistakes were added.

Model for students how to produce a final copy. You might write your final copy on the board, or you might use one of the publishing ideas listed in the student book. As you work, talk with students about who the audience for your book report will be. Encourage students to think of ways to publish that the audience will find interesting.

Go over the rest of the page. Talk with students about how they will publish their own book reports. Then allow time for students to make their final copies. Remind students to write slowly and carefully, and to check each sentence to make sure they do not make any new mistakes. Allow time for students to create artwork or other items to accompany their published pieces.

When students have finished, distribute copies of the student's Book Report scoring rubric. Help students understand what each item means and how to apply it to their own writing. Then allow time for students to self-evaluate their book reports.

Remind students to keep a copy of their final book reports in their portfolios. Point out that having a portfolio will help students keep track of the improvements they are making in their writing throughout the year.

Put all the book reports in a class magazine.

Put your book report on the class bulletin board.

Draw an ad for your book. Attach it to your book report.

Pretend you are selling the book on TV.

CHAPTER 6
Word Study and Research Reports

Introducing the Chapter
Pages 176–177

Chapter 7 of the student book provides lessons and activities that teach students how to use reference tools. You may find it helpful to teach Chapter 7 prior to or concurrently with Chapter 6 in order to prepare students to write their research reports.

Students Should
- have a basic understanding of research reports
- have a basic understanding of synonyms, antonyms, and homophones

Reading the Model
Read aloud the quotation. Write on the board *research* and explain that research happens when someone looks for information. Talk with students about places where they might look for information. *(Examples: the library, books, encyclopedias, magazines, the Internet)* Next to *research* write *report*. Remind students that when they wrote book reports, they shared with an audience what they knew about a book. Say: *A research report is a kind of report where you share research. First you look for information about a topic. Then you share that information with readers.*

Invite volunteers to talk about books or articles they have read that taught them about a topic. Ask students to name some things they learned from those books and articles. Say: *The things that you have learned are called facts. A fact is a piece of true information.* Share with students other examples of facts. *(Examples: The United States of America has 50 states. George Washington was the first president of the United States. Nigeria is a country on the continent of Africa.)* Point out that each fact tells

something that is true. Say: *When you do research, you look for facts about a topic. You use the facts in your research report.*

Encourage students to look for facts as you read aloud the model research report on page 177. When you have finished, invite a volunteer to tell what this research report is about. *(the blue whale)* Explain that the blue whale is the topic of the research report. Ask students which sentence tells what the topic of the research report is. *(the first sentence)* Explain that the first sentence of this research report is the topic sentence because it tells the topic of the report. Invite volunteers to tell facts they learned about the blue whale from the research report.

Write on the board the sentence *Krill are very tiny animals that are like shrimp.* Underline the word *tiny*. Invite volunteers to name other words they could use in place of *tiny*. *(Examples: small, little)* Write students' suggestions on the board. Say: *These words mean almost the same thing. Words that mean the same or almost the same thing are called synonyms.*

Invite volunteers to name words that mean the opposite of *tiny*. *(Examples: big, giant, large, enormous)* List students' suggestions on the board. Draw a line from each word to the word *tiny*. Say: *These words mean the opposite of* tiny. *Words with opposite meanings are called antonyms.*

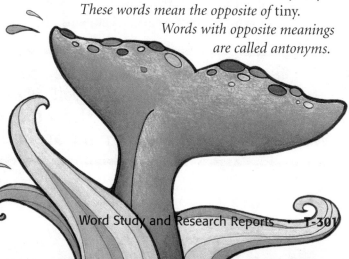

Read aloud the last sentence of the model. Then write on the board *The blew whale is the largest animal, but it eats some of the smallest food.* Read the sentence aloud and guide students to find the mistake. (blew *should be* blue) Erase *blew* and write *blue*. Talk about what the words *blue* and *blew* mean. Point out that the sentence sounds the same with the incorrect word. Say: *These words sound the same. Words that sound the same but have different spellings and different meanings are called homophones.*

Synonyms
and
Synonym Practice   Pages 178–179

Students Should
- recognize synonyms

Teaching the Lesson
Show students a picture of something large, such as an elephant or a mountain. Invite volunteers to tell what words they would use to describe the size of the objects in the pictures. Write students' responses on the board. (*Examples: large, giant, big, huge*) Point out that these words have the same or almost the same meaning. Invite a volunteer to use one of the words in a sentence about the picture. (*Example: The big elephant stomped through the jungle.*) Write the student's sentence on the board and underline the adjective. Invite other volunteers to say the sentence, substituting synonyms for the underlined word. Repeat with a picture showing someone happy. (*Examples: happy, glad, excited, pleased*) Explain that words that have the same or almost the same meaning are called synonyms.

Go over the teaching on page 178. Then have volunteers read aloud the examples. For each synonym pair, invite volunteers to explain what the two words mean.

Go over the activity directions on pages 178 and 179. When students have finished each activity, review their answers.

Extension
Have students recite the poem on page 178. Help them decide on a pantomime for each pair of synonyms in the poem. (*Example: pumping arms as if running for* quick *and* fast) Then have students recite the poem again, pantomiming each word in each synonym pair as they say it. Invite volunteers to say sentences using the synonyms in the poem.

More Synonyms
and
More Synonym
Practice   Pages 180–181

Students Should
- identify synonyms

Teaching the Lesson
Review that synonyms are words that have the same or almost the same meaning. Write on the board the following sentences: *That is a big sandwich. Are you glad we came?* Invite volunteers to name synonyms that might replace the underlined words. (*large, huge; happy, excited*)

Synonyms, synonyms, we know quite a few.
Quick and *fast*, *shout* and *yell*, *glad* and *happy* too.
Synonyms, synonyms, how our list will grow.
Words that we call synonyms are jolly friends to know.

Then review the synonyms that students studied on pages 178 and 179. Invite volunteers to use these words in sentences. Tell students that many words have synonyms. Write on the board the following sentences: *There is a spot on the wall. Let's pretend that we are astronauts. Linda shut her eyes. This homework is easy. The horses gallop away.* Read aloud each sentence and ask students to name words that have the same or almost the same meaning as the underlined words. *(mark, imagine, closed, simple, run)* Accept other correct synonyms students may suggest.

Go over the activity directions on pages 180 and 181. When students have finished each activity, review their answers.

Read aloud the Writer's Corner on page 181. Have students draw pictures of themselves performing each activity. Then allow time for students to write their sentences. Invite volunteers to share their pictures and sentences with the class.

Extension

Invite eight students to the front of the room. Assign each student one of the following words: *quiet, talk, afraid, find, hurt, pull, begin, hard.* Have each student say a sentence using his or her word. Then tell students to listen to your sentences and to raise their hands if they hear a word that means the same as the word they were assigned. Say sentences that use synonyms of the words students were assigned. *(silent, speak, scared, discover, harm, tug, start, difficult)* If a student does not raise his or her hand or if a student raises his or her hand at the wrong time, have that student sit down and pick a replacement student to come to the front of the room. Assign that student one of the following words: *spot, pretend, shut, easy, gallop.* Say additional sentences. Continue until all synonym pairs have been used.

Working with Synonyms *and* Synonyms Review Pages 182–183

Students Should

- identify synonyms

Teaching the Lesson

Use flash cards to review the synonyms that students have studied. Show students one word of a synonym pair and invite a volunteer to use the word in a sentence. Then have another volunteer identify the word's synonym and use the synonym in a sentence. Write on the board the following sentences: *Debbie is happy to be here. Your dog is little. I ride the bus with my pal. My dad drives a large truck.* Read aloud each sentence and ask students to name words that have the same or almost the same meaning as the underlined words. *(glad, small, friend, big)* Accept other correct synonyms students may suggest.

Go over the activity directions on pages 182 and 183. When students have finished each activity, review their answers.

Read aloud the Writer's Corner on page 183. Have students draw pictures of their bedrooms. Then allow time for students to write their sentences. Invite volunteers to read aloud their sentences and to use their pictures to identify the big and the large things in their bedrooms.

Extension

Students may benefit from learning other synonyms. Write on the board the following sentences and ask students for words that have the same or almost the same meaning as the underlined words: *Tam keeps his papers in a folder.* (saves, stores) *I was unhappy when the trip was called off.* (sad, disappointed) *Mom fixed my bicycle wheel.* (repaired) Encourage students to list in their notebooks new synonyms they find for words they use over and over.

Antonyms and More Antonyms   Pages 184–185

Students Should

- recognize antonyms

Teaching the Lesson

Show students a picture of something light and a picture of something heavy. (Examples: a feather and a brick) Talk about what is different about the items in the pictures. Write on the board light and heavy and explain that these words have opposite meanings. Tell students that words that have opposite meanings are called antonyms. Then write on the board the words strong, always, wrong, inside, come, night, and open. For each word, invite volunteers to suggest a word that means the opposite.

Go over the teaching on page 184. Then have volunteers read aloud the antonym pairs. For each antonym pair, invite volunteers to each say a sentence using one of the antonyms.

Go over the activity directions on pages 184 and 185. When students have finished each activity, review their answers.

Read aloud the Writer's Corner on page 185. Have students draw a horizontal line on a sheet of paper. Have students draw a night scene on one half and a day scene on the other half. Then allow time for students to write their sentences. Invite volunteers to share their work with the class.

Extension

Assign one of the 16 words on page 184 to each student. Then allow students to find their antonym partners. When students have found their partners, have pairs find in magazines, or draw, pictures of things that illustrate the meanings of their words. Have partners present their antonym pictures to the class.

Antonym Practice and Working with Antonyms   Pages 186–187

Students Should

- identify antonyms

Teaching the Lesson

Remind students that antonyms are words that have opposite meanings. Say aloud words that students have studied and invite volunteers to name an antonym for each word. Then write on the board the following sentences: The elevator went up. Look at the happy clown. The sponge is under the sink. I'll take a small apple. That is a short cowboy! The peaches are on the high branches. The next town is near. Those wires are thin. Read each sentence aloud and guide students to identify the antonym of each underlined word.

Go over the teaching and the antonym pairs on page 186. Invite volunteers to say aloud the sentences on the board, replacing each underlined word with its antonym.

Go over the activity directions on pages 186 and 187. When students have finished each activity, review their answers.

Extension

Draw a tick-tack-toe grid on the board. Write in each square of the grid one of the words students have studied on pages 184–187. Ask the class to form two teams, Xs and Os, to play a game of tick-tack-toe. Have one team choose a square. To claim a square, the team must say the antonym of the word in that square and use it in a sentence. Continue until one team has claimed three squares that form a line horizontally, vertically, or diagonally. Repeat with additional words from pages 184–187.

Antonyms Review *and* Synonyms and Antonyms Review   Pages 188–189

Students Should

- recognize antonyms
- recognize synonyms

Teaching the Lesson

Review that synonyms are words that have the same or almost the same meaning. Then review that antonyms are words that have opposite meanings. Write examples of synonym pairs and antonym pairs on the board. Invite volunteers to say whether the word pairs are synonyms or antonyms.

Go over the activity directions on pages 188 and 189. When students have finished each activity, review their answers.

Extension

Have the class form an Antonym team and a Synonym team. Then say aloud words that have both synonyms and antonyms. *(Examples: small-little-big; happy-glad-sad; bright-sunny-dark; pretty-beautiful-ugly; pull-tug-push)* Have the Antonym team say an antonym of your word and have the Synonym team say a synonym of your word. Give each team a point for using a correct synonym or antonym.

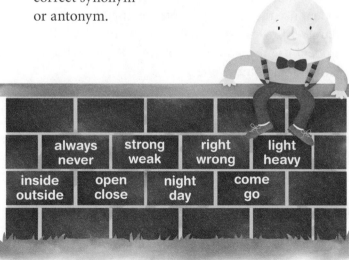

always	strong	right	light
never	weak	wrong	heavy
inside	open	night	come
outside	close	day	go

Homophones *and* Homophone Practice   Pages 190–191

Students Should

- recognize homophones

Teaching the Lesson

Write on the board the following sentences: *I knew your bike was new. Do you buy sweaters by color? Our favorite show lasts one hour. Meet me at the meat market.* Invite volunteers to read aloud the sentences. Then ask volunteers to underline the two words in each sentence that sound alike. Explain that some words sound alike but are spelled differently and have different meanings. Tell students these words are called homophones.

Go over the teaching and example sentences on page 190. For each example sentence, invite a volunteer to spell the homophone and to tell what it means. Point out that these words are easy to confuse because they sound the same. Explain that writers have to make sure that they write homophones correctly.

Go over the activity directions on pages 190 and 191. When students have finished each activity, review their answers.

Read aloud the Writer's Corner on page 190. Allow time for students to write their sentences. Invite students to share their sentences with the class.

Extension

Have eight students come to the front of the room. Say a sentence that uses one of the homophones listed on page 190. Then have the first student spell the homophone. If he or she is correct, allow that student to proceed to the next round. If he or she is incorrect, have that student return to his or her seat. Repeat with each student in line, using a different homophone from the list in each sentence. Continue by using the same homophones in new sentences until one student is left. Repeat with a new group of volunteers.

More Homophones *and* Working with Homophones

Pages 192–193

Students Should
- recognize homophones

Teaching the Lesson
Review that homophones are words that sound the same but have different spellings and meanings. Write on the board the words *new, knew, our, hour, buy, by, meet,* and *meat.* Invite volunteers to use each word in a sentence. Then write the following sentences: *He told a funny tale about a rabbit's tail. My sister ate eight peanuts. I hear that the band is coming here. A bee will be a good costume for you.* Invite volunteers to underline the homophones in each sentence.

Go over the teaching on page 192. Then have volunteers read aloud each pair of example sentences. For each homophone pair, invite volunteers to tell what the two words mean.

Go over the activity directions on page 192. When students have finished each activity, review their answers.

Read aloud the teaching on page 193. Then have students read aloud each pair of example sentences. Invite volunteers to tell what the words in each homophone pair mean.

Go over the activity directions on page 193. When students have finished the activity, review their answers.

Read aloud the Writer's Corner on page 193. Allow time for students to write their sentences. Invite volunteers to share their sentences with the class.

Extension
Have students fold a sheet of paper into quarters. Ask students to select two sets of homophones. Have them draw a picture in each quarter to illustrate each homophone and write the appropriate homophone underneath the picture. Invite volunteers to share their work with the class.

Practice Working with Homophones *and* Homophones Review

Pages 194–195

Students Should
- distinguish between homophones

Teaching the Lesson
Review that homophones are words that sound alike but are spelled differently and have different meanings. Say a homophone students have studied and invite a volunteer to write on the board one of the two homophone spellings. Then have the student use the word in a sentence. Invite another volunteer to write the other homophone. Have that student use the word in a sentence. Repeat with additional homophones.

Go over the activity directions on pages 194 and 195. When students have finished each activity, review their answers.

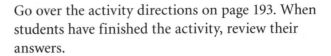

Homophones, homophones,
we know quite a few.
Dear and *deer*, *here* and *hear*,
to and *two* and *too*.
Homophones, homophones,
how our list will grow.
Words that we call homophones
are jolly friends to know.

Extension

Have students recite the poem on page 194. Then divide the class into three groups. Assign each group one of the following names: Synonym Searchers, Antonym Adventurers, and Homophone Hunters. Have students in each group underline in magazines and newspapers words that have synonyms, antonyms, and homophones. Have students record the words they find and their synonyms, antonyms, or homophones. Then invite the groups to share their words with the rest of the class.

Show What You Know
Pages 196–197

Students Should
- identify synonyms and antonyms
- distinguish between homophones

Teaching the Lesson
Explain the directions for each activity. Assist students if necessary. When students have finished each activity, review their answers. Show What You Know may be used as a review or a test.

Get Ready to Write
What Is a Research Report?
Page 198

Chapter 7 of the student book provides lessons and activities that teach students how to use reference tools. You may find it helpful to teach Chapter 7 prior to or concurrently with Chapter 6 in order to prepare students to write their research reports.

Students Should
- identify the elements and characteristics of a research report
- understand the purpose of writing a research report

Teaching the Lesson
Talk with students about wild animals that they know about. Invite students to explain what the animal looks like, where it lives, and what it eats. Say: *These animals would all be good topics for a research report. A research report tells facts about something. Research reports are written to teach others about a topic. A research report might be about an animal, a famous city, or a president of the United States. Research reports can be about almost anything.*

Invite a volunteers to read aloud the title. Then go over the first paragraph. Emphasize that the topic of a research report can be a person, a place, a thing, or an event. Invite students to name possible research-report topics. List appropriate suggestions on the board. *(Examples: George Washington, the state of Michigan, beagles, Paul Revere's ride)* Point out that any of these might be a good topic for a research report.

Go over the next three paragraphs. Explain that the beginning of a research report must tell the topic in an interesting way. Explain that the middle of a research report tells facts about the topic. Tell students that facts about a topic can be found in different sources, such as books, encyclopedias, and the Internet. Then explain that the ending of a

Word Study and Research Reports • T-307

research report sums up the report's information. Emphasize that summing up a research report means retelling what the topic was and reminding readers about the most important information in the report.

Go over the model research report. Direct students' attention to the sentences labeled Beginning, Middle, and Ending. Point out the beginning and emphasize how it identifies the topic of the report. Then ask students to tell some facts they learned about the brachiosaurus. Explain that these facts were researched and that the writer probably looked on the Internet or in books about dinosaurs to find the facts. Then ask which sentence is the ending. *(The brachiosaurus was a huge, gentle dinosaur.)* Explain that the ending retells the topic and sums up the report.

Go over the activity directions. Guide students to complete the first item as a class. Then have students complete the rest of the activity independently. When they have finished, invite volunteers to share their answers with the class.

Extension

Distribute to small groups a variety of research materials about the brachiosaurus. Have students work together to find two additional facts about the brachiosaurus and to write the facts on a sheet of paper. When students have finished, invite each group to share their facts with the class. Talk with students about how the facts might be added to the research report on page 198.

The Topic of a Research Report   Page 199

Students Should

- identify an appropriate topic for a research report
- understand how to write a topic sentence

Teaching the Lesson

Remind students that a research report is a report that tells facts about a topic. Ask a volunteer to tell where facts can be found. *(in different sources, such* as books or the Internet) Then review the beginning, the middle, and the ending of a research report.

Read aloud the title and go over the first paragraph. Emphasize that the topic of a research report is what the report is about. Ask students to name possible topics and list their suggestions on the board. *(Examples: racehorses, the Empire State Building, Abraham Lincoln)* As students suggest topics, help them understand that a narrow, specific topic is better than a broad topic. Say: *It is easier to write a research report about Abraham Lincoln than about all the presidents. There have been many presidents, so it would take a long time to tell about all of them. A report about Abraham Lincoln would be better, because it would tell about only one president.*

Go over the second paragraph. Point out that a topic sentence tells readers what the report will be about. Explain that an interesting topic sentence will make readers want to read more about the topic. Then go over the next paragraph and the example topic sentences. Ask students why the sentences on the right are more interesting than those on the left. *(Examples: The first sentence gives a fun fact. The second sentence helps readers imagine what the insect looks like. The third sentence tells where the Statue of Liberty is located.)*

Go over the activity directions. Invite volunteers to suggest appropriate topic sentences for the first item. Write their answers on the board. Then have students complete the second item independently. When they have finished, ask volunteers to share their sentences with the class.

Extension

Distribute age-appropriate magazines, such as *Highlights, National Geographic for Kids,* or *Ranger Rick.* Have students look through the magazines and list topics about which they might write a research report. Then have students each choose one topic and draw a picture of it. Tell them to write at the bottom of the picture a topic sentence that might be the beginning of a research report. When students have finished, invite volunteers to share their work with the class.

Fact and Opinion   Page 200

Students Should
- distinguish between fact and opinion

Teaching the Lesson

Remind students that a topic sentence tells the topic of a research report. Invite volunteers to name topics that would be good for a research report. Write their responses on the board. Help students to choose appropriate topics. Then ask volunteers to say a topic sentence for each topic.

Invite a volunteer to read aloud the title. Then go over the first paragraph. Point to a common object in the classroom that has one color. Ask students what color the object is. Tell students that the color of the object is a fact about that object. Tell students that facts are things that are true about a topic. Explain that writers find facts by researching. Explain that researching is reading and learning about a topic.

Go over the next paragraph and the examples. Explain that opinions tell what people think or feel. Say: *People can have different opinions about something. One person might think that a baseball team is great. Another person might think that the same team is terrible.* Tell students that the first example is a fact because an expert has examined polar bears and found this fact to be true. Emphasize that the second example is an opinion because it tells how one person feels about polar bears.

Go over the directions for activity **A**. Help students complete this activity as a class.

Go over the directions for the second activity. Have students complete the activity independently. When students have finished, invite volunteers to share their answers with the class.

Extension

Ask each student to write on a sentence strip one opinion about penguins. *(Example: Penguins are cute.)* Then distribute to small groups a short encyclopedia or magazine article about penguins.

Have each student write on a sentence strip one fact about penguins. Place all the sentence strips in a bowl. Then divide the class into two teams. Invite volunteers to choose a strip, read it aloud, and tell whether it is a fact or an opinion. If the student answers correctly, award his or her team one point. Repeat until each student has had a turn.

Finding Facts   Page 201

You may wish to teach pages 201–202 in the library.

Students Should
- use sources to find facts

Teaching the Lesson

Review what facts are. Write on the board two facts and two opinions about the same topic. Help students identify which are facts and which are opinions.

Invite a volunteer to read aloud the title. Then go over the first paragraph. Explain to students that fiction books are made-up stories and that nonfiction books tell facts. Invite students to describe their experiences using encyclopedias, nonfiction books, and the Internet. Ask students about things they have learned using these research tools. Say: *When you do research, you should use only sources that have true information. You probably wouldn't find true information about lions in a storybook about a talking lion. You would look for facts in sources about real lions.* Then reread the last line of the first paragraph. Explain that when students write facts in their own words, they show that they have learned the fact. Emphasize that it is not OK to copy facts word-for-word from a source.

Go over the next paragraph and the questions. Explain that these questions can help students find facts about their topics and can be helpful when doing research.

Go over the activity directions. Then allow time for students to complete the activity in small groups. When students have finished, invite them to share their facts with the class.

Extension

Have students answer at least two of the questions listed on this page about the topic that they researched in the activity. Provide students with assistance and support as they find additional facts about their topic.

Writing and Organizing Notes   Page 202

Students Should

- understand how to write and organize notes

Teaching the Lesson

Review where facts can be found. *(in sources such as encyclopedias, nonfiction books, and the Internet)* Remind students that facts are information that is true. Then review the difference between fact and opinion. Emphasize that students should not use opinions when writing research reports.

Ask a volunteer to read aloud the title. Then go over the first paragraph. Explain that note cards are where writers write facts. Tell students that writing facts on separate note cards is a good way to keep notes organized.

Go over the next paragraph and the three ways of writing a note card. Demonstrate on the board how to write each type of source on a note card. If your classroom resources allow, show students where to locate the information they must include when writing source information.

Go over the next paragraph. Direct students' attention to the model piles of note cards. Ask students to identify the fact on each card. *(Red*

Red pandas live in Nepal, Burma, and central China.

"Red Pandas." Encyclopedia Britannica. Vol. 2, p. 245

pandas live in Nepal, Burma, and central China. Red pandas weigh less than 20 pounds.) Go over the source information for each fact and ask students to identify what type of source each fact was found in. *(The left card has a fact from an encyclopedia. The right card has a fact from a Web site.)* Point out that while both cards are about red pandas, each pile has a different kind of information. Talk with students about what information each pile has. *(The left pile is about where red pandas live. The right pile is about what red pandas look like.)* Emphasize that organizing note cards will make writing their research reports easier.

Go over the activity directions. Have students complete the activity independently. As students work, assist them as they organize their note cards. When students have finished, have them share their work with the class.

Extension

Have students mix up their note cards from the activity and trade them with partners. Then have students organize the cards that they receive into piles according to information. Circulate among students to be sure they are organizing the cards properly.

Writing an Ending   Page 203

Students Should

- understand how to write an ending for a research report

Teaching the Lesson

Review writing and organizing notes on note cards. Emphasize the importance of writing facts in students' own words. Go over the information that belongs on a note card. *(the fact, the source, and the title, author, or web address)* Review how to organize note cards into piles. Remind students that taking notes and organizing those notes can help writers plan and organize their research reports.

Invite a volunteer to read aloud the title. Then go over the first two paragraphs and invite students to take turns reading each pair of sentences. Ask students to identify which ending is more interesting. *(the second sentence of each pair)* Say: *The second sentences sum up the information. They tell something interesting about the topics. The first sentences tell uninteresting information or information that the reader doesn't need to know. When you write a research report, always sum up your information in an interesting way.* Talk with students about ways they might write interesting endings. Suggest that students consider facts they have learned and think of something that sums up the facts.

Go over the activity directions. Read aloud each research report. Then have students complete the activity independently. When students have finished, invite them to share their answers with the class.

Extension

Have students take out the note cards they wrote for the activity on page 202. Ask students to draw a picture of their topic. Then have students use the facts that they have found to write at the bottom of their picture a research-report ending. Invite volunteers to share their work with the class.

Students Should

- brainstorm research-report topics
- identify appropriate topics for their research reports

Talk with students about animals, people, places, or events that they are interested in. *(Examples: poodles, John Adams, Boston, Kids Choice Awards)* Invite students to describe what they know about certain topics and things they might like to find out about each topic. Say: *When we write research reports, we choose a topic. All the things that we have talked about would make good topics for a research report. Research reports are a good way to learn more about a topic and to share with others what you learn.*

Invite a volunteer to read aloud the title. Then go over the first two paragraphs and Cady's notebook page. Say: *When we write a research report, we tell the reader the topic and we tell facts about the topic. When we do prewriting for research reports, we think about things we want to know more about. We write down our topic ideas. Then we decide which topic to write about.* Talk with students about the topics that Cady listed. Point out that Cady's topic ideas are about real things and that the topics are not too big to write about in a research report.

Model on the board brainstorming a list of topics for your own research report. Explain why you think each topic might be a good topic for a research report. Include a topic that might be too broad for a research report. Talk with students about why the topic might be difficult to write about in a short research report. Then choose your topic by circling it. Talk about why you have chosen the topic and emphasize why it will make a good topic for your research report.

Go over the last paragraph. Then allow time for students to write in their notebooks their topic ideas. As students work, circulate among them to provide support. Be sure that students are listing appropriate topics. Help students who list broad topics to narrow their topics. Guide students who are having trouble by asking the questions from the last paragraph. Emphasize that students do not have to choose a topic they know much about, because they will learn about the topic by doing research.

Prewriting—Plan Your Research Report   Page 205

Students Should

• plan their research reports

Review the importance of planning a research report. Talk about ways that students have planned their previous writing assignments. *(drawing pictures, making charts, writing on sentence strips)* Emphasize that planning a research report includes researching, writing note cards, and organizing those cards into piles.

Ask a volunteer to read aloud the title. Then go over the first paragraph. Talk with students about their experiences finding facts in encyclopedias and on the Internet. If necessary, review pages 218–221 to emphasize encyclopedia and library skills.

Go over the next paragraph and Cady's note cards. Invite volunteers to identify the fact on each card. *(Blue whales eat krill. Blue whales can weigh 200 tons.)* Then have students identify on the cards the sources where Cady found each fact. Point out that after Cady had found facts, she organized her note cards into piles. Remind students that when they write their own note cards, they should write only one fact on each card, and then they should organize similar information into separate piles.

Model for students how to research a topic for your research report. Be sure to have available research materials, such as nonfiction books, encyclopedias, and the Internet, from which to find your facts.

You may also consider conducting this part of the lesson in the library to optimize the resources available to you. As you work, explain your decisions for choosing and writing each fact that you gather. It may be helpful for you to draw note cards on the board or on a large sheet of paper for students to see how you write each fact. Demonstrate how to write facts in your own words. Emphasize how to write each source at the bottom of your note cards and explain how you found the required information.

Go over the rest of the page. Allow time for students to research their topics, to write their facts on note cards, and to organize the note cards. As students work, circulate among them to provide assistance and support. Help students make sure that they have written their notes correctly and have included complete information about the source of each fact. Assist students who are having trouble organizing their note cards into piles of related information.

Drafting   Page 206

Students Should

• use prewriting notes to write their first drafts

Talk with students about their experiences drafting previous writing assignments. Remind students that when they write a first draft, they use the notes they wrote during prewriting to help them. Explain that when they write research reports, their notes are very important, because they contain the facts that students will include in their reports.

Invite a volunteer to read aloud the title. Then go over the first paragraph and direct students' attention to Cady's draft. Invite a volunteer to identify Cady's topic sentence. *(The blue whale is the largest animal on earth.)* Point out that the topic sentence tells the reader right away what the report will be about. Guide students to identify in Cady's draft the facts that she wrote on her note cards on page 205. Remind students that Cady organized all her note cards into two piles, one pile of note cards about what the blue whale eats and one pile of note cards about the size of the blue whale. Invite volunteers to identify in Cady's draft other facts that came from the pile of note cards about what the blue whale eats. *(Krill are very tiny animals that are like shrimp. Blue whales can eat 12,000 pounds of krill a day.)* Then invite volunteers to identify in Cady's draft other facts that came from the pile of note cards about the size of the blue whale. *(The blue whale is the largest animal on earth. A blue whale's tongue can weigh as much as an elephant.)* Emphasize that grouping similar facts into piles helped Cady write her draft. Point out that similar facts are also grouped together in Cady's draft.

On the board, model for students how to use your note cards and facts to write your research report. Begin by writing a topic sentence and explaining your decision to include it at the beginning. Point out that your topic sentence names the topic. As you write, explain how the facts in the middle of your research report relate to the note cards you wrote in prewriting. Show students how you group related facts together in the middle of your report. Explain that facts should not be mixed up; similar facts should be grouped together in the middle of the report. Remind students of the difference between fact and opinion. Point out that opinions are not used in research reports. As you write the ending of your research report, explain how your ending sums up the report. Be sure to include in your draft at least one mistake from the Editing Checklist on page 207 and one mistake from the Proofreading Checklist on page 208. Explain to students that you will edit your draft later. Save your draft for use during the Editing stage.

Go over the last paragraph. Then allow time for students to complete their drafts. As students work, circulate among them to provide support. Help students who are having trouble grouping their facts appropriately in their drafts. Emphasize the importance of keeping related information together in a research report. Remind students that they will have time to fix mistakes in spelling and grammar later and that now is a time for them to capture their ideas.

Editing

Students Should
- edit their research reports

Talk with students about their previous experiences editing drafts. Invite volunteers to explain why editing is important. *(Editing is the time that writers fix mistakes in the ideas of a draft.)* Explain that when students edit research reports, they should look at how well the facts tell about the topic.

Invite a volunteer to read aloud the title. Then guide students through the first two paragraphs and the Editing Checklist. Help students to understand each question and how they might check for each question when editing their drafts.

Go over the next paragraph and the thought bubble. Ask students which item on the checklist helped Cady find the mistake in her draft. *(Did I leave out my opinion?)* Ask students how Cady fixed her draft. *(She took out the sentence* I think blue whales are really cool. *She added the sentence* The blue whale is the largest animal, but it eats some of the smallest food.*)* Help students understand how Cady's changes make the ending stronger.

Direct students' attention to your research report draft. Help students use the Editing Checklist to find the mistake in your draft. Ask students to suggest ways that you might fix your mistake.

Go over the next paragraph. Remind students that reading their drafts aloud is a good way to catch mistakes that were made while drafting. Then allow time for students to edit their drafts. Check that students are giving appropriate consideration to each item on the checklist. Check students' justifications for making or not making changes to their work. Have students pay particular attention to making sure their research reports include a topic sentence and that there are no opinions in the drafts.

If partners read each other's drafts, remind them of the proper language and behavior for peer-editing sessions. Remind students to check their friends' changes, using the checklist. Emphasize that they can also ask a teacher, a parent, or another friend for help.

Students Should

- use editing changes to revise their drafts

Review with students the purpose of revising. Remind students that some of the changes we include in revised drafts are our ideas, while others might come from a friend or a teacher. Emphasize that writers make a new copy of their drafts to more clearly see other possible mistakes when they proofread.

Go over the title and the first paragraph. Then demonstrate how you will revise your draft. Talk about how your editing change improves your draft. Then rewrite your draft on the board, incorporating into the new copy your marked change. Remember to include your mistake from the Proofreading Checklist on page 208.

Go over the last paragraph. Then allow time for students to revise their drafts. As they work, circulate among students to be sure that they are correctly writing their editing changes on their drafts.

I didn't leave out my opinion!

Students Should

- proofread their revised drafts

Remind students that when we do proofreading, we make sure that the sentences are written correctly and that there are no misspelled words. Talk about students' previous experiences proofreading. Invite volunteers to describe how proofreading improved their drafts.

Invite a student to read aloud the title. Then go over the first paragraph and the Proofreading Checklist. Talk with students about what each checklist item means and how they might check for it in their drafts.

Direct students' attention to the partial student model. Then go over the next paragraph. Talk about how the proofreading marks function within the draft. Then ask students to identify which question on the checklist helped Cady to find her mistake. *(Are all homophones used correctly?)*

Using your revised draft, model for students how to proofread. Demonstrate how you use the Proofreading Checklist to find your mistake. Show how to mark your change. Remind students that proofreading helps make drafts better.

Go over the last paragraph. Then allow time for students to proofread their drafts. Remind students to check for only one kind of mistake at a time. As students work, check that they are giving appropriate consideration to each item on the checklist. Remind students to use references such as a picture dictionary, a word wall, or the student book to check and correct mistakes.

If time allows, have partners trade drafts and proofread each other's work. Remind students that a friend might catch mistakes that they have missed. If you choose this option, circulate among students to be sure that they are using appropriate peer-conferencing language. When students have finished, remind them to double-check their friend's suggestions.

Publishing

Page 209

Page 176e provides a full-sized, reproducible copy of the student's Research Report scoring rubric. Students can use the rubric when assessing their own research reports.

Page 176f provides a full-sized, reproducible copy of the Teacher's Scoring Rubric for research reports. The rubric can be used when assessing students' understanding of the genre.

Students Should

- produce final copies of their research reports

Review ways that students have published previous writing assignments. Talk about why publishing is important. *(because it is when a writer shares his or her work with an audience)* Explain that textbooks, magazine articles, news stories, movies, and TV shows require research. Say: *The audience for a research report is someone who is interested in reading about your topic. This person is interested in learning the facts that you wrote about.*

Invite a volunteer to read aloud the title. Then go over the first paragraph. Remind students that reading a report aloud is publishing because Cady is sharing her work with an audience. Emphasize that Cady was careful writing her final copy because she was going to share it with her audience.

Model for students how to produce a final copy. You might write your final copy on the board, or you might use one of the publishing ideas listed in the student book. As you work, talk about who the audience for your report might be.

Go over the rest of the page. Allow time for students to make final copies of their research reports. Remind students to write slowly and carefully, and to check each sentence to make sure they do not make any new mistakes. Encourage students who are familiar with computers to type their final copies.

When students have finished, talk about how the class will publish their research reports. Allow time for students to create any artwork or other items that might help readers understand the facts in their reports.

When students have finished, distribute copies of the student's Research Report scoring rubric. Guide students to understand what each item means and how to apply it to their own writing. Then allow time for students to self-evaluate their research reports.

Have students add to their portfolios their finished research reports. Remind students that their portfolios have helped them to see how their writing has improved throughout the year. Encourage students to examine their portfolios at this time to view their progress from the beginning of the year.

CHAPTER 7
Research Tools

Introducing the Chapter
Pages 210–211

Students Should
- have a basic understanding of the library
- have a basic understanding of research tools

Using the Model

Read aloud the quotation. Say: *When we write, we are talking to our readers. Since our readers can't respond to us, we can explain or tell things without being interrupted. A good back-and-forth talk can be fun, but sometimes we need to talk without being interrupted so that we can explain topics in a way that people will understand them.* Explain to students that this quotation is especially true when writing research reports. Tell students that learning to use research tools in the library will help them write better research reports.

Direct students' attention to the picture on pages 210 and 211. Tell students that libraries may look a little different from one another, but that every library has the things in the picture. Ask students what a library is. *(a place to borrow books and to find facts and other true information)* Invite volunteers to talk about times they have gone to a library and to explain why they went. Tell students that the library contains many research tools, such as dictionaries, encyclopedias, nonfiction books, and computers.

Point out the Librarian callout. Ask students what they think the librarian does. *(He or she helps people find what they need in the library.)* Say: *Librarians go to school to learn how libraries are organized, what the rules of the library are, and how to help people who use the library. Librarians are one of the best research tools that we have.* Tell students

that they should ask a librarian whenever they need help finding materials in the library.

Go over the Circulation Desk callout. Tell students that the circulation desk is where people check books and other materials out of the library. Explain that checking out a book means borrowing the book for a period of time. Emphasize that students should take good care of materials they check out of the library so that others can use those materials later. Then point out the Book Return slot. Explain that if students have books to return to the library, they can drop the books into the slot and the librarians will check them in later.

Direct students' attention to the Fiction Section, the Nonfiction Section, and the Reference Area callouts. Explain that books are usually put in certain parts of a library to make them easier to find. Tell students that in the fiction section they will find made-up stories. Ask students to name some fiction books they have read. Tell students that in the nonfiction section they will find books with true information about real topics. Then tell students that in the reference section they will find special books such as dictionaries, encyclopedias, and books of maps. Explain that because these materials are used often by many people, they usually can't be taken out of the library. Emphasize that if students need to use books found in the reference section, they should take notes or make photocopies of the pages they need because they cannot take the books home.

Point out the Computer Area callout. Say: *Most libraries have computers so that people can use the Internet and do research. Computers at the library can also help you find books about a topic. These computers are called electronic card catalogs. You can type a topic into a computer, and it will list books that the library has about that topic.*

Go over the Reading Area callout. Explain that the reading area is for everyone, but that people must be quiet when in the reading area. Tell students that noise in the library makes it hard to read and to study. Emphasize that when students go to any library, they should remember to be quiet at all times.

Alphabetical Order Page 212

Students Should

- understand how to put words in alphabetical order by the first letter

Teaching the Lesson

Display the following groups of items: several books, a handful of pencils, and a stack of paper. Ask students how the items displayed are grouped together. *(They are grouped together by kind of thing.)* Tell students that we group things together to organize them. Explain that organizing things makes them easier to find. Then tell students that one of the most common ways to organize things is alphabetically. Invite students to talk about their experiences with alphabetical order.

Go over the teaching. Emphasize that words in alphabetical order are put in the order of the letters of the alphabet. Call to the front of the room five students whose last names begin with different letters. Have students line up in alphabetical order by the first letter of their last names. Explain that using alphabetical order is an easy way of organizing because most people know the order of the letters in the alphabet. Then show students a dictionary. Say: *This book has thousands of words in it. The words in a dictionary are arranged in alphabetical order to make finding words easier.*

Go over the activity directions. When students have finished the activity, review their answers.

Extension

Have students draw on separate sheets of paper three different animals whose names begin with different letters. Tell students to write at the bottom of each picture the name of the animal.

Circulate among students to be sure they are spelling the names of their animals correctly. Then have students exchange their drawings. Tell students to put the drawings they receive in alphabetical order. When students have finished, invite them to share their answers with the class.

More Alphabetical Order *and* Practice with Alphabetical Order Pages 213–214

Students Should

- understand how to put words in alphabetical order by the second letter

Teaching the Lesson

Write on the board two lists of five words that begin with different letters. Invite the class to help you write each list alphabetically. Ask students how they knew where to put each word in the list. *(according to where the first letter is in the alphabet)* Talk about things that can be organized by using alphabetical order. *(Examples: words, books, people's names)*

Go over the teaching and examples on page 213. Invite students who have names with the same first letter to the front of the room. Ask these students if they know how to put themselves in alphabetical order. Explain that when names or words begin with the same letter, they are put in alphabetical order by using the second letter. Then help students alphabetize themselves by second letter.

Go over the activity directions on pages 213 and 214. When students have finished each activity, review their answers.

Extension

Distribute to small groups several common objects. *(Examples: penny, chalk, marker, paper clip)* Make sure that the names of at least two of the items begin with the same letter. Allow time for students to work together to line up the items in alphabetical order. If students have difficulty, encourage them to write down the names of the items and to alphabetize the words on paper. Then have students line up the objects. Visit each group to make sure that the objects are correctly lined up. Then allow groups to trade objects and to alphabetize their new sets.

Dictionary Skills   Page 215

Students Should

- understand the purpose of a dictionary

Teaching the Lesson

Write on the board the following words: *arena, garret, lounge, inspire, sift.* Ask students whether they know what each word means. Tell students that if they don't know the meaning of a word, they can find out the meaning in a dictionary. Explain that dictionaries have the meanings of many words. Read aloud from a dictionary the meaning of each word on the board. Tell students that they can also use a dictionary to check the spelling of a word. Point out that knowing the meanings and spellings of words can help them better understand what they read and will make them better writers.

Go over the teaching. Then guide students to read the example dictionary page. Point out that the words on the dictionary page are listed in alphabetical order. Help students understand that each word, its meaning, and its example sentence make up one dictionary entry. Ask students how many dictionary entries are on this page. *(four)* Tell students that dictionaries have many words and that each word has its own entry.

Allow time for students to answer the questions. When they have finished the activity, review their answers.

Extension

Write on the board three words, such as *hurl, minnow,* and *salary.* Have pairs of students find the words in the dictionary and write each word's definition. Then have students work together to write for each word one sentence that correctly uses the word. When students have finished, invite volunteers to share their sentences with the class.

Dictionary Skills— Parts of an Entry   Page 216

Students Should

- identify the parts of a dictionary entry

Teaching the Lesson

Review why people use dictionaries. Ask a volunteer to explain how entries in a dictionary are arranged. *(alphabetically)* Then distribute a photocopied page from a book that you are reading with the class. Invite volunteers to name words that they do not know the meanings of. Write those words on the board. Then read aloud from a dictionary the meaning of each word. Talk about how knowing the meaning of the word makes the story easier to understand. Emphasize that dictionaries help people understand what they read and write.

Go over the teaching. Explain to students that although entries can look different depending on the dictionary, every dictionary entry has an entry word and the meaning of the entry word. Talk about how sentences or pictures in a dictionary can help people understand the meaning of a word. Then direct students' attention to the example entry. Help students identify which part of the entry each callout refers to.

Go over the activity directions. When students have finished the activity, review their answers.

Extension

Have partners choose two words from a dictionary. Tell students to write on separate sheets of paper each entry word and its meaning. Have students write their own example sentence for each word and a picture that helps illustrate the word's meaning. Then have students label their entry, using the same callouts used on page 216. Invite students to share their dictionary entries with the class.

Dictionary Skills— Guide Words

Page 217

Students Should

- understand the purpose of guide words in a dictionary

Teaching the Lesson

Review the parts of a dictionary entry. Ask a volunteer to explain why knowing the meaning of a word is important. *(Knowing the meaning of a word helps people understand what they are reading. It also helps make people better writers.)* Remind students that dictionary entries are arranged alphabetically.

Go over the first paragraph of the teaching. Then have students turn back to page 215. Point out the guide words *garden* and *gym*. Explain that all the words on that dictionary page come alphabetically between the guide words. To illustrate this point, write on the board each entry word in alphabetical order, circling the two guide words. Explain that because the words are written in alphabetical order, the words *germ* and *give* come between the guide words. Point out that when students look in a dictionary to find a word, they should use the guide words to find the page that has the word they are looking for.

Go over the rest of the teaching. Demonstrate finding the word *valley* in a dictionary, using each step listed. Emphasize that using guide words to find a word is faster and can make finding the word easier than by looking through all the words on each page.

Go over the activity directions. When students have finished each activity, review their answers.

Extension

Write the words from activity **A** on the board. Have students look up each word in a dictionary. For each word, have them write the guide words found on that page.

Encyclopedia Skills

Page 218

Students Should

- understand the parts and function of an encyclopedia

Teaching the Lesson

Talk with students about times they have seen or used an encyclopedia. Explain that encyclopedias are groups of books that have information about many different topics. Tell students that when they write research reports, they may use an encyclopedia to find facts about their topic. Then look up the entry for *knight* in an encyclopedia. Read aloud the first paragraph of the entry. Talk about some facts about knights that students have learned from the entry. Say: *We know that we use dictionaries to find out what words mean. We use encyclopedias to find information about topics. Encyclopedias are organized like dictionaries, but they have a lot more information.*

Go over the teaching and direct students' attention to the picture of the spine of a volume. Point out the title of the encyclopedia, the volume letter, and the volume number. Then display for students an encyclopedia volume. Point out that the volume has topics that all begin with the same letter or letters. Tell students that other volumes of the encyclopedia cover topics that start with other letters. Say: *Most encyclopedias have one volume for each letter of the alphabet. Letters that may not have as many topics, such as X, Y, and Z, might be put together in the same volume.*

Open an encyclopedia to the beginning of an entry and display the entry for students. Talk with students about how an encyclopedia is similar to a dictionary.

Go over the example encyclopedia entry on page 218. Invite volunteers to tell facts they learned about northern cricket frogs. Emphasize that the information in an encyclopedia can be used to learn more about a topic and that it can also be used in a research report to teach others about a topic.

Go over the activity directions. When students have finished the activity, review their answers.

Extension

Have students form small groups. Assign each group an invention. *(Examples: TV, light bulb, automobile, airplane)* Have students use encyclopedias to do an Invention Investigation to find out who invented each item. Have groups share with the rest of the class who invented their assigned item and any other interesting facts they found in the encyclopedia.

Fiction and Nonfiction Books   Page 219

Students Should
- distinguish between fiction and nonfiction books

Teaching the Lesson

Display a selection of age-appropriate fiction and nonfiction books. Talk about books that students have read. Invite students to tell whether the books were made-up stories or if they had true information. Talk about how students know that a story is made up. Tell students that books with made-up stories are called fiction books. Invite a volunteer to look up the meaning of the word *fiction* in a dictionary.

Go over the first paragraph of the teaching. Point out the fiction books that you have displayed. Emphasize that fiction books are stories that are made up by the writer. Invite students to name fiction books with which they are familiar. Explain that because the information in fiction books is made up, we do not use fiction books when we write research reports. Ask students to turn back to the picture on pages 210 and 211. Point out the area labeled Fiction Section. Say: *Librarians don't want people to get confused when they try to find books. So they put fiction books in a special part of the library. All the fiction books are put together. That way when you need to find a fiction book, you can go to that part of the library.*

Go over the second paragraph of the teaching. Then ask students to recall what they have learned about encyclopedias. *(Encyclopedias are groups of books that have true information about a lot of different topics.)* Explain that just like encyclopedias, nonfiction books do not have made-up information. Say: *When you put* non- *at the front of a word, it's like saying* not. *So if* fiction *means "made up,"* nonfiction *means "not made up." Nonfiction books are books with true information.*

Explain that encyclopedias have entries with information about a topic, while in most nonfiction books, the whole book is about one topic. Emphasize this point by displaying an encyclopedia entry and a nonfiction book that are about the same topic. Then have students turn back to the picture on pages 210 and 211. Point out the Nonfiction Section. Explain that librarians put all the nonfiction books in a different part of the library than the fiction books so that people can find what they're looking for more easily.

Go over the activity directions. When students have finished the activity, review their answers.

Extension

Make a list of book titles in the library from the fiction and nonfiction sections. Play a game with students in which you say the title of a book and students guess whether the book is fiction or nonfiction. Talk about clues in book titles that can help students distinguish between fiction and nonfiction books.

Parts of a Book   Page 220

Students Should
- identify the cover and contents page of a book

Teaching the Lesson

Display the cover of a nonfiction book that contains a contents page. Ask volunteers to say the title of the book and to identify the book's author. Tell students that books have many important parts, and that the cover, title, and author's name are only a few of them.

Go over the teaching. Explain that covers are important parts of books because they tell what the book's title is and who wrote it. Then direct students' attention to the contents page. Explain that the contents page tells what kind of information is in the book and where readers can find it. Have students read the contents page. Point out each chapter title and explain that a reader can use the chapter titles to find information about each kind of worm.

Go over the activity directions. When students have finished the activity, review their answers.

Extension

Ask students to find a book in the classroom that has a contents page. Ask students to write the title, author, and topic of the book. Then invite students to use the contents page to find a chapter title and to write the chapter title and one fact from that chapter. Invite students to share their work with the class.

Using the Internet   Page 221

Students Should

- understand how to use the Internet to do research

Teaching the Lesson

Talk with students about their experiences using the Internet. Invite volunteers to describe how they use the Internet. *(Examples: e-mail friends, read book or product reviews, play games)* Invite volunteers to name other things that the Internet allows people to do. *(find information, buy products)* Explain that the Internet is a powerful research tool because a great deal of information can be found on the Internet.

Go over the first paragraph. Explain that the Internet has billions of Web pages stored on computers for people to see. Tell students that these Web pages can be written and published by people, businesses, universities, and other organizations. Explain that there are Web pages on almost every topic and that people can find these Web pages from any computer. Tell students that using the Internet

can save a lot of time and work when doing research for a research report. Then say: *As helpful as the Internet is, we have to be careful when we use it. Anyone can make a Web site, and sometimes people make Web sites that have false information or information that we can't trust.* Tell students that when they use the Internet to do research, they should always check the facts that they find on at least two other Web sites or in a nonfiction book or an encyclopedia. Explain that by checking Internet facts, they can be sure the information isn't made up.

Direct students' attention to the example Web page. Talk about features of the Web page, such as the search field and links to information on other pages. Then go over the paragraph following the Web page. Point out that this example Web page is from a kid-friendly search engine. Emphasize that a kid-friendly search engine can find Web sites that have real facts and that have information that is OK for children to look at.

Go over the last paragraph. Then share with students the following rules for Internet safety:

1. *Never share personal information online.*

2. *Tell a parent or an adult if anything you see on the computer makes you feel scared, uncomfortable, or confused.*

3. *Never meet in person anyone you talk with on the Internet.*

Go over with students an Internet safety resource, such as NetSmartz.org, SafeKids.com, or iKeepSafe. org, that offers students, teachers, and parents guidelines for safe Internet use.

Extension

Supervise students as they use a kid-friendly search engine to find two facts about an animal of their choice. Have students write down each fact and the address of the Web site on which they found the fact. Then have students check the fact in a nonfiction book or an encyclopedia. Remind students that facts found on the Internet should be checked on at least two other Web sites or in a nonfiction book or an encyclopedia.

Index

Acknowledgments

Illustration

Anni Betts: 9, 14, 28, 30, 31, 46, 58, 59, 61, 89, 92, 102, 116, 127 top, 131, 156, 176–177, 204, 219, 221, T-226 left, T-290, T-301

Holli Conger: iii bottom, 18, 25, 32, 33, 42 top, 51, 57 top, 78, 79, 87, 112, 118, 132, 144–145, 170, 184, 189, T-233, T-263 right, T-273, T-305

Deborah Melman: iv top, v bottom, 10, 13, 40–41, 56, 77, 88, 95, 114, 122 top, 155, 158, 181, 195, 210–211, T-226 right

Cindy Revell: iii middle, 8, 11, 16, 19, 20, 21, 24, 27, 29, 42 bottom, 43, 45, 47, 49, 52, 57 bottom, 60, 62, 63, 76, 81, 84, 85, 86, 91, 94, 96, 99, 110–111, 117, 121, 122 bottom, 126, 127 middle, 128, 133, 146, 151, 159, 162, 163, 164, 178, 183, 188, 190, 192, 194, 196, 201, 212, T-224, T-227, T-231, T-237, T-240, T-243, T-244, T-246, T-248, T-249, T-253, T-254, T-259, T-263 left, T-264, T-267, T-268, T-277, T-278, T-280, T-289, T-291, T-292, T-293, T-296, T-302, T-306, T-307, T-311, T-318

Christine Schneider: 6–7, 48, 53, 64, 80, 93, 98, 113, 123, 129, 138–139, 149, 167, 179, 193, 203, 214, T-255

Melanie Siegel: iv middle, 17, 23, 44, 50, 54, 74–75, 97, 115, 124, 136, 154, 187, 198, 215

Photography

Phil Martin Photography: 74d, 37, 39, 41, 71, 73, 107, 109, 141, 143, 173, 175, 207, 209, T-238, T-252, T-271, T-284, T-286, T-300, T-314, T-315

© Lynda Richardson/CORBIS: 218

Literature

Quote from Joseph Addison found in *Scholastic Treasury of Quotations for Children*. Copyright © by Adrienne Betz. Published by Scholastic Inc. All rights reserved.

Acknowledgments for Literature Links

Chapter 1–Personal Narratives
Cover from *Celia's Island Journal*. Copyright ©1992 by Loretta Krupinski. Used by permission of Little, Brown and Company. All rights reserved.

Cover from *There's an Alligator Under My Bed*. Copyright © 1987 by Mercer Mayer. Used by permission of Penguin Books for Young Readers. All rights reserved.

Cover from *Tar Beach*. Copyright ©1991 by Faith Ringgold. Published by Crown Publishers, Inc., a Random House Company.

Chapter 2–Friendly Letters
Cover reprinted with the permission of Atheneum Books for Young Readers, an imprint of Simon & Schuster Children's Publishing Division from *Yours Truly, Goldilocks* by Alma Flor Ada, illustrated by Leslie Tryon. Illustrations copyright © 1998 Leslie Tryon.

Cover from *The Jolly Postman* by Janet and Allan Ahlberg. Copyright 1986 by Janet and Allan Ahlberg. First published in Great Britain 1986 by William Heinemann. Published by Little, Brown and Company, part of the Time Warner Book Group.

Cover reprinted with the permission of Margaret K. McElderry Books, an imprint of Simon & Schuster Children's Publishing Division from *Dear Mr. Blueberry* by Simon James. Copyright © 1991 Simon James.

Chapter 3–How-to Articles
The Kids' Multicultural Cookbook: Food & Fun Around the World by Deanna F. Cook. Copyright © 1995 by the author. Cover image used by permission of Williamson Books, an imprint of Ideals Publication.

Easy Art Fun: Do-It-Yourself Crafts for Beginning Readers by Jill Frankel Hauser. Illustrations by Savlan Hauser. Copyright © by the author. Published by Williamson Books, an imprint of Ideals Publications.

Cover from *My First Book of How Things Are Made* by George Jones. Copyright © 1995 by Pond Press. Reprinted by permission of Scholastic Inc.

Chapter 4–Descriptions
Cover from *Alice Ramsey's Grand Adventure*. Written and illustrated by Don Brown. Copyright © 1997 by Don Brown. Used by permission of Houghton Mifflin Company. All rights reserved.

Cover from *Abuela* by Arthur Dorros, illustrated by Elisa Kleven, copyright © 1991 by Elisa Kleven, illustrations. Used by permission of Dutton Children's Books, A Division of Penguin Young Readers Group, A Member of Penguin Group (USA) Inc., 345 Hudson Street, New York, NY 10014. All rights reserved.

Cover from *Frog and Toad All Year*. Copyright © 1976 by Arnold Lobel. Published by HarperCollins Children's Books.

Chapter 5–Book Reports
Cover from *Chang's Paper Pony* by Eleanor Coerr. Copyright © 1988 by Deborah Kogan Ray. Used by permission of HarperCollins Publishers.

Cover from *Babe the Gallant Pig* by Dick King-Smith, illustrated by Mary Rayner, copyright © 1983 by Dick King-Smith. Illustrations copyright © 1983 by Mary Rayner. Used by permission of Crown Publishers, an imprint of Random House Children's Books, a division of Random House, Inc.

Cover from *Days with Frog and Toad* by Arnold Lobel. Copyright © 1979 by Arnold Lobel. Published by HarperCollins Publishers, Inc.

Chapter 6–Research Reports
Cover from *Beacons of Light: Lighthouses* by Gail Gibbons. Copyright © 1990 by Gail Gibbons. Published by William Morrow & Company, Inc.

Cover from *What's It Like to Be a Fish?* Text copyright © 1996 by Wendy Pfeffer. Illustrations copyright © 1996 by Holly Keller. Published by HarperCollins Children's Books.

Cover from *Cheetahs* by Linda C. Wood. Part of the Zoobooks Series. Copyright © 1990. Published by Wildlife Education, Ltd.